Official Schedule

ToolBox

Mock up Window Mgr	
Mock up Menu routines (w/ I	
Mock up Buttons & Dials	Dec 25
ToolBox Document	Jan 2
code window mgr in assembly	Jan 29
code menu routines in assembly	Feb 12
code buttons & dials in assembly	Feb 26
code font manager in assembly	March 12
implement desk ornaments	April 2
alpha release ToolBox	March 19
Integrate into ROM	April 16

Finder

1st Finder MockUp	Jan 2
2nd Finder MockUp	March 5
Finder Document	April 7

Problem with LisaGraf →

Since its not re-entrant, cant write to screen from completion routines or async drivers, which is a minor bummer

One Solution →

make LisaGraf a driver. Requests will be queued up so only one can be processed ✓

at a time [trivial to make HideCusor / ShowCusor re-entrant. Just set sema & ignore if locked

---

Long Term Schedule   10/25/81

Async Disk Driver
Event Manager
Mouse Driver
Integrate File System   ← Nov 16, 1981

ToolBox Queing Routines
ToolBox Document
Menu Manager
Screen Manager
Font Manager

ToolBox Things to do   6/14/82

→ Code & type in NewWindow, BeginUpdate, EndUpdate, SetWTitle

→ Integrate with GrafFolders & debug

→ Code & type in WindowProc for documents

→ Integrate & debug

[Wed]

Mon, June 21

Code & type in icons

Fri, June 26

33
code & type in menus

July 5   ←

code & type in buttons

July 19

July 23rd ? code & type in dials

July 31   Desk] Mgr
            Scrap]

Should we do the
folder drag the
new Lisa way →
[saves about 300-500
bytes & handles
top folder quicker]
doesn't go transparent

~~Possible~~? I vote yes

Scrap Issues:
How does it exist between applications

6/15 Memory ~~manager~~ is a bitch.

Application heap + system heap is the only solution

28
44K
—
84

2K
4K
10K
—
36

never gets grown or cut back

holds system **data structures** [sysinit non-relocatables] [in RAM] make $ nop a r

Single segment, can chain ← AS

- desk ornaments
- fonts
- RAM Drivers
- scrap

Typically the system uses 8K so at least 8K is available for (su desk ornaments, fonts + RAM ~~State~~ Based Drivers. We could even make system heap size a parameter in clock chip (4 choices? 8?) or make in "sys gen" able on disk (latter is better)

The secret is that system heap is hard allocated (but changable)
by WXRENSTART

We never need to CLEAN Heap or Shrink Heap
This saves significant code.

Application heap gets **obliterated** by loader at load end, finder ~~inits its out heap~~ reinits it for app

Solves all the problems nicely except it introduces

REVOLUTION
in The Valley

REVOLU
in The Valley

O'REILLY®

Beijing Cambridge Farnham Köln Sebastopol Tokyo

TION

Andy Hertzfeld

with contributions by Steve Capps, Donn Denman, Bruce Horn, and Susan Kare

Revolution in The Valley
by Andy Hertzfeld

Copyright © 2005 Andy Hertzfeld.
All rights reserved.
Printed in Canada.

Published by O'Reilly Media, Inc.,
1005 Gravenstein Highway North,
Sebastopol, CA 95472.

O'Reilly books may be purchased for educational,
business, or sales promotional use. Online editions
are also available for most titles (*safari.oreilly.
com*). For more information, contact our corporate/
institutional sales department:
800-998-9938 or *corporate@oreilly.com*.

Editor	Allen Noren
Production Editor	Philip Dangler
Art Director	Michele Wetherbee
Cover Designer	Ellie Volckhausen
Interior Designer	Melanie Wang

December 2004: First Edition.

Revision History

2004-12-06:	First release
2011-09-09:	Second release
2012-01-17:	Third release

ISBN: 978-1-449-31624-2
[TI]

For my wife, Joyce,

my stepson, Nick,

my "best friend," Burrell Smith,

and the rest of the original Macintosh team.

Contents

Part Three

Foreword

There are occasionally short windows in time when incredibly important things get invented that shape the lives of humans for hundreds of years. These events are impossible to anticipate, and the inventors, the participants, are often working not for reasons of money, but for the personal satisfaction of making something great.

The development of the Macintosh computer was one of these events, and it has changed our lives forever. Every computer today is basically a Macintosh, a very different type of computer from those that preceded it. Who were the people who developed this revolutionary computer? What motivated them? What advancements did they make? How were tradeoffs made? What was the environment like where it happened?

The answers to some of these questions can be derived from other books. But they too often have the flavor of highly edited reality TV shows scripted by outsiders who weren't there. I occasionally read an article based on good, exhaustive reporting that gets to the heart and soul of this computer and of the people who created it, but none do it as well as this book.

Revolution in The Valley: The Insanely Great Story of How the Mac Was Made is a collection of stories by the actual personalities who gave life to this amazing computer, and it's more captivating than any book or article I have read. As you'll soon discover, these are people whose passion for doing great things has never before been captured, until now.

It's chilling to recall how this cast of young and inexperienced people who cared more than anything about doing great things created what is perhaps the key technology of our lives. Their own words and images take me back to those rare days when the rules of innovation were guided by internal rewards, and not by money.

Steve Wozniak

Introduction

The best purchase of my life occurred in January 1978 when I spent $1295 plus tax, most of my life savings at the time, on an Apple II microcomputer (serial number 1703) with 16K bytes of RAM. I was instantly delighted with it, and the deeper I dug into it, the more excited I became. It had incredible features, such as seven expansion slots and high-resolution color graphics. But it also had an ineffable quality that went beyond mere features. Not only could I finally afford to have my own computer, but the one I got turned out to be magic; it was better than I ever thought it could be.

I started spending most of my free time with my Apple, and then most of my not-so-free time, exploring various technical aspects of the system. As I taught myself 6502 assembly language from the monitor listing that came with the machine, it became clear to me this was no ordinary product: the coding style was crazy, whimsical, and outrageous, just like every other part of the design—especially the hi-res color graphic screen. It was clearly the work of a passionate artist. Eventually, I became so obsessed with the Apple II that I had to go to work at the place that created it. I abandoned graduate school and started work as a systems programmer at Apple in August 1979.

Even though the Apple II was overflowing with both technical and marketing genius, the best thing about it was the spirit of its creation. It was not conceived or designed as a commercial product in the usual sense. Apple cofounder Steve Wozniak was just trying to make a great computer for himself and impress his friends at the Homebrew Computer Club. His design somehow projected an audacious sense of infinite horizons, as if the Apple II could do anything, if you were just clever enough.

Most of the early Apple employees were their own ideal customers. The Apple II was simultaneously a work of art and the fulfillment of a dream, shared by Apple's employees and customers. Its unique spirit was picked up and echoed back by third-party developers, who sprung out of nowhere with innovative applications.

Making the transition from an ardent Apple II hobbyist to an Apple employee was like ascending Mount Olympus, walking among the gods, working alongside my heroes. The early team at Apple was full of amazing individuals, people like Steve Wozniak, Rod Holt, and Mike Markkula. It was a privilege to get to know them and learn the company mythology firsthand.

Apple's other co-founder, Steve Jobs, had no shortage of vision or ambition. Flush with the rapidly growing success of the Apple II, Apple initiated two new projects in the fall of 1978 (codenamed Sara and Lisa), which were aimed beyond the hobbyist market. Sara was a souped-up successor to the Apple II, using the same microprocessor with an

80-column display and additional memory, intended for small businesses. Lisa was an ambitious, more expensive, easy-to-use, next generation office computer featuring a revolutionary graphical user interface (GUI). By the time I started at Apple in August 1979, both projects were staffed up and well underway.

The Sara and Lisa teams were organized in a conventional fashion, with seasoned computer industry veterans recruited from companies like Hewlett-Packard coordinating dozens of engineers and marketing folks across multiple layers of management. I was afraid Apple's original freewheeling style was waning when I heard about Jef Raskin's Macintosh project, a tiny research effort to design an easy-to-use, low-cost, consumer-oriented computer. Jef recruited a brilliant young technician named Burrell Smith from Apple's service department to be his Macintosh hardware designer, and Smith quickly came up with a stunning design.

Burrell worshiped Woz's Apple II design and forged his own idiosyncratic design style that was even crazier than Woz's, using many clever tricks to coax enormous functionality out of the minimum number of chips. Somehow, Burrell's embryonic Macintosh board reeked of the same creative spirit so prevalent in the Apple II; as soon as I saw that board, I knew that I had to work on the project.

Steve Jobs also became enamored with Burrell's logic board and quickly took over the project, moving it to a remote location and inspiring us with a grand vision. The Apple II had broken through an important price barrier, making a useful personal computer affordable to ordinary individuals, but it was still much too hard for most non-technical people to master. The Macintosh would harness the potential of Motorola's 68000 microprocessor to provide a GUI and become the first personal computer that was both easy-to-use and affordable. We thought that we had a chance to create a product that could make computers useful to ordinary people and thereby truly change the world.

Most users today have never experienced what computing was like before the graphical user interface. Applications were usually controlled via a command line, where the user typed terse, cryptic commands that had to be memorized. There was no standard user interface, so a new method of interaction had to be mastered for each application. For many users, it simply wasn't worth the effort.

The Macintosh design team was inspired by Woz's original design and tried to recapture its innovative spirit. Again, we were our own ideal customers, designing something that we wanted for ourselves more than anything else. Although Apple was already a large company, Steve's unique position as co-founder enabled him to maintain the Macintosh group as a little island where Apple's original values could flourish and grow.

This book contains numerous anecdotes about the development of the original Macintosh computer, from its inception in the summer of 1979, through its triumphant introduction in January 1984, until May 31, 1985, when Steve Jobs was forced off the Macintosh team. They are arranged in roughly chronological order, but are also interlinked, and classified by topic and characters. The stories cover the full gamut of Macintosh development. I hope they will impart to the reader a sense of what it was like to be there at the time.

I've been regaling my friends and colleagues with these tales for years, but I had some trepidation about writing them down. I was afraid that my account would be limited, biased and self-serving, like so many others, no matter how hard I tried to get down the truth. Eventually, I had the idea of using the web to air out the anecdotes, allowing others to contribute comments and stories of their own. I began writing them in June 2003 in Hawaii, and I had over sixty stories written when I unveiled my web site in time for the 20th anniversary of the Macintosh launch in January 2004.

That web site, *http://www.folklore.org*, currently has over 115 stories, and will hopefully continue to grow over time. It has lots of relatively short anecdotes rather than a monolithic narrative because the anecdotal approach is inherently extensible, and multiple authors can elaborate the story indefinitely, without compromising their individual voices. The size of the web site is unlimited, but the book had to meet tighter constraints. We decided to include some stories written by other key original Mac team members (Steve Capps, Donn Denman, Bruce Horn, and Susan Kare), to provide a taste of the broader range of perspectives presented on the web site.

The accomplishments of the original Macintosh team are a crucial link in a long chain of development that stretches back to the work of Ivan Sutherland and Doug Englebart in the 1960s, and the efforts of Alan Kay and his amazing team at Xerox PARC in the 1970s. There are also many great stories about the continuing evolution of the Macintosh platform, with surprising twists and turns as it switched to the PowerPC without skipping a beat in 1994 and, against all odds, was reunited with Steve Jobs a few years later. Hopefully, all of that folklore will eventually be collected somewhere.

The Macintosh became very successful, although not quite in the way we imagined. Today, twenty years later, the user interface that we pioneered is ubiquitous, and used by hundreds of millions of people on a daily basis, even though most experience it through non-Apple platforms. But I also think in the largest sense we substantially failed, because computers remain frustratingly difficult to use for ordinary users. There is still a long way to go before the Macintosh dream is fully realized, and perhaps the best stories are yet to come.

Cast of Characters

Bill Atkinson Jef Raskin recruited Bill to work for Apple in the spring of 1978. His work on the QuickDraw graphics package was the foundation of both the Lisa and the Macintosh user interfaces. Later, he single-handedly wrote MacPaint, the first great application for the Macintosh, followed by HyperCard in 1987. He co-founded General Magic in 1990 to develop personal intelligent communicators. Since 1996, he's been a full-time nature photographer and has recently published a beautiful book of mineral photographs titled *Within the Stone*.

Bob Belleville After a stint at Xerox where he was one of the main hardware designers of the Xerox Star, Bob joined the Mac team in May 1982 as the software manager. In August 1982, he replaced Rod Holt as the overall engineering manager for the Macintosh division. He was one of the driving forces behind Apple's LaserWriter printer, which introduced Steve Jobs to the Adobe team. He left Apple in June 1985 and worked at Silicon Graphics in the 1990s. He is currently retired from the computer industry.

Steve Capps Steve joined the Lisa Printing team in September 1981 after computerizing his high school library and learning about GUIs at Xerox in Rochester, NY. He joined the Mac team in January 1983, and was an invaluable contributor during the home stretch, writing the text editing routines in the ROM and helping Bruce Horn finish the Finder. He left Apple in 1985, but he returned in 1987 to become one of the main creators of Apple's Newton PDA. He is now the founder and principal developer at Onedoto.

George Crow George joined the Mac team from HP in the summer of 1981 and designed the Macintosh analog board, which contained the Mac's power supply and video generator. He was also instrumental at convincing the Mac team to adopt the Sony 3.5" disc drive. He left Apple in September 1985 to co-found NeXT with Steve Jobs. He is currently working at Apple again.

Donn Denman Donn started at Apple in July 1979 to work on BASIC for the Apple III and joined the Macintosh team in September 1981 to write the first BASIC interpreter for the Macintosh. He also wrote some of the initial desk accessories, including the Notepad and the Clock. Later, Donn was one of the authors of Apple's end-user scripting environment, AppleScript. He currently works at the Open Source Application Foundation.

Chris Espinosa Chris grew up at Apple, starting work there as employee number #8 in 1976 when he was 14 years old, getting paid $3.00 an hour to write BASIC demo programs after school in Steve Job's garage. He has worked there ever since, except for a brief period when he left Apple to attend UC Berkeley. Steve Jobs talked Chris into dropping out of school to become the Macintosh publications manager in September 1981, and he has worked in a wide range of positions at Apple over the years. He was recently the AppleScript engineering manager and currently works on developer support.

 Andy Hertzfeld Andy started at Apple in August 1979, working on Apple II peripherals. He joined the Mac team in February 1981 and became one of the main authors of the Macintosh system software, working on the core operating system and the User Interface toolbox, as well as many of the original desk accessories. He later went on to co-found three innovative companies: Radius (1986), General Magic (1990), and Eazel (1999). He is also the author of the book you're currently reading and the creator of the Mac Folklore web site (*http://www.folklore.org/*).

 Joanna Hoffman Joanna Hoffman started on the Macintosh project in October 1980, while it was still a research project, and constituted the entire Macintosh marketing team for the first year and a half of the project. She wrote the first draft of the *Macintosh User Interface Guidelines* and later led the International Marketing team, where she was instrumental in making the Mac suitable for Europe and Asia from its earliest incarnations. She was vice president of Marketing for General Magic in the 1990s, and retired from the industry to devote her time to her family in 1995.

 Bruce Horn Bruce practically grew up at Xerox PARC, working there during summer break from the age 14. Bruce became one of the main architects of the Macintosh system software after starting at Apple in January 1982: he wrote the resource manager, dialog manager, and the Finder. After leaving Apple in the summer of 1984, he attended graduate school at Carnegie Mellon, earning his Ph.D. in Computer Science. In 1999, he co-founded Marketocracy, Inc.

 Brian Howard Brian Howard was Jef Raskin's close friend and collaborator, starting at Apple in January 1978 and working on the Macintosh project from its inception. Originally, Brian's official job was writing documentation, but he soon became indispensable as Burrell Smith's assistant, helping Burrell interface with the rest of the organization. He's worked at Apple continuously since 1978, co-designing many of the best Macintoshes over the years, such as the Macintosh IIci.

 Steve Jobs Steve Jobs co-founded Apple Computer with Steve Wozniak in 1976, when he was twenty-one years old. After being rebuffed by the Lisa team in the fall of 1980, he took over the Mac project from Jef Raskin in January 1981, and led the Macintosh team until John Sculley ousted him in May 1985. He left Apple in September 1985 to co-found NeXT, Inc, and returned to Apple in 1997 after Apple bought NeXT in December 1996. He is currently the CEO of Apple, as well as Pixar, a leading computer animation studio.

 Susan Kare Susan started working on the Mac Team in January 1983. She designed most of the icons and fonts for the Macintosh, as well as lots of the original marketing material, and helped to craft the overall look and personality of the system. After leaving Apple in the fall of 1985, she was one of the first ten employees at NeXT. Since 1988, she has been a successful independent graphic designer.

 Larry Kenyon Larry Kenyon began working at Apple in the summer of 1980 to work on Apple II peripheral cards, and joined the Mac team in January 1982 to work on low-level software. He wrote many of the device drivers for the Macintosh ROM. He also worked on the memory manager and file system. He is probably the most underrated important contributor to the Macintosh system software.

 Jef Raskin Jef was hired at Apple in January 1978 to start Apple's publications department. He conceived of the Macintosh project in early 1979, and formed a small team to pursue his ideas in September 1979. He put together an amazing team consisting of Burrell Smith, Bud Tribble, Joanna Hoffman and Brian Howard, and led the project until January 1981. He left the Mac team in the summer of 1981, and left Apple entirely in February 1982. Jef founded Information Appliance in 1982, which designed the Canon Cat, a small computer that embodied more of his ideas than the Macintosh. He is also the author of *The Humane Interface*, a book about user interface design, and is currently a professor at the University of Chicago.

 Caroline Rose Caroline started working on the Mac Team in June 1982. She wrote and edited the first three volumes of *Inside Macintosh*, the crucial Macintosh developer documentation. After leaving Apple in 1986, she managed the publications group at NeXT for a while and later returned to Apple to become the editor of Develop, Apple's technical journal for Mac developers. Since 1997, Caroline has been a successful independent technical writer and editor, working for Adobe and others.

 Burrell Smith Burrell started at Apple in February 1979 as a lowly service technician. His brilliant digital board provided the seed that the rest of the team coalesced around, its Woz-inspired creativity setting the tone for the rest of the project. Besides five different Macintoshes, Burrell also designed the digital board for the LaserWriter printer. He left Apple in February 1985. In 1986, he co-founded Radius, Inc. and created their first two products, the Radius Full Page Display and the Radius Accelerator. He retired from the computer industry in 1988.

 Bud Tribble Bud met Bill Atkinson and Jef Raskin at University of San Diego in the early 1970s. Jef convinced him to take a one-year leave of absence from medical school at the University of Washington to become the first Macintosh programmer in September 1980. He was instrumental in convincing Burrell to switch from the 6809 to the 68000 microprocessor, which turned Jef's research project into the future of Apple. A year and a half later, in December 1981, he had to leave the project to return to finish his M.D./Ph.D. degree, but he eventually returned to Apple in the summer of 1984. He left Apple to co-found NeXT with Steve Jobs in September 1985, and after a seven-year stint at Sun and year and a half at Eazel, he returned to Apple as a vice president of software technology in January 2002.

 Steve Wozniak Steve Wozniak co-founded Apple Computer with Steve Jobs in 1976. His brilliant design for the hardware and software of the Apple II created the foundation for Apple's initial success. While he didn't work directly on the original Macintosh, his engineering genius, impeccable integrity and playful sense of humor were a primary inspiration for the Macintosh team. He also founded Cloud 9 in 1985, where he created the first universal remote control, and Wheels of Zeus in 2001, which is creating wireless technology to "help everyday people find everyday things."

"Gallery" desk ornament is resource based

PICT + TEXT, prefers pictures

CUT, PASTE, COPY, scrolling

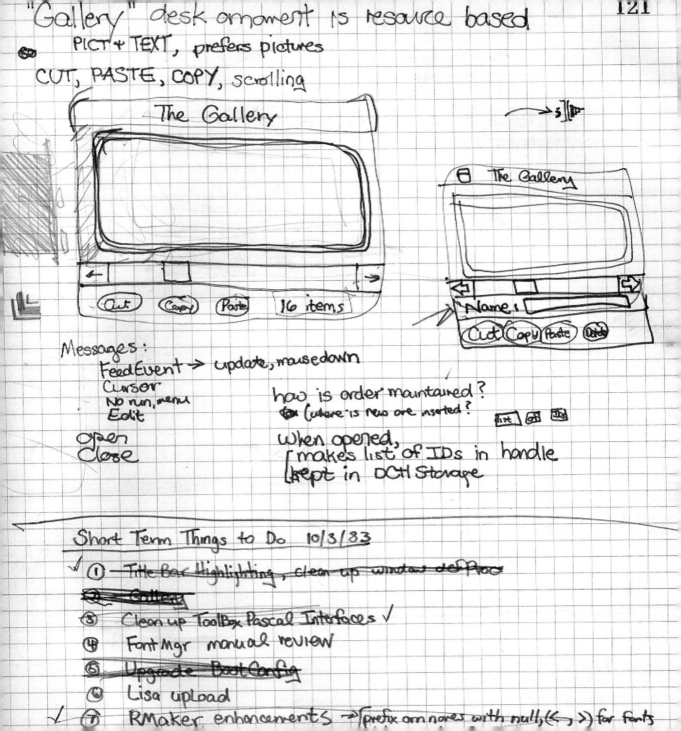

The Gallery

The Gallery

Cut Copy Paste 16 items

Name:

Cut Copy Paste Delete

Messages:
    FeedEvent → update, mousedown
    Cursor
    No run, menu
    Edit

    open
    Close

how is order maintained?
(where is new one inserted?)

When opened,
┌ makes list of IDs in handle
└ kept in DCtl Storage

Short Term Things to Do 10/3/83

✓ ① ~~Title Bar Highlighting, clean up window def Proc~~

② ~~Gallery~~

③ Clean up ToolBox Pascal Interfaces ✓

④ Font Mgr manual review

⑤ ~~Upgrade Boot Config~~

⑥ Lisa upload

✓ ⑦ RMaker enhancements → prefix own names with null, (<, >) for fonts

partone

The best way to predict the future is to invent it.

Alan Kay

I'll Be Your Best Friend   August 1979

Burrell Smith was creative in more than just engineering

Toward the end of my first week as an Apple employee in August 1979, I noticed that someone had left a black binder on my desk, with a handwritten title that read, *Apple II: Principles of Operation.* The binder contained a brilliant, concise description of how the Apple II hardware worked, reverently explaining details of Steve Wozniak's epic creative design hacks in a clearer fashion than I'd ever read before. I didn't know who left it there, but the title page said it was written by "Burrell C. Smith."

Later that same day I was approached by a young, animated, slightly nervous guy with long, straight, blond hair, who entered my cubicle and walked right up to me.

"Are you Andy Hertzfeld?" he asked. "Wow, it's amazing to meet you. I read your articles in *Call A.P.P.L.E.* and *Dr. Dobb's.* Apple's lucky they got you to work here. I want to shake your hand."

With exaggerated formality, he extended his right arm stiffly, almost in a parody of a handshake offer. "I'm Burrell. Burrell Carver Smith. Pleased to meet you. I wrote that manual and left it on your desk," he said, pointing to the black binder. We shook hands and then he suddenly turned around nervously and darted off, without explanation. "See you later!" he said, without looking back.

My cubicle in Bandley 1 was in the hardware engineering section because my first project was writing the firmware for the Silentype thermal printer. It was across the aisle from Wendell Sander's office. Wendell was the designer of the Apple III and an extremely brilliant and seasoned engineer who used to design RAM chips for Fairchild and who understood the Apple II hardware design inside out. All the other hardware engineers on the team, except for Woz, usually came to Wendell for advice.

I noticed that Burrell, even though he was supposed to be working in the service department in a different building, often hung around outside of Wendell's office. Sometimes he waited hours for Wendell to have a free moment, so he could ask him to verify his latest insight about the Apple II timings. At times, when Wendell was busy, he would try the insight out on me instead, or discuss a fine point of the Apple II firmware. Soon, we started to occasionally go out for lunch together.

The first time we went to lunch, I found out that Burrell's creativity extended beyond his engineering work. He would often try to convince our waitress to concoct variations of the standard fare on the menu, thinking of something different every time.

Facing page: Andy Hertzfeld, Burrell Smith, and Brian Howard in 1987

For example, after he successfully persuaded a waitress to divide his pizza toppings into thirds, he asked her to do fifths the next time. Or he ordered mixed sodas, as if they were cocktails, in ever varying proportions, like three-quarters Coke and one-quarter Sprite. The waitress often balked, but Burrell was sometimes charming enough to convince her to comply. He also obsessed on certain foods, becoming fixated on Bulgarian Beef sandwiches from Vivi's for a while, then going through a Pineapple Pizza phase (see "Pineapple Pizza" on page 43), before evolving to his most enduring favorite, sushi, which provided a new range of interesting choices and combinations.

Burrell also had a distinctive way of expressing himself, often by applying technical jargon to ordinary life—like describing a situation as *meta-stable*, or someone being a *state machine*—mixed with a dash of baby talk, such as adding plurals to people's names. An attractive woman was referred to as a *good prototype*, or a *good proto* for short. Burrell had a great sense of humor and periodically performed hilarious impressions of everyone else on the team, caricaturing their personality quirks with an incisive phrase or nickname (see "I Invented Burrell" on page 8). He also liked to make fun of various language conventions; for example, when pleased with new software, he'd say "Happiness comma software."

One of his favorite expressions was, "I'll be your best friend." He offered "best friendship" for a wide range of activities, like making some change in the software for him or getting him a Coke from the gas station. "Best friendship takes place," he would declare if pleased with the results. He also had a habit of reducing phrases to initials, like "B.F.R." for "Best Friendship Relationship."

Once, right after Burrell conferred best friendship upon me, I heard him offer best friendship to someone else for a different favor. "Wait a second," I challenged Burrell. "How can you give out best friendship to someone else? There can be only one best friend at a time, can't there?"

Burrell had a quick reply, delivered with a smile. "Of course there can be only one *best* friend at a given instant of time. But best friendship relationships may be highly dynamic. The average length of a best friendship is three to five milliseconds. So there's no problem in having a new B.F.R. a second or two later."

We'll See About That   November 1979
Burrell proves his mettle with the 80K language card

Burrell Smith was a 23-year-old, self-taught engineer, without a college degree, who was drawn to Apple by the sheer elegance of the Apple II design. Apple hired him in February 1979 as employee #282, a lowly service technician responsible for fixing broken Apple IIs that were returned by customers. As he debugged broken logic boards, sometimes more than a dozen in a single day, he developed a profound respect and empathy for Steve Wozniak's unique and creative design techniques.

Meanwhile, the Lisa software team was writing their first code in Pascal running on Apple IIs because the Lisa hardware wasn't ready yet. They had been at it for almost a year and had written more code than would fit in the 64K bytes of memory in a standard Apple II. In fact, the Apple II had only 48K bytes on its main board, but it used a "language" card to give it an extra 16K bytes to run Pascal. To accomplish this, the language card had to *bank switch* its RAM over to the ROM on the Apple II motherboard.

Bill Atkinson was the main programmer for both the Apple II Pascal system, as well as the new Lisa system. He was in the service department picking up some extra language cards when Burrell heard him lamenting about overflowing the Apple II's memory limitations.

"Well, why don't you add more memory to the language card?" Burrell suggested.

Bill was intrigued, but he complained, "You can't add any more memory because we're out of address space. 64K is the limit of what we can address."

Burrell had already thought of that. "Well, the language card is already bank-switching the RAM, even double-banking the last 2K where the monitor ROM is. We'll just make it bank-switch another bank."

Bill was enthusiastic, so Burrell built him a prototype while Bill modified the Pascal runtime to support the extra bank-switching. It worked like a charm, so soon Burrell was busy manufacturing 80K language cards for all the Lisa programmers.

Around this time, Bill ran into Jef Raskin. Jef had written a series of papers about a consumer-oriented computer that would be extremely inexpensive and radically easy to use. He was ready to start building a hardware prototype and was looking for a talented hardware designer who could pull off his vision of a brutally simple, ultra low-cost machine.

"I've got someone who you ought to meet," Bill told Jef. He made arrangements to bring Burrell over to Jef's house in Cupertino over the weekend.

Bill and Burrell showed up at Jef's house at the appointed time, and Bill introduced Burrell to Jef by saying "Jef, this is Burrell. He's the guy who's going to design your Macintosh for you." "We'll see about that," Jef replied. "We'll see about that."

Andy and Burrell in 1983

"I Invented Burrell"

Burrell had a great sense of humor, and he was capable of performing devastating impersonations of everybody else on the Mac team, especially the authority figures.

Whatever idea that you came up with, Jef Raskin had a tendency to claim that he invented it at some earlier point. That trait was the basis of Burrell's impersonation of Jef.

Jef had a slight stammer, which Burrell nailed perfectly. Burrell began by folding his fingers together like Jef and then exclaiming in a soft, Jef-like voice, "Why, why, why, I invented the Macintosh!"

Then Burrell would shift to his radio announcer voice, playing the part of an imaginary interviewer. "No, I thought that Burrell invented the Macintosh", the interviewer would object.

He'd shift back to his Jef voice for the punch line.

"Why, why, why, I invented Burrell!"

Scrooge McDuck February 1980
The very first image on the very first Macintosh

Burrell Smith liked to do intensive design work over the Christmas break, so the very first prototype of the very first Macintosh sprung to life early in the first month of the new decade, in January 1980. It wasn't really a standalone computer yet because the prototype resided on an Apple II peripheral card, but it already contained the essential hardware elements of Jef Raskin's Macintosh dream: a Motorola 6809E microprocessor, 64K of memory, and a 256 × 256 bitmapped graphic frame buffer, which was hooked up to a cute, 7-inch, black-and-white display. Burrell used the Apple II host to poke values into the memory of the prototype so he could initialize the control registers and run small programs with the 6809.

I went out to lunch with Burrell a few weeks later, and, knowing my appreciation for Woz-like hardware hacks, he explained the crazy way he'd contrived for the Apple II to talk with the prototype. He didn't want to waste time designing and wiring up hardware to synchronize the memory of the two machines, since it wouldn't be needed by the real product. Instead, he delegated the memory synchronization to the software, which required the Apple II to hit a special memory address to tell the prototype how many microseconds later to grab data off of the common data bus. It was weird enough to make me interested to see if it really worked.

By now, Burrell thought he had the graphics running properly, but he wasn't really sure; he still needed to write some software to try it out. I told him that I'd look into it when I had some time. He gave me a copy of a handwritten page that contained the magic addresses that I'd have to use and hoped I'd get around to it soon.

I was used to coming back to the lab at Apple after dinner to see if anything interesting was going on and working on various extracurricular projects. I had some spare time that night, so I got out Burrell's instructions and wrote an Apple II (6502) assembly language routine to do the necessary bit-twiddling to transfer whatever was on the Apple II's hi-res graphic display to the Mac prototype's frame-buffer, using Burrell's unusual synchronization scheme.

One of my recent side projects involved using Woz's new, one-to-one interleave floppy disk routines to make very fast slideshow disks on the Apple II. I had just made one full of Disney cartoon characters that were scanned by Bob Bishop, one of the early Apple software magicians. Bob adored the work of Carl Barks, the Disney artist who specialized in Donald Duck, and he had scanned dozens of Barks' Donald Duck images for the Apple II.

```
LDA C520    ; set time delay to 3 µs
LDA $0      ; READ on both busses
LDA C500    ; Get d_ _ from MACINTO_
```

After each DMA transfer, the value on the bus ?
available at C500. This does not initiate a time _
as to the other addresses in the C500- C5FF spa_

TIME DELAY ADDRESS TABLE

ADRS	# µS delay	Used with this ADRS mo_
C500	—	ANY, reads the register has last transferred value
C580	1	—
C540	2	E —
C520	3	Z P
C510	4	ABS
C508	5	(IND),Y Y=0 OR NO PAGE CROSS
C504	6	(IND,X) NO PAGE CRO_
C502	7	—
C501	8	—

I selected an image of Scrooge McDuck sitting on top of a huge pile of moneybags, blithely playing his fiddle with a big grin on his beak. I'm not sure why I picked that one, but it seemed to be appropriate for some reason.

Even though it was starting to get late, I was dying to see if my routine was working properly, and thought it would be very cool to surprise Burrell when he came in the next day with a detailed image on the prototype display. But when I went to try it, I noticed that Burrell's Apple didn't have a disk controller card, so there was no way to load my program. Damn! I couldn't shut the computer down to insert the card, because I didn't know how to reinitialize the Macintosh board after power-up; Burrell hadn't left the magic incantation for that. I thought I was stuck and would have to wait until Burrell came in the next morning.

The only other person in the lab that evening was Cliff Huston, who saw the trouble I was having. Cliff was another early Apple employee and was Dick Huston's (the heroic programmer who wrote the 256-byte Apple II floppy disc boot ROM) older brother and an experienced though somewhat cynical technician. I explained the situation to him and was surprised when he started to smile.

Cliff told me he could insert a disk controller card into Burrell's Apple II with the power still on without glitching it out, a feat I thought miraculous. He'd have to be incredibly quick and steady not to short-circuit any of the contacts while inserting the disk controller, or he'd run the risk of burning out both the Apple II and the card. But Cliff said he'd done it many times before. All that was required was the confidence that you could actually do it. So I crossed my fingers as he approached Burrell's Apple like a samurai warrior and concentrated for a few seconds before holding his breath and slamming the disk card into the slot with a quick, staccato thrust.

I could barely make myself look, but amazingly enough Burrell's machine was still running, and the disk booted up so I could load the Scrooge McDuck image and my new conversion routine. And even more surprising, my routine actually worked the first time and displayed a crisp rendition of Uncle Scrooge fiddling away on the Mac's tiny monitor. The Apple II only had 192 scanlines, while the embryonic Macintosh had 256, so I had some extra room at the bottom where I rendered the message "Hi Burrell!" in a nice-looking 24-point, proportional font.

Facing page:
Burrell's DMA instructions

By the time I came in the next morning, an excited Burrell had already showed the image to everyone he could find. But then he accidentally reset the prototype somehow and didn't know how to get the image back on the screen. I loaded it again so he could show it to Tom Whitney, the engineering VP. I think Jef was pretty pleased to see his new computer start to come alive, but I don't think he was very happy about me giving the demo because he thought I was too much of a hacker, and I wasn't supposed to be involved with his pet project.

Some Disney collectors have tried to track down the original image, with Uncle Scrooge fiddling, but they didn't have any luck. I also asked Bob Bishop to go through his collection, but he couldn't find the image I described. So I guess it's possible that my memory is faulty here.

It's the Moustache that Matters   September 1980
Burrell wants to get promoted to engineer

Apple hired Burrell (employee #282) in February of 1979 as a lowly service technician, one of the lowest-paying jobs at the company. Even though he'd been doing genius-quality work as a hardware designer on the Macintosh project for more than nine months, and was even filling in for Steve Wozniak on the low-cost Apple II project, he still hadn't been officially promoted to engineer as he requested and was getting pretty frustrated.

Burrell started thinking about what it would take to get promoted. It obviously wasn't a matter of talent or technical skill because he was already far more accomplished in that regard than most of the other hardware engineers. And it wasn't a matter of working harder because Burrell already worked harder and was more productive than most of the others. Finally, he noticed something that most of the other engineers had in common that he was lacking: they all had fairly prominent moustaches. And the engineering managers tended to have even bigger moustaches. Tom Whitney, the engineering VP, had the largest moustache of all.

So Burrell immediately started growing his own moustache. It took around a month or so for it to fully come in, but he finally pronounced it complete. And sure enough, that very afternoon, he was called into Tom Whitney's office and promoted to "member of technical staff" as a full-fledged engineer.

Steve Jobs, Jerry Manock,
Steve Capps, and Bill Atkinson

Good Earth   October 1980
The original Mac team's original office

In 1979 and 1980, Jef Raskin's Macintosh project was a four-person research effort with a tenuous existence. It wasn't considered important within Apple, and was almost cancelled a couple of times. When Apple had another major reorganization in the fall of 1980, it was terminated again, but Jef pleaded with Mike Scott and Mike Markkula for more time and was granted three more months to show that he was really onto something. As part of the re-org, the four-person Macintosh team (Jef Raskin, Brian Howard, Burrell Smith, and Bud Tribble) relocated to a small office building a few blocks from the main Apple campus. The new office, located at 20863 Stevens Creek Boulevard in Cupertino, California, was called the Good Earth building because it was adjacent to a Good Earth restaurant. In fact, the office was Apple's very first office in Cupertino after they moved out of Steve Jobs' parents' house, and it was later used as the first office of the Lisa project when the Lisa team had fewer than 10 employees. The Mac team moved in and outfitted it with lots of beanbag chairs and all kinds of interesting toys.

Jef was very playful and always encouraged his team to express themselves creatively, so the office quickly began to look more like a day care center than an engineering lab. Periodically, work would cease and the entire team, plus any visitors who might be on the premises, would play some organized game, usually led by Jef and Brian.

Their favorite game, which was usually played just after lunch, was a form of tag played with Nerf balls. There were dozens of brightly colored Nerf balls scattered around the office. The rules would be improvised, but usually the person who was *it* had to confer "it-hood" on someone else by hitting them with a Nerf ball. This inspired everyone to surround his work area with barricades made out of cardboard to provide cover during the game, making part of the office look like a cardboard maze.

Jef and Brian were both serious musicians, so the office was also littered with a variety of musical instruments, and sometimes, spontaneous concerts would erupt. Jef was also interested in model airplanes and automobiles—especially radio-controlled ones. It wasn't unusual to see a radio-controlled car dart underneath your desk, and occasionally, everyone would go outside to see the maiden voyage of the latest radio-controlled plane.

Jef was writing his *Book of Macintosh* during much of 1979 and all of 1980, articulating his vision in ever-finer detail. Burrell's 6809-based prototype came alive in the early part of 1980, but then he went off to work on the low-cost Apple II project. Jef hired Marc Lebrun to write software in early 1980, but Marc was more interested in Lisp machines than in a limited memory microcomputer like the Mac, so nothing much happened until Bud Tribble replaced him in September of 1980.

Bud knew Jef from UCSD, and was also good friends with Bill Atkinson. They had a part-time, two-person consulting company in Seattle called Synaptic Systems while they were both graduate students. Bill and Jef convinced Bud to take a one-year leave of absence from the M.D./Ph.D. program he was pursuing at University of Washington at Seattle. Bud was in the fifth year of a seven-year program. Instead of returning to med school, Bud moved into a spare room at Bill Atkinson's house and started work on the Mac project at Apple. He quickly began to breathe life into Burrell's languishing prototype by writing some graphics routines for the 6809.

With a new but limited lease on life, and software finally starting to happen, the move to Good Earth in October 1980 came at an interesting time. But the Good Earth era was rather short lived.

Around two months after the move, Bud convinced Burrell to consider using the 68000 processor instead of the 6809. Burrell came up with a brilliant design that caught the attention of Steve Jobs. Steve took over the project and quickly recruited most of the early Apple II crew that he trusted (including Steve Wozniak and Rod Holt), and moved the project to larger offices a half-mile away, in Texaco Towers (see "Texaco Towers" on page 26).

Black Wednesday

I could tell there was something wrong the moment I stepped into the building on the morning of Wednesday, February 25th, 1981. Instead of the normal office buzz there was a muted sadness hanging in the air. People were standing around, huddled in small groups. I ran into Donn Denman, who had a cubicle near mine, and asked him what was going on.

"Didn't you hear? Scotty fired almost half of the Apple II engineering team this morning. He started calling people into his office around 9 A.M., one at a time, and telling them that they were being fired. I think over 30 people have been fired so far. No one knows why, or who's going to be next. There's going to be a meeting out back around noon when he's supposed to tell us what's going on."

Apple had gone public a couple of months before and was still growing at a frenzied pace. Sales were booming and there was no financial reason to pare back. I wondered what was going on.

"Do you know who they fired?" I asked Donn.

"Yeah, it's amazing. Scotty fired three out of the four managers, so almost everyone's boss is gone. And believe it or not, they fired Rick Aurrichio."

I thought the managers were more or less incompetent, so that didn't bother me. But the Rick Aurrichio part was shocking because Rick was clearly one of the most talented programmers in the Apple II division. He would usually do a week's worth of work in a day or two, and then spend the rest of the week messing around with whatever caught his fancy, usually one of the latest games. I understood how he could be a management challenge, but it made no sense to fire him. He was also my partner on the new DOS 4.0 project, which was just getting underway. He was the only other programmer besides me working on it, so it was especially distressing they would fire him so abruptly.

So I joined the ranks of the shell-shocked and listened numbly to the basement meeting where Scotty explained his rationale. He said that the company had grown much too fast over the last year and had made a few key bad hires, who themselves had hired even worse people. He thought the Apple II division had become too complacent, and that we had lost the start-up hustle that was the basis of our success. He wanted to shake us out of our complacency and prune out the bad hires, so we could start growing again in the right direction.

Scotty himself seemed a little shaken and unsure. Some of the other senior executives were standing off to the side, but they didn't participate in the meeting. There was a Q&A session at the end of the meeting where a couple employees told Scotty how horribly he handled the situation, but in general everyone seemed listless, as if we didn't know how we should react. Within a few days, everyone was referring to the incident as "Black Wednesday."

Later in the day, I talked to Dick Huston about what had happened. Dick was an early Apple programmer who had written the boot ROM for the disk controller card. He was also an astute observer of Apple politics and was friendly with Scotty. He told me he knew that the purge was going to happen and had even met with Scotty a couple of times in the last week to help him draw up the list of dead weight. He also told me Scotty had asked for the approval of Mike Markkula and the board of directors, and hadn't received it yet, but decided to do it anyway.

I told Dick I agreed that Apple had made some poor hires over the last year, especially some of the managers, but a Stalin-like purge was not a valid way to run a company. I complained about Rick's firing and told him the situation made me feel alienated from the company. I was the type of programmer who had to believe in what I was doing, and I wasn't so sure about Apple's values anymore.

When I came in to work the next morning there was a message on my desk from Mike Scott's secretary, saying he wanted to talk to me. Obviously, Dick must have talked to him. I called Mike's secretary back and arranged to show up at his office in an hour. Scotty looked harried, and our conversation was interrupted a few times by various phone calls. Scotty told me he had heard I was upset and was thinking about leaving, and said he wanted me to stay. He asked what he could do to get me excited about Apple again. I told him I might like to work on the Macintosh, with Burrell and Bud.

Later that afternoon, Scotty's secretary called to tell me she'd arranged for me to talk with Steve Jobs. Steve had been involved with the Mac project for more than a month now and, although I didn't know it at the time, had dismissed the founder of the project, Jef Raskin, the day before. He'd made Jef take a mandatory leave of absence after Jef had complained about Steve's leadership.

"Who cares about the Apple II? The Apple II will be dead in a few years. Your OS will be obsolete before it's finished. The Macintosh is the future of Apple, and you're going to start on it now!"

Lots of people at Apple were afraid of Steve Jobs because of his spontaneous temper tantrums and his proclivity to tell everyone exactly what he thought, which was often very unfavorable. But he was always nice to me, although sometimes a bit dismissive in the few interactions I had with him. I was excited to talk with him about working on the Mac.

The first thing he said to me when I walked into his office was, "Are you any good? We only want really good people working on the Mac, and I'm not sure you're good enough." I told him that, yes, I thought I was pretty good. I was friends with Burrell and had already helped him out with software a few times.

"I hear you're creative," Steve continued. "Are you really creative?"

I told him I wasn't the best judge of that, but I'd love to work on the Mac and thought I'd do a great job. He said he'd get back to me soon about it.

A couple of hours later, around 4:30 P.M., I was back to work on DOS 4.0 for the Apple II. I was working on interrupt handlers and dispatchers for the system when I noticed Steve Jobs peering over the wall of my cubicle.

"I've got good news for you," he told me. "You're working on the Mac team now. Come with me, and I'll take you over to your new desk."

"Hey, that's great," I responded. "I just need a day or two to finish up what I'm doing here, and I can start on the Mac on Monday."

"What are you working on? What's more important than working on the Macintosh?"

"Well, I've just started a new OS for the Apple II, DOS 4.0, and I want to get things in good enough shape so someone else can take it over."

"No, you're just wasting your time with that! Who cares about the Apple II? The Apple II will be dead in a few years. Your OS will be obsolete before it's finished. The Macintosh is the future of Apple, and you're going to start on it now!"

With that he walked over to my desk, found the power cord to my Apple II, gave it a sharp tug and pulled it out of the socket, causing my machine to lose power and the code I was working on to vanish. He unplugged my monitor, put it on top of the computer, and then picked both of them up and started walking away. "Come with me. I'm going to take you to your new desk."

I also recall the meeting in the Taco Towers basement. We'd heard about the firings, and then we were told to meet in the basement. We all filed in, and there was Scotty standing next to a keg of beer. We got beers and sat down and Scotty began to talk. What stuck with me was his opening line: "I used to say that when being CEO at Apple wasn't fun any more, I'd quit. But now I've changed my mind—when it isn't fun any more, I'll fire people until it's fun again." Standing there with a beer in his hand. Wow, I thought. In later years I witnessed many Apple layoffs—and now Scotty's way of talking to us seems like a class act, compared to all the mealy-mouthed HR-driven rhetoric that replaced it.

David Casseres

We walked outside to Steve's silver Mercedes and he dropped my computer into the trunk. We drove a few blocks to the corner of Stevens Creek and Saratoga-Sunnyvale, to a nondescript, brown-shingled, two-story office building next to a Texaco station, while Steve waxed eloquent about how great the Macintosh was going to be. We walked up to the second floor and through an unlocked door. Steve plopped my system down on a desk in an office near the back of the building and, before darting off, said, "Here's your new desk. Welcome to the Mac team!"

I started looking around the office and saw Burrell Smith and Brian Howard in the next room, huddled over a logic analyzer connected to a prototype board. I told them what happened and they said Steve had been over earlier, asking them if they thought I was any good. They were happy I had joined the team.

After helping them a bit with the disk diagnostic routines they were trying to debug, I returned to my new desk and looked inside the drawers. I was surprised to see it was still full of someone else's stuff. In fact, the bottom drawer had all kinds of unusual stuff, including various kinds of model airplanes and some photography equipment. I later found out Steve had assigned me to Jef Raskin's old desk, which he hadn't had time to move out of yet.

People To Give Macs To:

- Woz ✓
- Bill Budge ✓
- Bud Tribble ✓
- Bill Atkinson ✓
- Larry Tesler
- Lisa Printing Team (3)
- Steve Jobs
- Randy Wiggington
- Charlie Kellner
- MicroSoft (3)?
- Bruce Daniels
- Rich Page
- Rich Williams
- Rich Henderson Gregg (?)
- Rich Myers
- Dick Huston

part two

Hell, there are
no rules here—
we're trying
to accomplish
something.

Thomas Edison

Reality Distortion Field

February 1981
Bud defines Steve's unique talent

I officially started on the Mac project on a Thursday afternoon, and Bud Tribble—my new manager and the only other software person on the project—was out of town. Bud was on leave of absence from an M.D./Ph.D. program, and he occasionally had to return to Seattle to keep up his standing in the program.

Bud usually didn't come into work until after lunch, so I met with him for the first time the following Monday afternoon. We started talking about all the work that had to be done, which was pretty overwhelming. He showed me the official software development schedule that had us shipping in about 10 months, in early January 1982.

"Bud, that's crazy!" I told him. "We've hardly even started yet. There's no way we can get it done by then."

"I know," he responded in a low voice, almost a whisper.

"You know? If you know the schedule is off-base, why don't you correct it?"

"Well, it's Steve. Steve insists that we're shipping in early 1982 and won't accept answers to the contrary. The best way to describe the situation is a term from *Star Trek*. Steve has a reality distortion field."

"A what?"

"A reality distortion field. In his presence, reality is malleable. He can convince anyone of practically anything. It wears off when he's not around, but it makes it hard to have realistic schedules. And there are a couple of other things you should know about working with Steve."

"What else?"

"Well, just because he tells you something is awful or great, it doesn't necessarily mean he'll feel that way tomorrow. You have to low-pass filter his input. And then, he's really funny about ideas. If you tell him a new idea, he'll usually tell you that he thinks it's stupid. But then, if he actually likes it, exactly one week later, he'll come back to you and propose your idea to you, as if he thought of it."

I thought Bud was surely exaggerating, until I observed Steve in action over the next few weeks. The reality distortion field was a confounding mélange of a charismatic rhetorical style, an indomitable will, and an eagerness to bend any fact to fit the purpose at hand. If one line of argument failed to persuade, he would deftly switch to another. Sometimes,

"In his presence, reality is practically malleable. He can convince anyone of practically anything."

he would throw you off balance by suddenly adapting your position as his own, without acknowledging that he ever thought differently.

Amazingly, the reality distortion field seemed to be effective even if you were acutely aware of it, although the effects would fade after Steve departed. We would often discuss techniques for grounding it (see "Are You Gonna Do It?" on page 253), but after a while most of us gave up, accepting it as a force of nature.

Texaco Towers   January 1981
The office where the Mac became real

The main Apple buildings on Bandley Drive in Cupertino had boring numerical appellations—Bandley 1 and Bandley 3—but from the beginning, the Lisa team gave the buildings they inhabited interesting names. The original office for the Lisa team was adjacent to a Good Earth restaurant (in fact, it was Apple's original office in Cupertino), so it was called the Good Earth building. When the team grew larger and took over two nearby office suites, they were designated as Scorched Earth (because it housed the hardware engineers, who were all smokers), and Salt of the Earth (for unknown reasons).

The Lisa team moved to a larger, two-story office building a couple of blocks from the main building on Bandley Drive when they became a separate division in 1980. Everyone was so impressed at their having two stories (all the other Apple buildings were single story) that the building was dubbed Taco Towers, although I'm not sure where the "Taco" part came from.

In December of 1980, the embryonic Macintosh team resided in the Good Earth building, which had been abandoned by the Lisa team for Taco Towers earlier in the year. When Steve Jobs took over the Macintosh project, he moved it to a new building a few blocks away from the main Apple campus at the southeast corner of Stevens Creek Boulevard and Saratoga-Sunnyvale Road. It was large enough to hold about 15 or 20 people.

There was a Texaco gas station at the corner and a small, brown, two-story, wood-paneled office building that might house some accountants or insurance agents behind it. Apple rented the top floor, which had four little suites split by a corridor, two on a side. Because of

Burrell Smith, Dan Kottke, and Patti Kenyon at a reunion in January 1990

The Macintosh analog board, which contains the power supply and video generation circuitry

the proximity of the gas station and the perch on the second story, as well as the sonic overlap between *Taco* and *Texaco*, the building quickly became known as Texaco Towers.

Burrell Smith and Brian Howard took over the side of the building closest to the gas station and built a hardware lab, while Bud Tribble and Jef Raskin set up shop on the other side and installed desks with prototype Lisas to use for software development. Bud's office had four desks, but he was the only one occupying it at first. Steve didn't have an office there, though he usually came by to visit in the late afternoon.

In the corner of Bud's office, on one of the empty desks, was Burrell's 68000-based Macintosh prototype. Wire-wrapped by Burrell himself, it was the only one in existence, although both Brian Howard and Dan Kottke had started wire-wrapping additional ones. Bud had written a boot ROM that filled the screen with the word *hello*, rendered in a small bitmap that was 32 pixels wide for easy drawing, which showed off the prototype's razor-sharp video and distinctive black-on-white text.

When I started on the project in February 1981, I was given Jef's old desk in the office next to Bud's. Desk by desk, Texaco Towers began to fill up as more team members were recruited, like Colette Askeland (who laid out the PC boards), or Ed Riddle (who worked on the keyboard hardware). When George Crow started, there wasn't an office available for him, so he set up a table in the common foyer and began the analog board design there.

Burrell and I liked to have lunch at Cicero's Pizza, which was an old Cupertino restaurant just across the street. They had a Defender video game we'd play while waiting for our order. We'd also go to Cicero's around 4 P.M. almost every day for another round of Defender. Burrell was getting so good he would play for the entire time on a single quarter (See "Make a Mess, Clean It Up!" on page 168).

In May of 1981, Steve Jobs complained that our offices didn't seem lively enough, and gave me permission to buy a portable stereo system for the office at Apple's expense. Burrell and I ran out and bought a silver-colored cassette boom box before he could change his mind. After that we usually played cassette tapes at night or on the weekends when there was nobody around to bother.

The "Taco" part of the Taco Towers name was given because the brick facing of the building roughly paralleled the architecture of Taco Bell franchises being built around the same time. Or so we were told when we visited the building from one of the boring-numbered Bandley Drive offices.

Steve Hix

By the spring of 1982, the Mac team was overflowing Texaco Towers, and it was obvious we'd soon have to move to larger quarters. Steve decided to move the team back to the main Apple campus, into Bandley 4, which had enough space for more than 50 people. The 68000-based Macintosh was born in the Good Earth building, but I still think of Texaco Towers as the place where it came of age, transitioning from a promising research project into a real, world-changing commercial product.

More Like A Porsche   March 1981
The design of the Macintosh case

In March of 1981, I had been working on the Mac team for only a month. I was used to coming back to the office after dinner and working for a few hours. Even though many of the early Mac team members often worked late and went out to dinner together, I was by myself one evening when I returned around 8 P.M. to Texaco Towers. As soon as I entered the building I heard loud voices emanating from Bud's office, which was adjacent to mine.

"It's got to be different, different from everything else." I recognized Steve Jobs's voice before I saw him as I passed by the door of Bud's office. He was standing near the doorway, near our only working prototype, conversing with someone I didn't recognize. Steve introduced him to me as James Ferris, Apple's Director of Creative Services. "James is helping me figure out what the Mac should look like," he said.

The plan of record for the Macintosh industrial design was still the one conceived by Jef Raskin, which was a horizontally oriented, lunch-box-type shape, with the keyboard folding up into the lid of the computer for easy transportability. It was kind of like the Osborne I, though we weren't aware of it at the time. But Steve had a real passion for industrial design and never seriously considered following Jef's recommendations.

I went into my office and continued working on improving the code that drove the serial link between the Mac and Lisa. But I couldn't help but overhear the passionate discussion between Steve and James Ferris taking place next door. For some reason they were talking about cars.

"We need it to have a classic look that won't go out of style, like the Volkswagen Beetle," I heard Steve tell James.

"No, that's not right," James replied. "The lines should be voluptuous, like a Ferrari."

"Not a Ferrari, that's not right either," Steve responded, apparently excited by the car comparison. "It should be more like a Porsche!" Not coincidentally, in those days Steve was driving a Porsche 928.

I thought it was kind of pompous to compare computers with sports cars, even metaphorically. But I was impressed with Steve's passion for elegance in the industrial design, and his powers of discrimination continually amazed me as the design took shape.

"We need it to have a classic look that won't go out of style, like the Volkswagen Beetle."

"The lines should be voluptuous, like a Ferrari."

Steve recruited Jerry Manock to lead the industrial design effort. Jerry was the early Apple employee who had designed the breakthrough plastic case for the Apple II, initially as a contractor before signing up as an employee. For the Macintosh, Jerry recruited a talented designer named Terry Oyama to do most of the detailed drafting of the actual design. The hard tooling for the plastic case was the component with the longest lead time, so we had to get started right away.

A week or so after the car conversation, Steve and Jerry decided the Macintosh should defy convention and have a vertical orientation with the display above the disk drive instead of next to it. This was done in order to minimize the desktop footprint, which also dictated a detachable keyboard. That was enough of a direction for Terry to draft a preliminary design and fabricate a painted, plaster model.

We all gathered around for the unveiling of the first model. Steve asked each one of us, in turn, to say what we thought about it. I though it was cute and attractive. It looked a lot like an Apple II, but had a distinctive personality all its own. But after everyone else had commented on the design, Steve cut loose with a torrent of merciless criticism.

"It's way too boxy. It's got to be more curvaceous. The radius of the first chamfer needs to be bigger, and I don't like the size of the bezel. But it's a start."

I didn't even know what a chamfer was, but Steve was evidently fluent in the language of industrial design and was extremely demanding about it. Over the next few months, Jerry and Terry iterated the design and produced a new plaster model every month or so. Before a new one was unveiled to the team, Jerry lined up all of the previous ones so we could compare the new one with past efforts. One

"It's way too boxy. It's got to be more curvaceous. The radius of the first chamfer needs to be bigger, and I don't like the size of the bezel."

notable improvement was the addition of a handle at the top of the case that made it easier to carry. By the fourth model, I could barely distinguish it from the third one, but Steve was always critical and decisive, saying he loved or hated a detail that I could barely perceive.

At one point, when we were almost finished, Steve called up Jerry over the weekend and told him that we had to change everything. He had just seen an elegant new Cuisinart at Macy's and decided the Mac should look more like it. So Terry did a whole new design based on the Cuisinart concept. It didn't pan out, though, and we were back on the old track after a one-week diversion.

After five or six models Steve signed off on the design and the industrial design team shifted focus to the laborious engineering work necessary to convert the conceptual model into a real, manufacturable plastic case. In February 1982, it was finally time to release the design for tooling. We held a little party, complete with champagne (see "Signing Party" on page 68) to celebrate sending the design into the world, the first major component of the Macintosh to be completed.

It is quite obvious that the entire top part of the Macintosh was copied from the French Minitel terminal, especially the handle part. I wonder whether Steve is the one who liked it so much when he saw it in Paris.

Jean-Michel Decombe

SQUARE DOTS April 1981

The Lisa had a different screen resolution than the Macintosh

From the very beginning, even before it had a mouse, the Lisa was designed to be an office machine, and word processing was considered to be its most important use. In the late 70s, the acid test for an office computer (as compared with a hobby computer) was its ability to display 80 columns of text.

The Lisa team decided to optimize their display for horizontal resolution in order to display 80 columns of text in an attractive font. The vertical resolution wasn't as important because vertical scrolling works much better for text than horizontal scrolling. The designers decided to endow Lisa with twice as much horizontal resolution as vertical by using a 720 × 360 pixel display with pixels that were twice as high as they were wide. This was great for text-oriented applications like a word processor, but it made things somewhat awkward for graphics applications.

When Burrell redesigned the Macintosh in December 1980 to use the same microprocessor as the Lisa—the Motorola 68000—it set off shock waves within Apple. Not only was Burrell's new design much simpler than the Lisa's, with less than half the chip count, but it also ran almost twice as fast, using an 8-megahertz clock instead of a 5-megahertz clock. Among other advantages was the fact that the Mac's 384 × 256 pixel display had the identical horizontal and vertical resolution, a feature we called "square dots." Square dots made it easier to write graphical applications because you didn't have to worry about the resolution disparity.

Bill Atkinson, the author of QuickDraw and the main Lisa graphics programmer, was a strong advocate of square dots, but not everyone on the Lisa team felt the same way. Tom Malloy, who was Apple's first hire from Xerox PARC and the principal author of the Lisa word processor, thought it was better to have the increased horizontal resolution. But Burrell's redesign moved the debate from the theoretical to the pragmatic by creating a square dots machine to compare with the Lisa.

The Lisa hardware was scheduled to go through a final round of design tweaks, and Bill tried to convince the Lisa team to switch to square dots. He mentioned his desire to Burrell, who responded by working over the weekend to sketch out a scaled-up version of the Macintosh design that featured a full 16-bit memory bus with a 768 × 512 display and square dots. It would also run twice as fast as the current Lisa design. Bill convinced the

Lisa engineering manager, Wayne Rosing, that he should at least consider adopting some of Burrell's ideas. He arranged for the leadership of the Lisa team to get a demo of the current Macintosh and learn about Burrell's new scaled-up design.

Wayne Rosing led a delegation of his top hardware and software guys, including Rich Page and Paul Baker and software manager Bruce Daniels, over to Texaco Towers for a demo on a Monday afternoon. Bill Atkinson did the talking as we ran various graphics demos, and then Burrell gave a presentation on the Mac design and his ideas for scaling it up to 768 × 512 display. Everyone seemed pretty impressed and Bill was optimistic that they would make the change.

After a few days, Bill told us the disappointing news that Wayne had decided there wasn't enough time to embark on such a radical redesign because the Lisa was scheduled to ship in less than a year. It ended up shipping almost two years later, with the original 720 × 360 resolution. It also had a relatively slow microprocessor that became a problem when Apple decided to offer a Macintosh compatibility mode for Lisa in 1984. The emulation software didn't try to compensate for the different resolutions, so applications were distorted by the resolution disparity. It was almost like looking at a fun-house mirror. This problem wasn't resolved until the Lisa was discontinued in the spring of 1985.

Early Demos April 1981
Various demos showed off what the hardware could do

Bud Tribble wrote the first demo program for the 68000-based Macintosh as part of the original boot ROM. It filled the screen with the word "hello" more than a hundred times in tiny letters. When the Mac was switched on, it performed some hardware diagnostics, filled the screen with "hello," and then listened to its serial ports for commands to execute. The "hellos" told us that everything was working OK.

The boot ROM allowed us to download other programs from the Lisa to the Mac over a serial line in order to try out new code and test or demo the prototype. There was a ton of work still to do before launch. We had to write an operating system, hook up peripherals like the keyboard and mouse, and get Bill Atkinson's graphics and user interface routines, running, for example. But we also sometimes wrote demo programs just for the fun of it.

In early March of 1981, for example, I wrote a fast, disk-based slideshow for the Mac the same night that I got the disk routines going. It was exciting to see detailed, relatively high-resolution images parading across the display so quickly.

By April, I was experimenting with writing custom graphics routines to show off the raw graphical horsepower of the system. I had written a few ball-bouncing routines on the Apple II, and I thought it would be interesting to see how many balls the Mac could animate smoothly. I wrote some 68000 code to draw 16×16 images very quickly, and I found that I could keep more than 100 balls animating smoothly, which seemed pretty impressive. I also wrote a small sketch program with a seed fill using Bill Atkinson's 8×8 pattern bitmaps, as well as an entertaining Breakout game in which I implemented Bud's idea of dodging the bricks when they fell down after you hit them.

Bob Bishop had experimented with a variety of graphical special effects on the Apple II, and I thought I'd try some of them out on the Mac. The idea was to transfer an image onto the screen in an entertaining way. The one I liked best was a kind of waterfall effect that was achieved by copying an image onto the screen using a varying number of multiple copies of successive scan lines, and

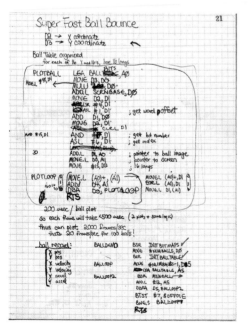

Assembly language code for bouncing balls

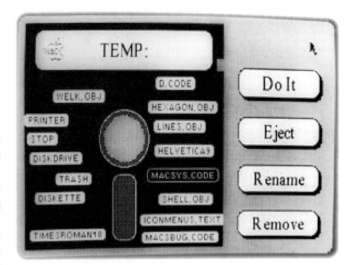

Early Finder prototype

then stretching the image vertically. The image looked like it poured onto the screen like water going over a waterfall; it was rather hypnotic. I often used it with an image of the Muppets I converted from the Apple II, and the "Stretching Muppets" demo became pretty well known.

In May 1981, Bud pulled an all-nighter and ported QuickDraw and some pull-down menu code from the Lisa to the Mac (see "Busy Being Born, Part 2" on page 153). For the first time, we were running mouse-based software with real pull-down menus. The best part of the demo was the pattern menu that showed off the extensibility of the menu routines to draw an entirely graphical menu.

In June 1981, we realized it would be worthwhile to create a standalone demo environment in which the Macintosh booted and ran programs from its own disk, even though we'd only use it temporarily. Our own operating system wasn't close to usable yet, but Rich Page had written a simple operating system called the "Lisa Monitor" that was based on UCSD Pascal and was pretty easy to port; all we had to do was integrate our I/O drivers. At last, using the Monitor, a Mac could boot up and run demos without help from a Lisa.

It was easy for us to run QuickDraw-based programs in the Lisa Monitor environment. Soon, we had a Window Manager demo that featured balls bouncing in multiple windows (see "Bouncing Pepsis" on page 149), as well as a nice icon editor and MacSketch (an early ancestor of MacPaint) running.

I think the most interesting demo was an early prototype for the Finder, written by Bruce Horn and myself in the spring of 1982, and pictured here. Its window was filled with an image of a floppy disc over which the files were represented as draggable tabs. You could select files and perform operations on them by selecting them and then clicking on a command button. Bruce also made a second mock-up with folder icons that influenced Bill's design for Lisa's Filer (see "Rosing's Rascals" on page 74), which we eventually adopted instead. The prototype provides an interesting glimpse of possibilities that we might have chosen instead of what seems so familiar today.

Bicycle   April 1981
Rod wants to change the name of the project

Jef Raskin chose the name *Macintosh*, after his favorite kind of apple. When Jef was forced to go on an extended leave of absence in February 1981, Steve Jobs and Rod Holt decided to change the name of the project, partially to distance it from Jef. They considered Macintosh to be a code name anyway and didn't want us to get too attached to it.

Apple had recently taken out a two-page ad in Scientific American that featured quotes from Steve Jobs about the wonders of personal computers. The ad explained how humans were not as fast runners as many other species, but a human on a bicycle beat them all. Personal computers were "bicycles for the mind."

A month or so after Jef's departure, Rod Holt announced to the small design team that the new code name for the project was *Bicycle* and that we should change all references from Macintosh to Bicycle. When we objected, thinking Bicycle was a silly name, Rod responded by saying it shouldn't matter "since it was only a code name."

Rod's edict was never obeyed. Somehow Macintosh just seemed right. It was already ingrained with the team, and the Bicycle name seemed forced and inappropriate, so no one but Rod ever called it Bicycle. For a few weeks Rod reprimanded anyone who called it Macintosh in his presence, but the new name never acquired any momentum. Finally, about a month after his original order, after someone called it Macintosh again, he threw up his hands in exasperation and told us, "I give up! You can call it Macintosh if you want. It's only a code name, anyway."

But it was a code name that proved to be sturdy and resilient. In the fall of 1982, Apple paid tens of thousands of dollars to a marketing consulting firm to come up with a themed set of names for Lisa and Macintosh. They came up with lots of ideas, including calling the Mac the "Apple 40" or the "Apple Allegro." After hearing all the suggestions, Steve and the marketing team decided to go with Lisa and Macintosh as the official names. They did manage to reverse engineer an acronym for Lisa, "Local Integrated Systems Architecture," but internally we preferred the recursive "Lisa: Invented Stupid Acronym," or something like it. Macintosh seemed to be acronym-proof.

But there was still a final hurdle to clear; the name was too close to a trademark from the McIntosh stereo company. I'm not sure how the situation was resolved (I suspect that Apple paid them a modest amount), but toward the end of our big off-site meeting held in

Carmel in January of 1983, Steve announced to the team we had gotten rights to use the name. He dashed a champagne bottle against one of the prototypes and declared, "I christen thee Macintosh!"

The tree-grown apple is spelled "McIntosh," but that's harder to type and was also the name of a maker of audio equipment. I had hoped the change of spelling would avoid trademark infringement as both the spelling and the field of commerce were different. The ploy didn't work: I was later told that Apple had to not only make a deal with McIntosh, but also with the Macintosh people who make the famous overcoats of that name.

Jef Raskin

Steve Jobs described personal computers as "bicycles for the mind." This image was used to promote the Apple University consortium.

A Message for Adam   April 1981

We encounter Adam Osborne at the West Coast Computer Faire

The Apple II was officially introduced at the First West Coast Computer Faire in April 1977, which was one of the very first trade shows dedicated to the newly emerging microcomputing industry. I loved the Computer Faires because passionate hobbyists attended them in the days before commercial forces completely dominated.

In April 1981, a few members of the Mac team took the afternoon off and drove up to San Francisco to visit the seventh West Coast Computer Faire at Brooks Hall. The biggest splash at the show was the unveiling of the Osborne I, from a brand new company named Osborne Computer, which was touted as the world's first portable computer.

The Osborne I was the brainchild of Adam Osborne, a well-known figure in the world of early microcomputers. Adam was a technical writer who founded a publishing company to publish crucial information about microprocessors and software that was sorely lacking at the time. The company was eventually sold to McGraw-Hill and Adam became a controversial columnist for opining on the industry from his pulpit in *InfoWorld* and other publications. He had a populist vision of computing that touted a no-frills, low-cost, high-volume approach to the business.

In 1980, he decided to put his theories into practice and founded the Osborne Computer Company to design, manufacture, and market the Osborne 1, a low-cost, one-piece, portable computer complete with a suite of bundled applications. He recruited Lee Felsenstein, already a microcomputing legend as the master of ceremonies for the Home Brew Computer Club, to design the hardware. Now they were introducing the fruits of their labor at the West Coast Computer Faire, just as Apple had done four years earlier.

The Osborne 1 was on display at their crowded booth near the center of Brooks Hall. It looked a lot like an oversized lunch box with a keyboard on the back of the lid. It was crammed full with two floppy drives and a tiny, 5" monitor in its center. We were a little surprised because it looked uncannily like some of Jef Raskin's early sketches for the Macintosh, which Steve had recently abandoned for a vertically oriented design. Portable was sort of a euphemism because the Osborne I weighed around 25 pounds; but at least it fit under an airline seat...barely. As Macintosh elitists, we were suitably grossed out by the character-based CP/M applications, which seemed especially clumsy on the tiny, scrolling screen.

Facing page:
Adam Osborne with his
creation, the Osborne I

We worked our way up to the front of the crowd to get a good look at the units on display. We started to ask one of the presenters a technical question and were surprised to see Adam Osborne himself standing a few feet from us, looking at our show badges, preempting the response.

"Oh, some Apple folks," he addressed us in a condescending tone. "What do you think? The Osborne 1 is going to outsell the Apple II by a factor of 10, don't you think so? What part of Apple do you work in?"

When we told him we were on the Mac team, he started to chuckle. "The Macintosh; I heard about that. When are we going to get to see it? Well, go back and tell Steve Jobs that the Osborne 1 is going to outsell the Apple II and the Macintosh combined!"

So, after returning to Cupertino later that afternoon, we told Steve about our encounter with Adam Osborne. He grinned with a sort of mock anger, grabbed the telephone on the spare desk in Bud's office, and called information for the number of the Osborne Computer Corporation. He dialed the number and a secretary answered.

"Hi, this is Steve Jobs. I'd like to speak with Adam Osborne."

The secretary informed Steve that Mr. Osborne would not be back in the office until the following morning. She asked Steve if he would like to leave a message.

"Yes", Steve replied. He paused for a second. "Here's my message: tell Adam he's an asshole."

There was a long delay as the secretary tried to figure out how to respond. Steve continued, "One more thing. I hear Adam's curious about the Macintosh. Tell him the Macintosh is so good that he's probably going to buy a few for his children even though it put his company out of business!"

PC Board Esthetics   July 1981
Steve is concerned with the esthetics of the PC board

The first Mac prototypes were hand-made using a technique called "wire-wrapping," where each individual signal is routed by wrapping an individual wire around two pins. Burrell wire-wrapped the first prototype himself, and others were done by Brian Howard and Dan Kottke. But wire-wrapping is time consuming and error prone.

By the spring of 1981, the Mac's hardware design was stable enough for us to make a printed circuit board, which allowed us to make prototypes much more quickly. We recruited Collette Askeland from the Apple II group to lay out the board; after working with Burrell and Brian for a couple of weeks, she taped out the design and sent it off for a limited production run of a few dozen boards.

We started having weekly management meetings attended by most of the team in June where we discussed the issues of the week. At the second or third meeting, Burrell presented an intricate blueprint of the PC board layout, which had already been used to build a few working prototypes, blown up to four times the actual size.

Steve started critiquing the layout on a purely esthetic basis. "That part's really pretty," he proclaimed. "But look at the memory chips. That's ugly. The lines are too close together."

George Crow, our recently hired analog engineer, interrupted Steve. "Who cares what the PC board looks like? The only thing that's important is how well it works. Nobody is going to see the PC board."

Steve responded strongly. "I'm gonna see it! I want it to be as beautiful as possible, even if it's inside the box. A great carpenter isn't going to use lousy wood for the back of a cabinet, even though nobody's going to see it."

George started to argue with Steve. He hadn't been on the team long enough to know it was a losing battle. Fortunately, Burrell interrupted him.

"Well, that was a difficult part to lay out because of the memory bus," Burrell responded. "If we change it, it might not work as well electrically."

"OK, I'll tell you what," said Steve. "Let's do another layout to make the board prettier, but if it doesn't work as well, we'll change it back."

So we invested another $5,000 or so to make a few boards with a new layout that routed the memory bus in a Steve-approved fashion. But sure enough, Burrell's prediction came true: the new boards didn't work properly, and we reverted to the old design for the next run of prototypes.

A designer knows that he has achieved perfection not when there is nothing left to add, but when there is nothing left to take away. **Antoine de St-Exupery**

The creation of art is not the fulfillment of a need but the creation of a need. The world never needed Beethoven's Fifth Symphony until he created it. Now we could not live without it. **Louis Kahn** I can't understand why people are frightened of new ideas. I'm frightened of the old ones. **John Cage** If you don't live it, it won't come out of your horn. **Charlie Parker** The details are not the details. They make the design. **Charles Eames** Less is more **Mies van der Rohe** Technique alone is never enough. You have to have passion. Technique alone is just an embroidered pot holder. **Raymond Chandler**

Pineapple Pizza   May 1981
We stay late to bring up the first printed circuit board

When I began working on the Mac project in February 1981, there was still only one 68000-based Macintosh prototype in existence, the initial digital board that was wire-wrapped by Burrell himself. It was now sitting in the corner of Bud Tribble's office on one of the empty desks, attached to a small, seven-inch monitor. When powered up, the code in the boot ROM filled the screen with the word *hello* in a tiny font, crisply rendered on the distinctive black-on-white display.

Dan Kottke and Brian Howard were already busy wire-wrapping more prototype boards, carefully following Burrell's drawings. About a week later I received the second prototype for my office so I could work on the low-level I/O routines, interfacing the disk and keyboard, while Bud worked on the mouse driver and ported Bill's graphics routines.

The next big step for the hardware was to lay out a printed circuit board. We recruited Collette Askeland, the best PC board layout technician in the company, from the Apple II group. Burrell spent a week or two working intensely with Collette, who used a specialized CAD machine located in Bandley 3 to input the topology and route the signals and eventually created a tape containing all the information needed to fabricate the boards.

Burrell and Brian checked and rechecked the layout, which was tediously expressed as thousands of node connections. After a day or two they decided they were ready to send it out for fabrication. We were hoping to get the first sample boards back before the weekend, but it looked as though they weren't going to make it. However, around 4:30 P.M. on Friday afternoon, they arrived.

Burrell figured it would take at least two or three hours to assemble a board, and then even longer to troubleshoot the inevitable mistakes, so it was too late to try to get one working that evening. Maybe Burrell and Brian would come in on Saturday to get started, or maybe they'd wait until Monday morning. While they were discussing it, Steve Jobs strolled into the hardware lab, excited as usual.

"Hey, I heard that the PC boards finally arrived. Are they going to work? When will you have one working?"

Burrell explained the boards had just arrived and that it would take at least a couple of hours to assemble one, so they were thinking about starting the next morning or waiting until Monday.

Burrell Smith
in downtown
Palo Alto, 1986

"Monday? Are you kidding?" replied Steve. "It's your PC board, Burrell. Don't you want to see if it works tonight? I'll tell you what. If you can get it to work this evening, I'll take you and anyone else who sticks around out for Pineapple Pizza."

Steve knew Pineapple Pizzas had recently replaced Bulgarian Beef as Burrell's latest food obsession (as a staunch vegetarian, he thought this was a positive development), and that Burrell wanted a Pineapple Pizza pretty much every chance he could get it. Burrell looked at Brian Howard and shrugged. "OK. We may as well give it a shot now. But I don't think we'll be able to get it working before the restaurants close."

So Burrell and Brian got busy. They selected a board, stuffed it with sockets, and carefully soldered them in place, while five or six of us, including Steve, sat around and kibitzed. Burrell was a little tense and impatient because he didn't like the pressure of bringing up a board in front of so many spectators. Every five minutes or so he referred to the awaiting Pineapple Pizza and speculated about how good it was going to taste.

Finally, around 8 P.M. or so, the board was assembled enough to try to power it up for the very first time. The prototype was hooked up to an Apple II power supply and a small monitor, and fired up as we held our breath. The screen should have been filled with "hellos," but instead all it displayed was a checkerboard pattern.

We were all disappointed, except for Burrell. "That's not too bad," he commented. "It means the RAM and the video generation are more or less working. The processor isn't resetting, but it looks like we're pretty close." He turned to look directly at Steve. "But I'm too hungry to keep working. I think it's time for some Pineapple Pizza."

Steve smiled and agreed that it was good enough for the first night and it was time to celebrate. The seven or eight of us who stayed late drove in three cars to Burrell's favorite Italian restaurant, Frankie, Johnny and Luigi's in Mountain View, where we ordered three large Pineapple Pizzas (which tasted great).

Round Rects Are Everywhere! May 1981
Steve inspires Bill by pointing out something about the real world

Bill Atkinson worked mostly at home, but whenever he made significant progress he rushed in to Apple to show it off to anyone who would appreciate it. This time, he visited the Macintosh offices at Texaco Towers to show off his brand new oval routines, which were implemented using a really clever algorithm.

Bill had added new code to QuickDraw (still called LisaGraf at this point) to draw circles and ovals very quickly. This was difficult to do on the Macintosh because the math for circles usually involved taking square roots, and the 68000 processor in the Lisa and Macintosh didn't support floating-point operations. But Bill had come up with a clever way to perform the circle calculation using only addition and subtraction.

Bill's technique used the fact that the sum of a sequence of odd numbers is always the next perfect square—for example, 1 + 3 = 4, 1 + 3 + 5 = 9, 1 + 3 + 5 + 7 = 16, etc. So he could figure out when to bump the dependent coordinate value by iterating in a loop until a threshold was exceeded. This allowed QuickDraw to draw ovals very quickly.

Bill fired up his demo and it filled the Lisa screen with randomly sized ovals faster than you'd think possible. But something bothered Steve Jobs. "Well, circles and ovals are good, but how about drawing rectangles with rounded corners? Can we do that now, too?"

"No, there's no way to do that," Bill said. "In fact, it would be really hard to do, and I don't think we really need it." I think Bill was miffed Steve wasn't raving over the fast ovals and still wanted more.

Steve suddenly got more intense. "Rectangles with rounded corners are everywhere! Just look around this room!" And sure enough, there were lots of them: the whiteboard and some of the desks and tables. Then he pointed out the window. "And look outside, there are even more practically everywhere you look!" He even persuaded Bill to take a quick walk around the block with him and pointed out every rectangle with rounded corners he saw.

When Steve and Bill passed a no-parking sign with rounded corners, it did the trick. "OK, I give up," Bill pleaded. "I'll see if it's as hard as I thought." He went back home to work on it.

Bill returned to Texaco Towers the following afternoon with a big smile on his face. His demo was now drawing rectangles with beautifully rounded corners blisteringly fast, almost at the speed of plain rectangles. LisaGraf called the new primitive "RoundRects." Over the next few months, RoundRects worked their way into various parts of the user interface, and soon became indispensable.

Apple II Mouse Card   June 1981
We hook up a mouse to the Apple II

Burrell's Macintosh design was elegant and clever and strove to use minimal hardware resources for maximal value. The mouse interface was a typical example. It used just a fraction of the general purpose 6522 VIA chip Burrell had incorporated. The mouse was hooked up to the Versatile Interface Adapter (VIA), an input/output chip on the digital board, so it generated an interrupt each time the mouse moved an increment horizontally or vertically, with an additional one-bit line to read the mouse button. That was it; the rest of the cursor positioning and rendering was done in software.

Mousepaint

Meanwhile, my good friend Bill Budge, an amazing Apple II games programmer, came up with an incredibly fast way to draw proportional text on the Apple II graphics screen using seven preshifted tables. He also wrote a very fast BitBlit routine (BitBlit was the most important graphics primitive in GUIs). It was crying out for a way to interface the mouse. An interface to the mouse would enable a complete graphical user interface on the Apple II.

Bud Tribble had written the initial code to drive the mouse on the Macintosh, but I had to maintain it and was familiar with how it worked. The Apple III had a 6522 chip that I'd programmed the previous year to shift bits out to the Silentype thermal printer. I realized that all that was required to interface a mouse to the Apple III was to make a simple connector to route the appropriate signals to the proper pins.

I asked Dan Kottke to wire up a connector. Once that was finished, it took only a few hours to write cursor routines and a driver. We had the beginnings of a full graphical user interface going on the Apple III, with no additional hardware required.

It was exciting enough that I started helping Bill Budge flesh out the program, careful to work on it only after regular hours so it didn't compromise my other work. Before long we had pull-down menus working, and then a simple proportional-text word processor. The only problem was that Apple IIIs weren't selling very well; we really needed to get it running on the Apple II somehow.

I talked to Burrell about the problem, which basically came down to making a peripheral card for the Apple II that included a 6522 VIA chip on it. Burrell came back the next day with a brilliant two-chip design that included just the VIA and a tiny dual flip-flop chip to synchronize it.

In order to move the mouse cursor without causing the screen to flicker, both the Mac and the Apple III code used a vertical blanking interrupt, which drew the cursor during the

Bill Budge in 1982

time interval when no video was being painted. Unlike the Mac and Apple III, the Apple II didn't have a vertical blanking interrupt. The most brilliant part of Burrell's design was how it synchronized with the video without running a wire to pick up the video signal.

The 6522 chip had a timer that could generate an interrupt at a specified interval. The problem was synchronizing it with the video, because the video generation was not accessible to the processor. Burrell solved the problem by wiring the spare flip-flop to the low bit of the data bus, and using it to latch whatever data the video was displaying so the processor could read it.

To synchronize with the video, Burrell had me write software to fill the Apple II's frame buffer so the low bit of each byte was on most of the time except at the end of the last scan line. I wrote a routine to sit in a tight loop and read the latch. When the low bit changed, we would know the vertical blanking interval had just begun.

The Apple II wasn't fast enough to keep up with its own frame buffer. A new byte of video data flew by every microsecond, which was only one processor cycle. It took at least 10 processor cycles to iterate through a loop, so we ran the risk of never seeing the low bit change. However, Burrell had a way around this: if the loop time was relatively prime to the display frequency, it eventually had to slip into place. I wrote a 17-microsecond loop that fit the bill, and we were delighted to see it work perfectly.

Apple II mouse card prototype

Bill Atkinson had told Steve a decent graphical user interface on the Apple II wasn't possible because of the weakness of its 6502 processor and the complexity of Woz's convoluted frame buffer. But, after a little more work on the software, we had a cool little GUI for the Apple II, including a proportional text word processor, in the summer of 1981. We thought we had a potentially valuable product on our hands.

We were reluctant to show it to Steve, knowing he would want to commandeer it, but he heard about it from someone and demanded to see it. We showed it to him, and, unfortunately, he loved it. But he also insisted that Apple owned all the rights to it, even though we had developed it in our spare time.

Steve couldn't insist that Apple owned all of it, though, because Bill Budge wasn't an Apple employee at the time. But Steve could claim complete ownership of the interface card, which he said was developed with Apple resources. Burrell and I were pretty upset because we did it on our own time and thought we should be compensated. But it was really hard to argue with Steve, especially about money.

We ended up turning over Burrell's design to the Apple II division, but they didn't think the Apple II could deal with interrupts properly even though we had demonstrated that it could. They ended up adding tons of hardware with more than a dozen chips. Steve made a deal with Bill Budge that eventually resulted in MousePaint, a MacPaint clone for the Apple II that was bundled with the mouse card. Burrell and I got over it quickly, but a bit of bitterness lingered, and the whole episode whetted our appetites for eventually working on our own.

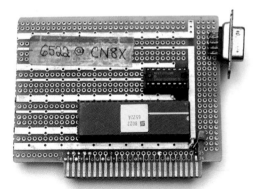

The mouse card prototype, with note

Diagnostic Port   July 1981

Burrell tries to sneak in some hardware expandability

Expandability, or the lack thereof, was far and away the most controversial aspect of the original Macintosh hardware design. Apple co-founder Steve Wozniak was a strong believer in hardware expandability, and he endowed the Apple II with luxurious expandability in the form of seven built-in slots for peripheral cards configured in a clever architecture that allowed each card to incorporate built-in software on its own ROM chip. This flexibility allowed the Apple II to be adapted to a wider range of applications and quickly spawned a thriving third-party hardware industry.

But Jef Raskin had a very different point of view. He thought slots were inherently complex, and that they were one of the obstacles holding back personal computers from reaching a wider audience. He thought hardware expandability made it more difficult for third-party software writers since they couldn't rely on the consistency of the underlying hardware. His Macintosh vision had Apple cranking out millions of identical, easy-to-use, low-cost appliance computers. Because hardware expandability would add significant cost and complexity, it was therefore avoided.

Apple's other co-founder, Steve Jobs, didn't agree with Jef about many things, but they both felt the same way about hardware expandability: it was a bug instead of a feature. Steve was reportedly against having slots in the Apple II back in the days of yore, and felt even stronger about slots for the Mac. He decreed that the Macintosh would remain perpetually bereft of slots, enclosed in a tightly sealed case, with only the limited expandability of the two serial ports.

Mac hardware designer Burrell Smith and his assistant Brian Howard understood Steve's rationale, but they felt differently about the proper course of action. Burrell had already watched the Macintosh's hopelessly optimistic schedule start to slip indefinitely, and he was unable to predict when the Mac's pioneering software would be finished, if ever. He was afraid that Moore's Law would make his delayed hardware obsolete before it ever came to market. He thought it was prudent to build in as much flexibility as possible, as long as it didn't cost too much.

Burrell decided to add a single, simple and inexpensive slot to his Macintosh design that made the processor's bus accessible to peripherals. He worked out the details and made a proposal at the weekly staff meeting, but Steve immediately nixed it. He stated there was no way the Mac would even have a single slot.

But Burrell was not easily thwarted. He realized the Mac was never going to have something called a slot, but perhaps the same functionality could be called something else. After talking it over with Brian, they decided to start calling it the "diagnostic port" instead of a slot, arguing that it would save money during manufacturing if testing devices could access the processor bus to diagnose manufacturing errors. They didn't mention that the same port would also provide the functionality of a slot.

Original Macintosh digital board

This was received positively at first, but after a couple weeks, engineering manager Rod Holt caught on to what was happening, probably aided by occasional giggles when the diagnostic port was mentioned. "That thing's really a slot, right? You're trying to sneak in a slot!" Rod finally accused us at the next engineering meeting. "Well, that's not going to happen!"

Even though the diagnostic port was scuttled, it wasn't the last attempt at surreptitious hardware expandability. When the Mac digital board was redesigned for the last time in August 1982, the next generation of RAM chips was already on the horizon. The Mac used 16 64 Kbit RAM chips, giving it 128K of memory. The next generation chip was 256 Kbits, giving us 512K bytes instead, which made a huge difference.

Burrell was afraid the 128 Kbyte Mac would seem inadequate soon after launch. On top of that, there were no slots for the user to add RAM. He realized he could easily support 256 Kbit RAM chips by routing a few extra lines on the PC board, allowing adventurous people who knew how to wield a soldering gun to replace their RAM chips with the newer generation. The extra lines would only cost pennies to add.

But once again Steve Jobs objected because he didn't like the idea of customers mucking with the innards of their computer. He also wanted them buy a new 512K Mac instead of buying more RAM from a third party. But this time Burrell prevailed because the change was so minimal. He just left it in and no one bothered to mention it to Steve, much to the eventual benefit of customers who didn't have to buy a whole new Mac to expand their memory.

Shut Up!

July 1981

The first demo of the Macintosh for Microsoft

Apple had already learned the value of having a thriving third-party software market with the Apple II, whose sales increased more than ten-fold when VisiCalc, the spreadsheet program developed by a tiny company called Software Arts, caught on in the business market. Apple intended to replicate the success of the Apple II with the Macintosh as an industry standard platform, so it was very important to bring third-party developers into the picture as soon as possible.

Microsoft was an obvious choice as one of the first companies to talk to. Both companies were started during the infancy of the personal computer industry, and a business relationship already existed because Apple licensed Microsoft's Applesoft Basic for the Apple II. Bill Gates and Steve Jobs were born in the same year and shared a similar vision for the potential of personal computers. Each one thought he was smarter than the other, but Steve generally treated Bill as someone who was slightly inferior, especially in matters of taste and style. Bill looked down on Steve because he couldn't actually program.

Steve had mentioned the Macintosh project to Bill at an industry conference in April, which led to a meeting in Seattle in June where Steve spun an intriguing vision of pumping out Macintoshes by the millions in an automated factory. The plan was for Microsoft to develop a series of applications for the Macintosh that would be ready at launch. Things went well enough to schedule a meeting in Cupertino in July, where we promised a demo of the actual machine.

Unfortunately, there was one small snag. We were using the Lisa as the development machine for writing the software for Macintosh, and we hadn't yet reached the point where the Macintosh could run as a standalone machine. The Macintosh needed to be hooked up to a Lisa in order to download software from it. But the Lisa group was writing all of its own applications for Lisa and made us promise we wouldn't let Microsoft see the Lisa.

We finally came up with a solution: we'd use a 25-foot cable and keep the Lisa in a different room—one the Microsoft guys weren't allowed to enter. I would start up the programs on the Lisa in the other room and Bud Tribble would operate the Macintosh. I would then run into the main room to see their reaction.

Steve generally treated Bill as someone who was slightly inferior, especially in matters of taste and style.

Bill looked down on Steve because he couldn't actually program.

Bill Gates showed up in the early afternoon with three colleagues: Charles Simonyi, who had recently joined Microsoft from Xerox PARC, Jeff Harbers, who would manage the Macintosh development team, and Mark Matthews, who was to be the technical lead on the project. They crowded around the prototype, and we started to run our various demos for them, with Steve doing most of the talking.

Bill Gates was not a very good listener; he couldn't bear to have anyone explain how something worked to him. He kept leaping ahead instead and guessing how he thought the Mac worked.

We showed him how the Macintosh mouse cursor moved smoothly in a flicker-free fashion.

"What kind of hardware do you use to draw the cursor?" he asked. Many current personal computers had special hardware to draw small bitmaps called *sprites*, and he thought we might be doing something similar.

Of course, the Macintosh didn't use any special hardware at all. It did everything in software, which was more flexible anyway, during the vertical blanking interval to eliminate the possibility of flicker. In fact, Burrell and I had recently gotten a mouse to run smoothly on an Apple II using a similar technique (see "The Apple II Mouse Card" on page 47).

"We don't have any special hardware for it!" I blurted out, probably with a proud sneer in my voice. "In fact…" I was about to mention that we got it running on an Apple II, which had one-tenth the processing horsepower of a Macintosh, when Steve guessed what I was about to say.

Bill Gates, Mitch Kapor, and Fred Gibbons: early third-party developers

Bill Gates in the early days

"Shut up!" he yelled as loud as he could, looking directly at me. He yelled it again, possibly trying to drown me out in case I kept on going. But I understood what he wanted and changed what I was going to say. "In fact, doing it in software is better anyway," I concluded.

The rest of the demo went pretty well, and both teams shared their excitement about how the Macintosh was going to take the industry to another level. We went to dinner at a fancy restaurant in Los Gatos to celebrate working together and agreed to a framework of a deal where we would give Microsoft a standalone Mac prototype to develop with in the fall. We were very excited to be working with a third-party company that seemed to understand and appreciate what we were doing.

Donkey
We discover who wrote an awkward game for the PC

The first version of the IBM PC was introduced in August 1981. Apple responded by running an ad in the *Wall Street Journal* with the headline "Welcome, IBM. Seriously." Even though he was usually tight with money, Steve Jobs allowed the Mac team to buy an early IBM machine to dissect and evaluate. The day it became available, we ran to the store and purchased one to take back to the lab.

Needless to say, we were not very impressed. From the perspective of the Macintosh that we were already in the midst of bringing to life, it seemed like ancient history the day it came out. There was little, if any, Woz-like cleverness in the hardware design. The IBM used dozens of extraneous chips without having any cool features. The 8088 was a decent processor compared to the 6502, but it paled next to the 68000 we were using in the Mac.

But the clunkiest part of the system was the software. MS-DOS seemed like a clone of an earlier system, CP/M, and even the demo programs lacked flair. It came with some games written in BASIC that were especially embarrassing.

The most embarrassing game was a driving game called Donkey that used low-resolution graphics. The player was supposed to drive a car down a slowly scrolling, poorly rendered "road," and had the ability to hit the space bar to toggle the jerky motion. Every once in a while a brown blob filled the screen, which was supposed to be a donkey manifesting in the middle of the road. If you didn't hit the space bar in time, you crashed into the donkey and lost the game.

We thought the concept of the game was as bad as the crude graphics it used. Since the game was written in BASIC, you could list it out and see how it was written. We were surprised to see that the comments at the top of the game proudly proclaimed the authors: Bill Gates and Neil Konzen. Neil was a bright teenage hacker who I knew from his work on the Apple II (and who would later become Microsoft's technical lead on the Mac project), but we were amazed such a thoroughly bad game could be co-authored by Microsoft's co-founder, and that he would actually want to take credit for it in the comments.

Desk Ornaments
A brief history of desk accessories

One of the first architectural decisions Bud and I made for the Macintosh system software in the spring of 1981 was that it would run only one application at a time. We barely had enough RAM or screen space to do even that, and we thought we'd benefit from the resultant simplifications. Besides, multitasking was supposed to be Lisa's forte, and we didn't want to usurp all of the reasons for buying a Lisa.

Bud Tribble was usually on an even keel, but one afternoon in the fall of 1981 he came into my office, unusually excited. "You know, I've been thinking about it. Even if we can only run one major application at a time, there's no reason we can't also have some little applications running in their own windows at the same time."

That sounded intriguing to me. "What kind of little programs? How are they different?" I asked.

Bud smiled. "You'd want tiny apps that were good at a specific, limited function that complements the main application. Like a little calculator, for example, that looked like a real calculator. Or maybe an alarm clock, or a notepad for jotting down text. Since the entire screen is supposed to be a metaphorical desktop, the little programs would be like desk ornaments, adorning the desktop with useful features."

"But where do we draw the line?" I asked. "What are the differences between an ornament and a real application?"

"Well, ornaments have to fit into the world of the main application," Bud responded, "but not the other way around. The main application owns the menu bar, for example, but maybe the ornaments can have a menu when they're active. The main application would still run its event loop, but it would occasionally pass events to the little guys. And, of course, you can cut-and-paste between them."

That sounded good to me, but we had plenty of other stuff to work on first. Bud left Apple in December 1981 to return to medical school, but I explained his concept to new team members and considered them to be part of our plan. Chris Espinosa liked the idea when we explained it to him, and he worked on a visualization of the calculator as part of learning to program with QuickDraw, culminating in a calculator construction set (see "Calculator Construction Set" on page 63). After getting the initial implementations of the window, menu, and event managers going, we eventually had enough of the rudiments done to give desk ornaments a try by May of 1982.

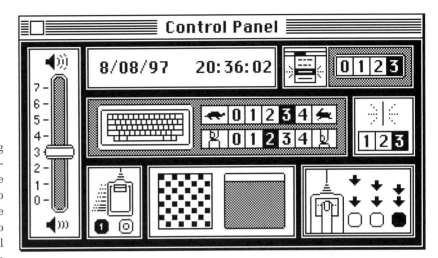

The control panel was compared to a "crib toy" by an early reviewer

The nascent Mac operating system already had an implementation of loadable device drivers, which allowed code to be loaded from disk to manage optional peripherals. I decided to cast desk ornaments as a special kind of driver, adding a few extra calls so they could maintain a window on the screen, receive events from the host application, and occasionally get some processing time to accomplish something. Applications were required to make a system call periodically to yield some time for ornaments to run, and had to occasionally pass events to them and follow a few other conventions for coexisting. The very first desk ornament was a boring example program called "TestOrn." It displayed a rectangular window with an incrementing counter, showing that it was capable of doing background processing, even when it wasn't the topmost window. It wasn't very impressive, but it became the template from which all the others sprang.

In the fall of 1982, the first pass of the User Interface Toolbox was completed, so I had time to work more on ornaments, which by this time had been renamed "desk accessories" by the pubs group—they thought the term "ornament" was, well, too ornamental. I wrote a simple clock and got the calculator going, modeled after Steve Jobs's design from the calculator construction set. The most interesting accessory I wrote in that spurt was a desktop pattern editor, which was a sort of miniature icon editor that let you edit an 8 × 8 pixel pattern by clicking to toggle the dots on and off. When you made a pattern you liked, you could make it the desktop pattern, filling the background of the screen with your new creation instead of the standard gray.

Within a couple of months, other people wanted to take a crack at writing desk accessories. Someone asked me if they could write one in Pascal. This wasn't easy because you had to pass parameters to the underlying driver in registers, which the Pascal compiler couldn't manipulate directly. I realized you could write a little bit of standard glue code in assembly language to do the dirty work and have most of your desk accessory written in Pascal. I wrote a number puzzle in Pascal as a test case, to prove it could be done (see "The Puzzle" on page 186).

But once again I had to get back to other things, and the desk accessories languished. By the spring of 1983, the ROM was beginning to stabilize, and we realized we had to get serious about the desk accessories that would ship with the initial system. Jerome assigned Donn Denman—who was taking a hiatus from working on Basic to help us finish the system—to help with desk accessories. Donn and I collaborated on finishing the calculator, with Donn doing the backend that interfaced with the floating-point routines. Donn was also responsible for the alarm clock and notepad.

Now that we had cut and paste working, I realized it would be useful to have a desk accessory that could hold commonly used snippets of text and graphics so they could be pasted into any application. I wrote a desk accessory called the "Gallery" that allowed you to manage a set of clippings using cut and paste, building it on top of the resource manager so it was easy to implement. Everyone seemed to like the functionality but not the name. I was explaining the situation to Larry Kenyon when he suggested we call it the "Scrapbook," which was perfect. And so the Scrapbook joined our growing armada of useful desk accessories.

The Macintosh's character encoding scheme allocated the upper half of the 8-bit character set to occasionally useful but rare characters, such as vowels with diacritical marks, that were not portrayed on the keyboard and were nearly impossible to remember. Steve Capps conceived of a desk accessory called "Key Caps" (named partially after himself?) that displayed a picture of the keyboard, with the keycaps changing depending on which meta-keys were pressed, and that allowed you to hunt for the special characters visually. He coded it up quickly and it became another great addition.

We needed a way to control various system parameters such as the sound volume and the mouse-scaling parameters. We decided a desk accessory would be perfect for this since it would be easy to access no matter what application a user was in. The last desk accessory I worked on before shipping, in November 1983, was the Control Panel. Susan Kare came up with a beautiful, highly graphical design (with no text whatsoever), which I implemented using a separate purgeable resource for each section so they didn't have to be in memory at once. It had a little rabbit and tortoise to represent a range of speeds, and lots of other graphical embellishments. After the Mac was released, one review described it as a crib toy, which I took more or less as a compliment.

The most controversial part of the Control Panel was the desktop pattern editor, which I had rescued from its earlier standalone incarnation. Users could select from a couple dozen prefabricated desktop patterns or edit their own. It was this latter capability that caused problems, as it was pretty easy to create abominably ugly patterns.

Bill Atkinson, the creator of MacPaint, complained to me that it was a mistake to allow users to specify their own desktop patterns because it was harder to make a nice one than it looked. He couldn't bear the thought of people creating ugly desktops. But I thought users should be free to do as they pleased because it was their desktop, plus they could always revert to one of the built-in patterns. In order to avoid having a potentially ugly desktop pattern mar MacPaint, he arranged it so MacPaint would allocate a window the size of the screen when it started up, and then fill it with the standard 50% gray pattern. This made his own desktop cover up the real one, and thus protected the poor users from their rash esthetic blunders, at least within the friendly confines of MacPaint.

contributed by
Bruce Horn

I Don't Have a Computer! December 1981
Bruce needs to find a computer, and fast

The Mac group was still very small when I joined it. We worked in what we called Texaco Towers, a nondescript office building behind a Texaco station at the corner of De Anza and Stevens Creek in Cupertino, long since gone (see "Texaco Towers on page 26").

The software group had offices on one side of the office building and the hardware group was on the other. Our offices were quite spare. One room toward the front of the building had a line printer (one of those big, noisy impact printers) that was driven by an Apple II. To print out your source code, you had to write them to an Apple II disk, run a program to swap the bytes or do some other manipulation, and then put the disk in the Apple II which would then run the line printer.

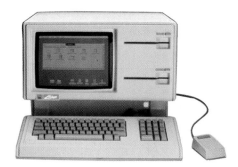

The Apple Lisa, which was the Macintosh's predecessor

Of course, to print out sources, you had to write some code. I had been on the Mac team for several weeks but still hadn't gotten a Lisa, the development machine we used. The Lisa was still under development, and the prototypes were very difficult to obtain.

I was starting to get a little frustrated and complained to Andy Hertzfeld at one point that maybe I should go work for a real company that could provide the appropriate tools for their software developers.

Andy mentioned this to Steve Jobs. Steve immediately said, "Well, should we fire him?" Andy replied, "No, just get him a computer!"

Later that day I received a note from Steve to go to a particular office in another Apple building; there would be a Lisa on the desk, and I could take that one and use it. I went over to the other building and found the office.

The nameplate on the office door said, "John Couch." John was the head of the group developing the Lisa. I wasn't sure this was really OK, but I had a note from Steve if anybody asked, so I walked into the office, unplugged the computer, and carted it away.

I still don't know to this day whether Steve had arranged this with John, or if John came back to the surprise of an empty desk, but I did get a lot of use out of that machine, maybe more than John ever did.

Hungarian   January 1982
A curious style of programming

The Macintosh used the same Motorola 68000 microprocessor as its predecessor, the Lisa, and we wanted to leverage as much code written for Lisa as we could. But most of the Lisa code was written in the Pascal programming language. Since the Macintosh had much tighter memory constraints, we needed to write most of our system-oriented code in the most efficient way possible. We did this using the native language of the processor: 68000 assembly language. Even so, we could still use Lisa code by manually translating it from the Pascal into assembly language.

We directly incorporated QuickDraw, Bill Atkinson's amazing bitmapped graphics package, since it was written in assembly language. We also used the Lisa window and menu managers, which we recoded in assembly language from Bill's original Pascal, thereby reducing the code size by a factor of 2 or so. Bill's lovely Pascal code was a model of clarity, so it was relatively easy to incorporate his programs.

The Mac lacked the memory-mapping hardware prevalent in larger systems, so we needed a way to relocate memory in software to minimize fragmentation as blocks got allocated and freed. The Lisa word-processor team had developed a memory manager with relocatable blocks that accessed memory blocks indirectly through "handles." The blocks could be moved as necessary to reduce fragmentation. We decided to use it for the Macintosh, again by recoding it from Pascal to assembly language.

The primary author of the Lisa word processor and its memory manager was Tom Malloy, an original member of the Lisa team and Apple's first recruit from Xerox PARC. Tom had worked on the Bravo word processor at PARC under the leadership of Charles Simonyi and had used many of the techniques that he learned there in his Lisa code.

Even though Bud Tribble had to leave the Mac team in December 1981 in order to retain his standing in the M.D./Ph.D. program at the University of Washington, he decided he could still do the initial implementation of the memory manager and was hoping to finish it quickly before classes started. He obtained a copy of the memory manager source from Tom Malloy, but he had a shock when he began to read the code.

Disappointingly, the memory manager source lacked comments. But the biggest obstacle was that the names selected for variables and procedures didn't include vowels! Every identifier was an unpronounceable jumble of consonants, making it much harder to understand the code because each variable's meaning was far from obvious. We wondered why the code was written in such an odd fashion. What happened to all of the vowels?

It turned out that Tom Malloy was greatly influenced by his mentor at Xerox, a strong-willed, eccentric programmer named Charles Simonyi. Charles held many strong opinions about the best way to create software, and developed and advocated a number of distinctive coding techniques that Tom brought to the Lisa team. One of the most controversial techniques was a particular method of naming the identifiers used by a program that mandated the beginning of each variable name be determined by the type of the variable.

However, most of the compilers in the early 80s restricted the length of variable names, usually to eight characters only. Since the beginning of each name had to include the type, there weren't enough characters left over to use a meaningful name describing the purpose of the variable. But Charles had a sort of workaround, which was to leave out all of the vowels out of the name.

The lack of vowels made programs look as though they were written in some inscrutable foreign language. Since Charles Simonyi was born and raised in Hungary (defecting to the west at age 17), his coding style came to be known as "Hungarian." Tom Malloy's memory manager was an outstanding specimen of Hungarian Pascal code in which the identifiers looked as though they were chosen by Superman's enemy from the 5th dimension, Mr. Mxyzptlk. Bud decided it would be too error prone to translate the Hungarian memory manager directly into assembly language. To get around this, he made a pass through it to strip the type prefixes and restore the vowels to all the identifier names (so you could read the code without getting a headache) before adding lots of block comments to explain the purpose of various subcomponents.

A few weeks later, when Bud came back to attend one of our first retreats, he brought with him a nicely coded, efficient assembly language version of the memory manager, complete with easy-to-read variable names. These immediately became a cornerstone of our rapidly evolving Macintosh operating system.

Calculator Construction Set   February 1982
Chris makes a Steve-approved calculator

Chris Espinosa was one of Apple's earliest and youngest employees, who started work for the company at the ripe age of 14. He left Apple in 1978 to go to college at UC Berkeley, but continued to do freelance work for them during the school year. This work included writing the official Apple II Reference Manual, the replacement for the legendary *Red Book*.

In the summer of 1981, Steve Jobs convinced Chris to drop out of school to come work on the Mac team full time, arguing that he could go back to school anytime, but there would be only one chance to help shape the Macintosh. Chris did so to become the manager of documentation for the Macintosh, starting in August 1981.

We needed technical documentation right away because we planned to seed third-party developers with prototype units in only a few months. Since the most important part of the Macintosh software was the QuickDraw graphics package, Chris decided to start documenting it.

In order to better understand QuickDraw, Chris wanted to write a demo program using it. He got excited about little utilities programs that we called "desk ornaments," which at that point were not yet implemented. He decided to work on a QuickDraw program to draw the calculator.

After playing around for a while, he came up with a calculator he thought looked pretty good. But the acid test was showing it to Steve Jobs, in his role as our esthetic compass, to see what he thought.

We all gathered around as Chris showed the calculator to Steve and then held his breath, waiting for Steve's reaction. "Well, it's a start," Steve said. "But, basically, it stinks. The background color is too dark, some lines are the wrong thickness, and the buttons are too big." Chris told Steve he'd keep working on its until Steve thought he got it right.

So, for a couple of days, Chris would incorporate Steve's suggestions from the previous day, but Steve continued to find new faults each time he saw it. Finally, Chris got a flash of inspiration.

The next afternoon, instead of a new iteration of the calculator, Chris unveiled what he called "The Steve Jobs Roll-Your-Own Calculator Construction Set." The included pull-down menus offered every possible choice regarding graphical attributes of the calculator. You could select line thickness, button sizes, background patterns, and everything else to design your own calculator.

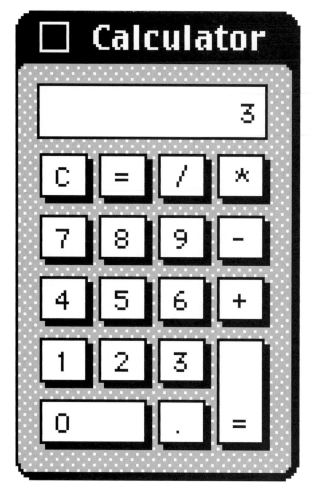

Steve took a look at the new program and immediately started fiddling with the parameters. After trying out alternatives for 10 minutes or so, he settled on something that he liked. When I implemented the calculator user interface (Donn Denman did the math semantics) for real a few months later, I used Steve's design. It remained the standard calculator on the Macintosh for many years, all the way up through OS 9.

–2000 Lines of Code
February 1982

It's hard to measure progress by lines of code

In early 1982, the Lisa software team was trying to buckle down for the big push to ship the software within the next six months. Some of the managers decided it would be a good idea to track the progress of each individual engineer in terms of the amount of code they wrote from week to week. They devised a form that each engineer was required to submit every Friday, which included a field for the number of lines of code written that week.

Bill Atkinson, the author of QuickDraw and the main user interface designer, who was by far the most important Lisa implementer, thought lines of code was a silly measure of software productivity. He thought his goal was to write as small and fast a program as possible, and the lines of code metric only encouraged writing sloppy, bloated, broken code.

He had recently worked on optimizing QuickDraw's region calculation machinery, and had completely rewritten the region engine using a simpler, more general algorithm—which, after some tweaking, made region operations almost six times faster. As a byproduct, the rewrite also saved around 2,000 lines of code.

He was just putting the finishing touches on the optimization when it was time to fill out the management form for the first time. When he got to the lines of code part, he thought about it for a second, and then wrote in the number: –2,000.

I'm not sure how the managers reacted, but I do know that after a couple more weeks they stopped asking Bill to fill out the form, and he gladly complied.

Mister Macintosh   February 1982
Steve has a unique idea for the software

Steve Jobs often came by Texaco Towers after dinner to see what was new, and we'd usually show him whatever recent progress we'd made. Sometimes he'd be pissed off about something, but other times he'd be really excited about a new idea.

I was the only one in the office one evening when he burst in, exclaiming that he'd had a flash of inspiration.

"Mr. Macintosh! We've got to have Mr. Macintosh!"

"Who is Mr. Macintosh?" I wondered.

"Mr. Macintosh is a mysterious little man who lives inside each Macintosh. He pops up every once in a while, when you least expect it, and then winks at you and disappears again. It will be so quick that you won't be sure if you saw him or not. We'll plant references in the manuals to the legend of Mr. Macintosh, and no one will know if he's real or not."

Engineers like myself always daydream about building surreptitious little hacks into software, but here was the co-founder and chairman of the company suggesting something really wild. I enthusiastically pressed him for details. Where should Mr. Macintosh appear? How often? What should he do when he shows up?

"One out of every thousand or two thousand times that you pull down a menu, instead of the normal commands, you'll get Mr. Macintosh, leaning against the wall of the menu. He'll wave at you, and then quickly disappear. You'll try to get him to come back, but you won't be able to."

I loved the idea and promised I would implement Mr. Macintosh, but not right away, since there were still so many more important things to get done. Steve told the idea to the marketing team, and eventually recruited the French artist Folon to do some renditions of Mr. Macintosh. I also asked my high school friend Susan Kare, who hadn't started with Apple yet, to try and draw some Mr. Macintosh animations.

Most of the Macintosh system software had to be packed into a 64 KByte ROM, and ROM space became scarcer as development proceeded and the system grew. It was eventually clear we'd never be able to fit bitmaps for Mr. Macintosh into the ROM, but I wasn't willing to give up on him yet.

I made the software that displayed the menus look at a special low memory location called the "MrMacHook" for an address of a routine. If the routine was present, it was called with parameters that let it draw in the menu box, and it returned a result that told the menu manager if it did anything. Using this, an application or system module could implement Mr. Macintosh (or perhaps his evil twin) if they saw fit.

I'm not sure if anybody ever actually implemented Mr. Macintosh or used the "MrMacHook" for something worthwhile.

Signing Party

The artists sign their work

The component of the Macintosh hardware that had the longest lead time was the tool that molded its distinctive plastic case. After tweaking the case design for more than six months, we built a small production run of 50 units with a soft-tooled case. The final design had to go out for hard tooling toward the end of February 1982 in order to meet the ship date we were aiming for at the time, which was January 1983.

The Mac team had a complicated set of motivations, but the most unique ingredient was a strong dose of artistic values. First and foremost, Steve Jobs thought of himself as an artist, and he encouraged the design team to think of themselves that way, too. The goal was never to beat the competition or to make a lot of money; it was to do the greatest thing possible, or even a little greater. Steve often reinforced the artistic theme. For example, he took the entire team on a field trip in the spring of 1982 to the Louis Comfort Tiffany museum because Tiffany was an artist who learned how to mass-produce his work.

Because the Macintosh team were artists, it was only appropriate that we sign our work. Steve came up with the awesome idea of having each team member's signature engraved on the hard tool that molded the plastic case so our signatures would appear inside the case of every Mac that rolled off the production line. Though most customers would never see them because a special tool was required to open the case, we would take pride in knowing our names were in there, even if no one else was aware of them.

We held a special signing party after one of our weekly meetings on February 10, 1982. Jerry Manock, manager of the industrial design team, spread out a large piece of drafting paper on the table to capture our signatures. Steve gave a little speech about artists signing their work, and then cake and champagne were served as he called each team member to step forward and sign their name for posterity. Burrell had the symbolic honor of going first, followed by members of the software team. It took 40 minutes or so for around 35 team members to sign. Steve waited until everyone else had signed before choosing a spot near the upper center and signed his name with a flourish, using all lower case letters as usual.

We were aware that the team was still growing rapidly, and in a few months there would be a new crop of key contributors who also deserved to sign the case. We decided to draw the line at the date of the signing party, but knew it would be tough to stick to that. We also wanted to add the signatures of a few major contributors who had left the project, including Steve Wozniak, Jef Raskin, and Bud Tribble. But that was supposed to be it.

Jerrell A. Ozama
Jerrold C. Manock
Daniel Kottke
Terry Cash
Pamela J. Wyman
Bill Atkinson
Vick Milledge
Bruce Horn
George Crow
Rod Holt
Andy Hertzfeld
Angeline Lo
Joanna Karin Hoffman
EDEN
HAP HORN
M.E. McCammon
Guy "tribble"
Peggy Alista
Patricia Sharp
steven jobs
Brian Robertson
Susan Kare
Larry Kenyon
Martin P. Haeberli
Colette Askeland
Larry Fidel
Christopher Espinosa
Mike Boich
Lynn Takahashi
Benjamin Pang
Bill Fernandez
Donn Denman
Patti King
David H. Roots
Ronald H. Nicholson
Matt Carter
Robert L. Belleville
Woz
Burrell Smith
Randy Wigginton
Linda Wilkin
Michael R. Murray

Over the next few months a few more signatures of people who weren't on the team at the time of the signing party managed to make it into the case. For a while Rod Holt held the line, but eventually Bob Belleville (who was hired in April 1982 as the software manager but soon became the overall engineering manager when Rod Holt retired) decided to add his own name. He also snuck in a few other key people, such as marketing manager Mike Murray and original evangelist Mike Boich.

And then, over time, names gradually began to disappear as Apple changed the case to make it easier to manufacture. Some design details were changed even before first ship, partially obscuring some of the signatures. Each time the case was revised, more names were left off, as dictated by the nature of the revision, until a substantial number of them were gone. I'm not sure which model was the last to have any names at all, but I'm pretty sure the Macintosh Classic, from the early 90s, didn't have any.

And Another Thing...

Friction between the Mac and Lisa teams

By early 1982, the Macintosh was beginning to be acknowledged as a significant project within Apple, instead of a quirky research effort. But it still remained somewhat controversial. Since the Mac was sort of like a Lisa that was priced like an Apple II, it was seen as potential competition from both groups. Also, Steve Jobs had a habit of constantly boasting about the superiority of the Mac team, which tended to alienate everybody else.

Larry Tesler, who came to Apple from Xerox PARC in the summer of 1980, was the manager of the Lisa Application Software team. He understood and appreciated the potential of the Macintosh and was very supportive of the project. He was concerned that some of the Lisa team didn't share his enthusiasm and thought it would be helpful for us to demonstrate the Mac to them and talk about our plans. He arranged for Burrell Smith and me to give a demo during a lunch meeting.

By this point, we had standalone Macintosh prototypes that no longer depended on an umbilical cord to a hosting Lisa. We didn't have the real plastic cases yet, but we were able to house the prototypes in plastic boxes of around the same size that were a passable imitation. The demo software environment was based on the "Lisa Monitor," a simple operating system cooked up by Rich Page (one of the main Lisa architects), that I got running on the Macintosh. The monitor was based on the UCSD Pascal system Filer and offered a simple, menu-based UI. We were able to boot the Mac into the monitor from an Apple II floppy, and then use it to launch various demo programs.

Burrell and I set up the prototype in a large conference room in the Lisa building. The Lisa applications team was seated around the table, but quite a few other team members had also gathered around—standing room only, perhaps 25 people in all. Larry Tesler gave us a nice introduction, and then we booted up the prototype and started to run through various demos while explaining the capabilities of the machine. Everything was going well, when suddenly there was a loud, insistent knock at the conference room door.

The door was flung open before anyone could respond, and in strode Rich Page, the systems wizard who was one of the main designers of the Lisa. Rich was a tall, bearded, ursine engineer who was equally adept at hardware and software. But I had never seen him looking as angry as he was at the moment.

Key members of the Lisa team:
Paul Baker, Bruce Daniels,
Chris Franklin, Rich Page,
Larry Tesler, and John Couch
(with arm on Lisa).

"You guys don't know what you're doing!" he growled, obviously in an emotional state of mind. "The Macintosh is going to destroy the Lisa! The Macintosh is going to ruin Apple!!!"

Burrell and I didn't know how to respond, and neither did anyone else in the room. Larry Tesler gave me an embarrassed glance, trying to figure out what to do. But Rich wasn't particularly interested in a response, he just wanted to vent his frustration.

"Steve Jobs wants to destroy Lisa because we wouldn't let him control it," Rich continued, looking as though he was going to start crying. "Sure, it's easy to throw a prototype together, but it's hard to ship a real product. You guys don't understand what you're getting into. The Mac can't run Lisa software; the Lisa can't run Mac software. You don't even care. Nobody's going to buy a Lisa because they know the Mac is coming! But you don't care!"

"You guys don't know what you're doing!

The Macintosh is going to destroy the Lisa!
The Macintosh is going to ruin Apple!!!"

With that, he turned around and strode out of the conference room as quickly as he had come in. He slammed the door as he left and the noise reverberated ominously in the stunned silence. There was some nervous laughter but nobody knew what to say. Larry Tesler started to apologize, explaining that Rich didn't speak for most of the Lisa team, when suddenly the door was flung open again and Rich Page was back, just as angry as before.

"And another thing," he said, before pausing to look directly at Burrell and myself. "I don't have any problem with you. I know it's not your fault. Steve Jobs is the problem. Tell Steve that I think he's destroying Apple!" Once again, he turned around and left abruptly, slamming the door for a second time. We steeled ourselves, wondering if he was going to return for a third round.

But this time Larry was able to finish apologizing, and then we finished the demo quickly and held a brief question-and-answer session, though everyone was still a bit shell-shocked from the unexpected outburst. We told Steve Jobs about Rich Page's oration later that afternoon, and he just shrugged, "That's Rich Page for you. He'll get over it."

The next morning Bill Atkinson called and told me that Rich Page felt bad about what happened and wanted to take Burrell and me out to lunch to apologize. So that afternoon the four of us went out for a long lunch during which Bill explained that Rich was just trying to do what he thought was right, and he didn't intend to get so emotional. Rich told us he really appreciated that Burrell and I were doing great work for the company, but he was frustrated that Steve was such a loose cannon and wasn't working for our mutual success. We left on decent terms, but in the back of my mind I was still worried that such obvious resentment would be a problem for us in the future.

Rosing's Rascals   March 1982
The Lisa Filer is radically redesigned with no time to spare

By the spring of 1982, the Lisa User Interface was finally settling down, and the software team was working feverishly to get everything ready to ship by their deadline in the fall. Though myriad problems remained, most of the applications were shaping up, and the team could finally sense a glimmer of light at the end of the long tunnel.

Dan Smith and Frank Ludolph were working on the Lisa Filer, the key application that managed files and launched other applications. It was beginning to come together, but Dan was still unsatisfied with the current design.

The Filer was based on a dialog window that prompted the user to select a document from a list, and then select an action like Open, Copy, or Discard, and then answer more questions depending on the selected action. There was so much prompting that it became known as the "Twenty Questions Filer." Dan thought it wasn't easy or enjoyable to use, but there just wasn't enough time left in the schedule for further experimentation, so they were pretty much stuck with it.

One afternoon Dan mentioned his dissatisfaction to Bill Atkinson, the main designer of the Lisa User Interface. Bill suggested they meet that evening at his home in Los Gatos for a brainstorming session to see if they could come up with a better design, even though it was probably too late to implement for the initial release.

Bill favored a more graphical approach and wanted to use small graphical images to represent files that could be manipulated by dragging them with a mouse. He remembered an interesting prototype he saw at M.I.T. called Dataland that allowed data objects to be spatially positioned over a large area. He adapted the idea for Lisa by allowing icons representing files and directories to be positioned on a scrolling, semi-infinite plane.

After a couple nights of fiddling around, Dan and Bill had an interesting mock-up with icons representing documents and folders, including a trash can with flies buzzing around it. The icons used a mask bitmap to define their borders so irregular shapes could be rendered seamlessly on the gray desktop. The new design seemed to have the simplicity and elegance they were striving for, and they began to get excited.

They were both eager and afraid to show the mock-up to the rest of the team. The design of the Filer was supposed to be frozen, and embarking on such a major revision would surely slip the schedule, which was already precariously close to unrealizable. They gathered up their courage and approached Wayne Rosing, the Lisa Engineering Manager, and explained their dilemma.

Wayne appreciated the potential of the new approach, but wasn't ready to slip the schedule to accommodate it. He thought it was barely possible to go with both the new design and the current schedule, if they could turn the mock-up into a solid working prototype in record time. He proposed a deal: he gave them permission to work on the new design in secret for the next two weeks. If they had a robust, stable prototype by then, he promised to support it. If they didn't, Bill and Dan promised to forget it and work to finish the earlier design.

Wayne extracted one additional promise from Bill. Under no circumstances was he to show the mock-up to Steve Jobs. Wayne knew Steve would have a strong reaction and would probably wreak havoc with the schedule accordingly. He didn't want Steve to see it until they knew they could pull it off.

Bill was used to showing off his latest advances to the Mac team, and this new, icon-based approach to file management was a particularly important one. Bruce Horn had started working on the Mac team the previous month and was already starting to develop our file manager, which Bud had christened "The Finder." Bruce had similar ideas about spacial filing, and he and I had created a prototype called the "micro-finder" that represented files as tabs that were spatially organized on a picture of a diskette. Bill thought it was important for us to see the new direction as soon as possible, so he left us a copy of his prototype with strict instructions not to show it to Steve.

We had a few close calls over the next couple of weeks as we played with the prototype, frantically quitting it when we heard Steve approaching. Finally, on the last day before the deadline expired, we must have cut it too close because Steve knew we were hiding something from him. We explained our promise to Bill, but Steve demanded to see it. We had to show it to him. He immediately fell in love with it and ran off to talk to Bill and Wayne, just as we feared.

Luckily, the development had gone well the last two weeks, and Wayne was ready to commit to the new approach and unveil it to the entire team. He called an all-hands meeting, to which Bill, Dan, Frank, and Wayne wore newly minted T-shirts labeled "Rosing's Rascals." Wayne explained the surreptitious nature of the two-week effort to the team while Bill set up the demo. Rosing's rascals had pulled it off, endowing the Lisa with a much more intuitive file manager that quickly became a hallmark of Apple's new user interface.

Gobble, Gobble, Gobble   March 1982
We interview candidates for software manager

When Bud told us in early December of 1981 that he had to leave the Mac team to go back to Seattle to keep his place in medical school, both Burrell and I were pretty shaken. We were worried we couldn't pull it off without Bud and that to fill his place we'd get some authoritarian manager who would wreck the unique spirit of our team. We expressed our concerns to Steve, and he promised we'd have a big say in hiring the new manager. He also said he'd personally protect us if a situation like the one we feared ever arose.

In January, we began interviewing candidates for the software manager position. We had high standards and expectations and interviewed a number of outstanding people, like Ed Taft, who became one of the first employees at Adobe, and Tim Mott, who helped start Electronic Arts, though for one reason or another neither took the job. But we also interviewed some more mundane candidates, which got pretty wild if Steve decided he didn't respect someone.

For example, Burrell, Steve and I interviewed Angeline Lo's former manager, whom she highly recommended. I knew the interview was going to be problematic as soon as the guy walked into the room. He was extremely straight-laced and uptight, and was dressed more like an insurance salesman than a technologist. He also seemed very nervous as he fumbled at our first few questions.

I could tell Steve was losing patience when he started to roll his eyes at the candidate's responses. Steve began to grill him with some unconventional questions.

"How old were you when you lost your virginity?" Steve asked

The candidate wasn't sure he had heard correctly. "What did you say?"

Steve repeated the question, changing it slightly. "Are you a virgin?" Burrell and I started to laugh as the candidate became more disconcerted. He didn't know how to respond.

Steve changed the subject. "How many times have you taken LSD?"

The poor guy was turning varying shades of red, so I tried to change the subject and asked a straightforward technical question. But Steve got even more impatient when he started to give a long-winded response.

"Gobble, gobble, gobble, gobble," Steve said, making turkey noises. This was too much for Burrell and me, and we started cracking up. "Gobble, gobble, gobble," Steve continued, laughing himself now.

At this point the candidate stood up. "I guess I'm not the right guy for this job," he said.

"I guess you're not," Steve responded. "I think this interview is over."

How old were you when you lost your virginity?

Software Wizard   March 1982
The Mac group gets business cards

By the spring of 1982, the Macintosh project was beginning to transition from a research effort into a mainstream project. We had to get more organized as the team grew.

Initially, we didn't have formal titles in the Mac group, but we needed to figure out what they were in order to get business cards made. My title with the Apple II group was "Senior Member of Technical Staff," which sounded dull to me. Peggy Alexio, Rod Holt's secretary, was ordering the business cards, and I told her I didn't want any because I didn't like my title.

The next day Steve Jobs came by and said he had heard I didn't want business cards. He wanted me to have them, though, and he didn't care what title I used. I could pick any title I liked. After a bit of thought I decided on "Software Wizard" because you couldn't tell where it fit in the corporate hierarchy and because it seemed a suitable metaphor to reflect the practical magic of software innovation.

When I told Burrell about my new title he immediately claimed "Hardware Wizard" for himself, even though I discouraged him because it diminished the uniqueness of my title. And as soon as word got around, lots of other folks on the Mac team started to change their titles to something more creative. Bruce Horn chose "Trailblazer," for example, reflecting his work for the Sierra Club as well as his programming inclinations. My nomination for the weirdest Apple business card title goes to Ed Tecot, whose title was "Not Andy Hertzfeld." I never knew whether to take that as a compliment or a slur. The trend persisted at Apple for many years, and even spread to other companies. But as far as I know, that's how it got started.

I was "Boy Guru" and "Exception Handler," and, eventually, when I worked in a group called "Class," I was "Class Clown." Bill Dawson's card read "I have no pants on." Darin Adler was "Cheese Host."

Scott Knaster

Andy Hertzfeld sitting on his car in 1985

US Festival   September 1982
We travel to Woz's rock festival

UNUSON PRESENTS

The 'US' Festival

SPECIAL GUEST

Woz guest

name

VIPs, thanks to Woz

As soon as Steve Jobs took over the Macintosh project in January 1981, he recruited many of the crucial early Apple employees who had worked on the Apple II, including Rod Holt, Jerry Manock, Dan Kottke, Randy Wigginton, and Apple co-founder Steve Wozniak.

Woz was enthusiastic about the Macintosh and started hanging out at the Mac team's new office at Texaco Towers, reviewing Burrell's design and learning the 68000 instruction set. But he was only working on the project for a couple of weeks when he crashed his Beechcraft Bonanza airplane while taking off near his home in Scott's Valley, sustaining a serious head injury and knocking out a couple of teeth.

The accident put Woz out of commission for almost two months. While he was recuperating, he had time to rethink his priorities and he decided he wanted to go back to college to earn his undergraduate degree (he needed just one more year of classes) instead of returning to Apple. He enrolled in the engineering program at UC Berkeley in the summer of 1981 under the assumed name of Rocky Clark, in honor of his dog Rocky and his new wife, Candi Clark.

A couple of months after the crash, Woz was listening to his favorite radio station, KFAT, and had an inspiration about putting together a music festival, a "Woodstock West" featuring his favorite progressive country music performers. He realized that while he had the financial wherewithal, he didn't know the first thing about the music industry and filed the idea away, but not before mentioning it to a few friends.

Later that fall, while attending classes at Berkeley, Woz was introduced to a new age entrepreneur named Dr. Peter Ellis. Peter was a former college radical who had organized a "survival fair" at San Jose State University in the 60s, during which he presided over the burial of a Ford Pinto. He hit it off with Woz and was enthusiastic about Woz's Woodstock West idea. Peter came up with the name "The US Festival" (in reaction to the "me" decade), and threw in other ideas like incorporating a technology fair and featuring a satellite linkup with rock musicians in Moscow. Woz wrote a sizable check to fund a new corporation named Unuson, which stood for "Unite Nations Using Singing Over Network," to create and produce the US Festival. Peter was the executive director.

Peter put together a team and plans began to take shape for an impressive three-day music festival to be held over Labor Day weekend at Glen Helen park in San Bernardino, around an hour away from Los Angeles. Unuson paid top dollar to hire Bill Graham, the foremost rock promoter in the country, to put together a superlative bill of first-class bands, including the Police, Fleetwood Mac, Tom Petty, Santana, and many others.

Woz encouraged his Apple friends to come to the US Festival by giving us special gold passes that got us in for free and permitted us to hang around back stage. Burrell Smith, Bill Budge and myself rented a camper and drove down together, skipping work to leave Friday morning so we could be there by the start of festivities that evening.

After the long drive, we parked the camper a half mile away from the festival site and walked the dusty trail to the main concert area amid the gathering crowd. We arrived just as the sun was setting and the first band, The Gang of Four, was taking the stage. After their set ended, we made our way to the stage area to test out our gold passes and see if we could find Woz.

The security guard at the stage door verified our gold passes and let us in, but seemed to resent doing it. I had never been backstage at a rock concert before. There was a nice spread of cold cuts and beverages in front of a line of trailers that served as dressing rooms for the bands. Lots of people were milling around, including roadies, groupies, bodyguards and even the occasional rock star.

Suddenly I heard a very loud noise as someone rode into the backstage area on the largest motorcycle I had ever seen. At first I thought it was a Hell's Angel, but it turned out to be Bill Graham in a black leather jacket and sunglasses, scowling as he ordered people around. We didn't feel very welcome and were frequently asked to show our passes. It seemed as though the festival staff was resentful that Woz's friends were allowed to be there.

We finally spotted Woz and waved to get his attention. He came over to us, looking happy and excited.

"Do you guys want to introduce a band? Which one? I've got it worked out with Bill Graham so my friends can introduce their favorite band if they want to. We still have plenty of slots left."

I was intrigued since one of my favorite groups, the Kinks, were scheduled for Saturday afternoon. But getting up on stage in front of hundreds of thousands of people sounded utterly terrifying to me. I declined, but then I noticed Burrell's eyes had lit up and he was very excited.

"Santana? Can I introduce Santana? That would be so cool..." Carlos Santana was one of Burrell's favorite guitarists.

That evening, when we got back to the camper, Burrell wrote a brilliant short, sweet and humorous introduction of Santana to use the next day, and started to memorize it by reading it aloud. It was all he could talk about until we made our way backstage early on Saturday morning. Burrell waited expectantly until Woz showed up. He read Woz his introduction, which Woz really liked.

Woz led Burrell up onto the stage to introduce him to Bill Graham and tell him about the upcoming Santana intro. But lots of people wanted to talk with Woz and he got distracted, leaving Burrell alone on stage for a few minutes, just as Bill Graham appeared, looking pissed off as usual.

Bill Graham took one look at Burrell and grimaced. "Who the #$*! are you? What are you doing on the goddamn stage?"

Burrell explained he was a friend of Woz's and was waiting onstage to introduce Santana. He pulled out his notes for the introduction from his pocket and waved them for Bill Graham to see.

"Sure you are," Bill Graham responded sarcastically. "I'm going to introduce Santana. And you're gonna get the #%$*! off the stage right now, this instant!"

Burrell looked around for Woz but couldn't spot him. He started to argue but stopped short when he saw how furious Bill Graham became.

Bill Graham motioned to one of his ubiquitous bodyguards, a huge guy with long hair and tattoos covering his forearms. "Please escort this gentleman from the premises," he ordered peremptorily, "and don't let him return!" The bodyguard literally picked Burrell up off the ground by the back of his shirt collar and carried him off the stage and then completely out of the backstage area.

That was the last we saw of Burrell for the next six hours, and we wondered what had happened to him. Finally, he reappeared just before Tom Petty started the final set of the day. Bill Graham's thug had dragged him outside the festival gates and confiscated his

Crowd at the US Festival at Glen Helen Regional Park in San Bernardino, California Facing page: gold pass for the US festival

gold pass. Burrell didn't know what to do, but eventually he obtained another gold pass by walking a few miles to the house that Woz had rented for the weekend. Woz was sorry about what had transpired and asked Burrell if he wanted to try again on Sunday to introduce another band, but this time Burrell was wary and quickly declined. In fact, he had had enough of the US Festival and persuaded Bill and me to drive back home early on Sunday morning without attending the last day of shows.

part
three

The future is here.
It's just not evenly
distributed yet.

William Gibson

And Then He Discovered **Loops!** April 1982

Bob has written many lines of code

We interviewed quite a few candidates to replace Bud Tribble as the software manager before encountering Bob Belleville, who was one of the main hardware designers of the Xerox Star, the first commercial computer with a graphical user interface. He was intelligent, soft-spoken, and dryly skeptical about human nature. One of his many aphorisms was "The Law of Conservation of Misery," which said no matter what course of action is taken, the total human misery in any given situation is maintained. It seemed particularly applicable to large computer companies.

It looked as though Bob's background was stronger in hardware, so we were somewhat skeptical about his software expertise, but he claimed to be equally adept at both. His latest project was a rebellious, skunk works effort to make a low-cost version of the Star called "Cub," which used an ordinary Intel microprocessor (the 8086). This was heresy to the PARC orthodoxy that felt you needed custom, bit-slice processors to get sufficient performance for a Star-type machine. Bob had written much of the software for Cub himself.

"I've got lots of software experience," he declared. "In fact, I've personally written over 350,000 lines of code."

I thought that was pretty impressive, although I wondered how it was calculated. I couldn't begin to honestly estimate how much code I had written since there are too many different ways to construe lines of code.

That evening, I went out to dinner with my friend Rich Williams, who started at Apple around the same time I did. Rich had a great sense of humor. I told him about the interview with Bob and how he claimed to have written over 350,000 lines of code.

"Well, I bet he did," said Rich. "But then he discovered loops!"

busy being born

A visual history of the development of the Lisa/Macintosh user interface

The Macintosh User Interface wasn't designed all at once; it was actually the result of almost five years of experimentation and development at Apple, starting with graphics routines Bill Atkinson began writing for Lisa in late 1978. Like any evolutionary process, there were many false starts and blind alleys along the way. It's a shame these tend to be lost to history, since there is a lot we can learn from them.

Fortunately, the main developer of the user interface, Bill Atkinson, was an avid, lifelong photographer, and he had the foresight to document the incremental development of the Lisa User Interface (which more or less became the Mac UI after a few tweaks) with a series of photographs. He kept a Polaroid camera by his computer and took a snapshot each time the user interface reached a new milestone, which he collected in a loose-leaf notebook. I'm excited to be able to reproduce and annotate them here because they offer a fascinating, behind-the-scenes glimpse of how the Mac's breakthrough user interface was crafted.

. . . .

The first picture in Bill's notebook is from Bill's previous project, just before starting work on the Lisa: Apple II Pascal. The high-performance graphics routines Bill wrote for Apple II Pascal in the fall of 1978 led right into his initial work on the Lisa.

The center and right photos, from the spring of 1979, were rendered on the actual Lisa Display system,

Apple II graphics for Pascal

First Characters on Lisa

Hand-Built Font Proportional Spacing

featuring the 720 × 360 resolution that remained constant all the way through to the shipping product. No Lisa existed at this point; these were done on a wired-wrapped prototype card for the Apple II. The middle picture shows the very first characters ever displayed on a Lisa screen; note the variable-width characters. The rightmost picture has more proportional text about the Lisa display system, rendered in a font Bill designed by hand.

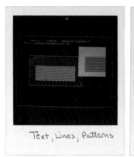

Text, Lines, Patterns

25×80 + softkeys
80×9 · 720 dots wide
Scanline pointers

Patterns

The leftmost picture illustrates the first graphics primitives Bill wrote for LisaGraf (which was eventually renamed to QuickDraw in 1982) in the spring of 1979, rendering lines and rectangles filled with 8 × 8 one-bit patterns. The power and flexibility of the patterns are illustrated in the rightmost shot, which were our poor man's substitute for color. Color was too expensive (at the required resolution) in the early 80s.

The middle picture depicts the initial user interface of the Lisa, based on a row of "soft-keys" drawn at the bottom of the screen, which would change as a user performed a task. These were inspired from work done at HP, where some of the early Lisa designers hailed from.

Faster Lines

Polygon Fill

Here are some more demos of the initial graphics routines. Bill made line-drawing blindingly fast with an algorithm that plotted "slabs" of multiple pixels in a single memory access. The rightmost picture shows how nonrectangular areas could also be filled with patterns.

Halftone Images

Here are some scanned images, showing off Lisa's impressive resolution for the time, which Bill scanned using a modified fax machine. He was always tweaking the half-toning algorithm, which mapped grayscales into patterns of monochrome dots. Bill had made versions of these for the Apple II that Apple distributed on demo disks, but these higher resolution Lisa versions were much more impressive.

The left and middle pictures show off the first sketch program, an early ancestor of MacPaint, that allowed mouse-based drawing with patterns and a variety of brush shapes. I think these are perhaps a bit out of sequence, done in early 1980. The rightmost picture shows the final soft-key-based UI, which is about to change radically…

…into a mouse/windows-based user interface. This is obviously the biggest single jump in the entire set of photographs, and the place where I most wish Bill had bothered to date them. It's tempting to say the change was caused by the famous Xerox PARC visit, which took place in mid-December 1979, but Bill thinks the windows predated that, although he can't say for sure.

The leftmost picture shows different fonts in overlapping windows, but we didn't have a window manager yet, so they couldn't be dragged around. The middle window shows the first pop-up menu, which looks just like Smalltalk, as does the simple, black title bar. The rightmost picture shows we hadn't given up on the soft-keys yet.

First SketchPad

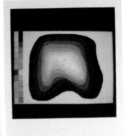

Initial Lisa
User Interface

windows

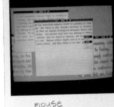

mouse
& pop-up menu

windows + soft keys
pop-up menu

"Thing & Place"

First Scroll Bar

Folder with menu at bottom

By now, it was the spring of 1980 and things were happening fast. The leftmost picture shows the earliest text selection, using a different highlighting technique than we ended up with. It also shows a "command bar" at the bottom of the screen. We had also started to use non-modal commands (make a selection, then perform an action, instead of the other way around).

The middle picture shows the very first scroll bar, on the left instead of the right, before the arrow scroll buttons were added. It also has a folder-tab style title bar, which would persist for a while before being dropped (Bill says that at that point, he was confusing documents and folders). The rightmost photo shows we adopted the inverse selection method of text highlighting.

· · · · · · · · · · · ·

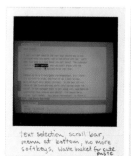

text selection, scroll bar, menu at bottom, no more softkeys, Waste basket for cute paste

Scroll box not proportional
I-Beam Cursor for text
Commit to One-Button Mouse

early Spline algorithm

By the summer of 1980, we had dropped the soft-keys. The leftmost photo shows we had mouse-based text editing going, complete with the first appearance of the clipboard, which at that point was called "the wastebasket." Later, it was called the "scrap" before we finally settled on "clipboard." There was also a Smalltalk-style scrollbar, with the scroll box proportional to the size of the document. Note there are also two sets of arrows, since a single scrollbar weirdly controlled both horizontal and vertical scrolling.

The next picture shows that we dropped the proportional scroll box for a simpler, fixed-size one, since we were afraid users wouldn't understand the proportionality. It also shows the I-Beam text cursor for the first time. At this point, we were finally committed to the one-button mouse, after a long, protracted, internal debate.

The rightmost picture shows Bill playing around with splines, which are curves defined by a few draggable control points. QuickDraw didn't end up using splines, but the picture is still notable for the first appearance of the "knobbie" (a small, draggable, rectangular affordance for a point).

· · · · · · · · · · · ·

By now, it was the fall of 1980. The middle picture shows us experimenting with opened and closed windows, which were eventually dropped (but made a comeback in the 90s and are in most systems today one way or another). The rightmost picture shows the first window resizing by dragging a gray outline, although it's not clear how resizing was initiated.

· · · · · · · · · · · ·

The middle picture shows that windows can be repositioned by dragging a gray outline. We wanted to drag the whole window, like modern user interfaces do today, but the processors weren't fast enough in those days. As far as I know, NeXTStep was the first system to drag the entire window.

The rightmost picture shows the first appearance of pull-down menus, with a menu bar at the top of the window instead of the top of the screen, which

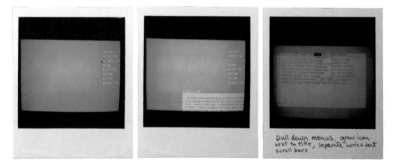

Pull down menus, grow icon next to title, separate horizontal vert scroll bars

is the way it's still done in Windows. By this point, we also gave up on using a single scroll bar for both horizontal and vertical scrolling; it's looking very much like what the Mac shipped with in 1984 now.

This set of pictures illustrates the Lisa desktop, circa the end of 1980, with a tab-shaped title, followed by a menu bar attached to the window. Windows could be reduced to tabs on the desktop. We've also changed the name of the clipboard to "the scrap," an old typesetting term.

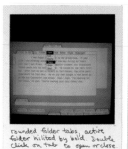  

rounded folder tabs, active folder hilited by bold. Double click on tab to open or close

Menus moved to top. Grow icon in bottom right. Both scroll bars required

The leftmost picture mentions the first use of double-clicking to open and close windows. The middle picture represents a real breakthrough by putting the menu bar at the top of the screen instead of the top of each window. The menu bar contains the menus of the "active folder," which is the topmost window. By this point, the grow icon found its way to the bottom right, at the intersection of the horizontal and vertical scrollbars, which stuck. This is the first picture that is really recognizable as the shipping Macintosh.

· · · · · · · · · · · ·

By now, it was early 1981, and the UI was beginning to shape up. The leftmost picture shows a window with scrollbars that look a lot like the ones in the final UI. The middle folder illustrates split views, which were used by Lisa's spreadsheet

split folder

the dialog box

application. The rightmost picture contains the first appearance of a dialog box, which at the time ran the entire length of the screen, just below the menu bar.

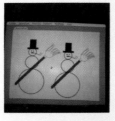

SketchPad in a Folder

Normal Text

Bold

Now that the basic window structure was stabilizing, Bill turned his attention back to the graphics routines. He worked more on the Sketch program (the forerunner of MacPaint); the snowman drawing on the left is a clue that it's now winter 1981. He added algorithmic text styles to the graphics, adding styles of bold (pictured on the right), as well as italic, outline, and shadow.

. . . .

At this point Bud Tribble was living at Bill's house, and he tended to sleep during the day and work all night, so Bill drew the phase diagram on the left with the sketch program. The middle picture shows fast ovals, which were added to LisaGraf as a basic type in Spring 1981, using a clever algorithm that didn't require multiplication. They were quickly followed by rectangles with rounded corners, or "roundrects", illustrated on the right, which were suggested by Steve Jobs (see "Round Rects Are Everywhere!" on page 46).

. . . .

By May 1981, the Lisa user interface was beginning to solidify. The leftmost photo shows scrollable documents of different types in overlapping windows, still sporting folder tabs for titles.

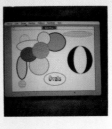

rounded-corner pull-downs

Sketchpad & graphical menus

The middle picture shows how roundrects began to creep into various UI elements, such as menus, providing a more sophisticated look, especially when combined with drop shadows. The rightmost photo shows how menus could be graphical, as well as text-based.

"THE TRAY"
Check marks in menus
no closed tabs on desk

Ideas for Graphics Editor

Office / Desk filer
lower box is exploded view

graphical diskette
directory.

The Lisa team was worried about the closed window tabs being obscured by other windows on the desktop, so Bill added a standard menu on the extreme left called "the tray," which could show and hide opened windows. The middle and right pictures portray a prototype Bill created for the Lisa Graphics Editor (which eventually evolved into MacDraw), to demonstrate that modes could sometimes be useful; it was the first program to select modes with a graphical palette, which eventually became the main user interface of MacPaint.

. . . .

The last major change in the Lisa User Interface was moving to an icon-based file manager in March 1982. The leftmost picture is an early mock-up done in the graphics editor, using a two-level hierarchy; selecting an icon in the top pane displays its contents in the bottom one. By the middle photo, Bill had arrived at something very similar to the shipping design, complete with a trash can at the lower right (see "Rosing's Rascals" on page 74). Note that the folder tab on windows had disappeared, replaced by a rectangular title bar that's partially inverted when highlighted.

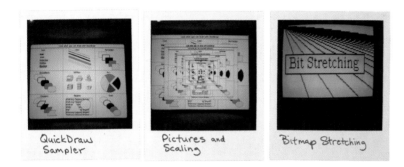

QuickDraw Sampler   Pictures and Scaling   Bitmap Stretching

Finally, Bill renamed "LisaGraf" to "QuickDraw" in the spring of 1982 because he wanted a name that was also suitable for the Macintosh. He added two related features to meet the burgeoning needs of the Lisa applications: pictures and scaling. Pictures were a way of recording graphics operations into a data structure for later playback; this became the basis of both our printing architecture and cutting and pasting graphics. Since pictures could be drawn into an arbitrarily sized rectangle, it also caused Bill to add bitmap-scaling features as well.

Most users and developers experienced the user interface as a completed whole only, so they tended to think of it as static and never changing, when in fact these pictures show it was always evolving as we gained more experience and tackled more application areas. A user interface is never good enough, and, while consistency between applications is an important virtue, the best developers will continue to innovate when faced with new problems or when they see a much better way to accomplish something. As usual, Bob Dylan said it best when he wrote in 1965: "He not busy being born, is busy dying."

I Still Remember Regions   April 1982
We almost lose Bill in a car accident

The single most significant component of the original Macintosh technology was QuickDraw, the graphics package written by Bill Atkinson for the Lisa project. QuickDraw pushed pixels around the frame buffer at blinding speeds to create the celebrated user interface. One of QuickDraw's main jobs was to provide the primitives for quickly drawing text and graphics into overlapping windows whenever the window a user was drawing into was partially obscured by other windows. Applications could just draw without worrying if their window was obstructed because QuickDraw, with a little help from the Window Manager, took care of the clipping to make sure pixels stayed inside of their window.

Overlapping windows could form complex shapes, especially if their corners were rounded. The key data structure in QuickDraw was called a "region," which compactly represented an area of the screen. QuickDraw provided routines that allowed the programmer to define regions by using the built-in drawing primitives, and to perform operations with them such as union and intersection. Most importantly, all of the QuickDraw drawing primitives clipped to the intersection of three different regions to allow drawing into obscured windows. We considered QuickDraw's speed and deftness at region handling to be the most significant "crown jewel" in Apple's entire arsenal.

The region data structure was a variable-sized list of what Bill called "inversion points," the coordinate values where black changed to white or vice versa. Since most regions were mostly rectangular, there weren't many inversion points, so regions were quite compact. But occasionally there were lots of inversions, like in a circle, so regions grew as necessary.

QuickDraw was written entirely by Bill Atkinson, and in the spring of 1982, it was still evolving. He had recently sped up region operations by more than a factor of 4. The concept of "pictures," a set of drawing operations grouped together for easy playback, was recently added to the package and hadn't really settled down yet. At this point, the Lisa applications were beginning to come together and Bill was changing QuickDraw in response to what they needed.

One morning, we were shocked to hear Bill had gotten into a really bad car accident on his way into work. Apparently he had turned a corner and not seen a parked truck. He slammed his little Corvette into the truck, shearing the roof off the top of his car. Bill was knocked unconscious and got pretty banged up, but he was still in one piece. One of the

Facing page: Steve Jobs and
Bill Atkinson in January 1984

police officers who surveyed the wrecked Corvette commented that it was a miracle Bill wasn't decapitated. This was a little more than a year after Woz's plane crash, but it brought back memories of that.

When Steve Jobs heard about the accident he immediately jumped into his car and drove to the hospital where Bill had been taken. He was in a hospital bed, and had only recently regained consciousness by the time Steve arrived. He sustained a head injury and lost some blood, but luckily there were no major problems.

"Is everything OK?" Steve asked upon entering Bill's room. "We were pretty worried about you."

Bill turned his head and looked at Steve. He managed a painful smile. "Don't worry, Steve, I still remember regions."

I must add a few details to Andy's story of Bill's accident. The truck Bill hit straddled a road he drove on every day near his home. There had never before been a vehicle at that location. He didn't see it soon enough to stop. But he rolled his upper body onto the passenger seat and thus avoided decapitation. The Corvette emerged from the other side of the truck and proceeded down the road on its own. After a block or so, it crossed a major boulevard and came to rest on the other side. Bill regained consciousness just long enough to tell the police officer, "Call Larry Tesler and tell him I'll be late for the meeting." He then passed out and forgot the conversation. But I did get the call.

Larry Tesler

You Can't Fire Bruce!

May 1982

The software team has a personality clash

Even though he was only 22 years old when he joined the Mac team, Bruce Horn already had 7 years of experience tinkering with graphical user interfaces. He was recruited as a 14-year-old by Ted Kaehler to do some programming experiments in Smalltalk at Alan Kay's Learning Research Group in the mid-70s, and he took to it so well that he had worked part-time at Xerox PARC ever since. By the time he joined the Mac team in late 1981, he was an expert in object-oriented programming and graphical user interfaces.

Bruce was a bright, idealistic, and uncompromising programmer who fit right in with the prevailing values of the team, and he quickly became an important contributor to the Macintosh system software effort. He was slated to work on the application that graphically represented files, which Bud Tribble had dubbed the "Finder." But after a few weeks, he convinced us we were missing a crucial part of the system he called the "Resource Manager," which managed the various chunks of data—such as text strings and images— that an application relied on. According to Bruce, the Resource Manager would also be used by the Finder application for managing icons and bindings between documents and applications (see "Resource Manager Countdown" on page 116).

Bruce was busy implementing the Resource Manager when Bob Belleville arrived on the scene as the new software manager in April 1982, replacing Bud Tribble, who had returned to medical school at the end of 1981. Bob was also a Xerox alumnus, but otherwise he and Bruce couldn't have been more different. Bob was pragmatic and somewhat authoritarian, with a worldview substantially forged by his stint in the Navy. He immediately began to clash with Bruce's idealism.

I spent a lot of time helping Bob get up to speed when he first started on the project, and we got along well at first even though we had very different perspectives. Bob was a little bit older than most of the core team and had a wife and children. He was also naturally skeptical. He didn't understand why we were so excited about the Macintosh, which he saw as just another increment along a continuum. "I don't get it," he complained to me. "This computer will be obsolete in a year, and then there will be another one, and another one after that. What's so special about this one?"

The first software team meeting Bob presided over took place soon after we moved from Texaco Towers to Bandley 4. The meeting was held in the main conference room around a long table Burrell and I used for after-hours ping-pong. Up to this point, the software team had a very loose management style, without formal meetings, so this was something new for us. Bob went around the table and had each person tell the group what they were currently working on and when they were planning to complete it.

When it was Bruce Horn's turn, he described his Resource Manager work but refused to give a date as to when it would be finished. Bob visibly bristled and asked him to make the best estimate he could, which Bruce refused to do, claiming that it wouldn't be accurate. Bob wanted Bruce to put the Resource Manager aside to work on the Finder, which Bob thought had much higher priority, but Bruce refused to go along with him because of the dependence of the Finder design on the Resource Manager. They were at an impasse, but finally Bob said he'd resolve it by talking with Bruce privately, and the meeting was able to progress.

I was worried about how the obvious tension between Bruce and Bob would be resolved. A few days later, Bruce came to me in the late afternoon, visibly shaken.

"You wouldn't believe what just happened! I finally had my meeting with Bob about the Resource Manager."

"So what happened?"

"We started off talking about the work that was needed to finish it, but I guess I said something he didn't like. He started getting all weird, and told me I was insubordinate, that he was my manager, and that I had to follow his orders or else. 'Or else what?' I asked him. You wouldn't believe what he did!"

"What did he do?" I asked, not knowing what to expect.

"He threatened me! Can you believe that? For a second I thought we were going to have a fistfight, but he started smiling as if he was joking. I didn't know what to think. Finally, he said we'd talk more later and walked away."

The image of Bruce and Bob duking it out was ludicrous. Bruce was at least 8 inches taller than Bob and probably more than 60 pounds heavier. Bruce's father was an ex-professional football player before he became a doctor, and Bruce was built the same way. I tried to calm him down and told him I would help him get this resolved. The next morning I went to Bob Belleville's office as soon as I arrived at work.

"I don't get it," he complained to me. **"This computer will be obsolete in a year, and then there will be another one, and another one after that. What's so special about this one?"**

"Good. I'm glad you're here," Bob greeted me. "I need to talk to you about Bruce Horn."

"Yes, that's what I want to talk about," I responded. "Bruce told me about the conversation you had last night."

"Well, it's not a problem anymore," Bob said, flashing a cryptic smile.

"Why not?" I asked. Something didn't sound right to me.

"I decided to fire him. He doesn't respect authority enough to work on this team."

Now it was my turn to get upset. "You can't fire Bruce!" I said, stating something that I thought was obvious. "He's doing really important work for us, and losing him would set us back months."

"Keeping him will set us back even more, because he's a trouble maker, and he'll cause more trouble in the future."

But I was adamant, defending Bruce until Bob got frustrated with me. "Well, Andy, I am very disappointed in you. I thought you had more sense than that." I walked out of his office not knowing what was going to happen.

Later that day, when Steve Jobs came by for his usual early evening visit, I told him what had transpired and repeated how bad it would be if we lost Bruce. I don't know what Steve eventually said to Bob, but he apparently dropped his plan to fire Bruce since he never mentioned it again. But I never thought of Bob the same way after that, and I think that was when he started to have problems with me as well.

Alice   June 1982
The Macintosh's first great game

Even though Bruce Daniels was the manager of the Lisa software team, he was very supportive of the Mac project. He had written the mouse-based text editor we were using on the Lisa to write all of our code, and he even transferred to the Mac team as a mere programmer for a short while in the fall of 1981, before deciding he preferred managing for Lisa. He would sometimes visit us to see what was new, but this time he had something exciting to show us.

"You've got to see the new game Steve Capps wrote," he told me while he was connecting his hard drive to my Lisa. He booted up into the Lisa Monitor development system, which featured a character-based UI similar to UCSD Pascal, and launched a program named "Alice." Steve Capps, who started at Apple in September 1981, was the second member of the Lisa printing team. I had seen him around but not met him yet.

The screen turned black and then, after a few seconds delay, a three-dimensional chessboard in exaggerated perspective filled most of the screen. On the rear side of the board was a set of small white chess pieces arranged in their standard positions. Suddenly, pieces started jumping in long, slow parabolic arcs, growing larger as they got closer.

Soon there was one specimen of each type of piece, all rather humanoid looking except for the tower-like rook, lined up on the front rank of the board, waiting for the player to click on one to start the game. The player was able to move like the piece they chose, so it was prudent to click on the queen, at least at first.

The pieces jumped back to their natural positions on the far side of the board and an image of a young girl in an old fashioned dress floated down to the front row. It was Alice from Lewis Carroll's *Alice in Wonderland* and *Through the Looking Glass*, drawn in the style of the classic John Tenniel illustrations. The player controlled Alice and viewed the board from her perspective, facing away from the player so you saw her from the rear only.

A three-digit score, rendered in a large, ornate Gothic font, appeared centered near the top of the screen, and then the game began in earnest with opposing chess pieces suddenly leaping into the air, one at a time, in rapid succession. If you stood in one place for too long, an enemy piece would leap onto Alice's square, capturing her and ending the game.

It didn't take long to figure out that if you clicked on a square that was a legal move, Alice would leap to it, so it wasn't too hard to jump out of the way of an enemy piece. And, if you managed to leap onto the square of another piece before it could move out of the way, you knocked it out of action and were rewarded with some points. You won the game if Alice was the last one standing.

I was impressed at the prodigious creativity required to recast *Through The Looking Glass* as an action-packed video game that was beautiful to behold and fun to play. Alice was also addicting, although it took some practice to survive for more than a few minutes. Obviously, we needed to have it running on the Mac as soon as possible.

Bruce Daniels was pleased that we liked the game. "Capps could probably port Alice to the Mac," he said, anticipating what we were thinking. "Do you think you could get him a prototype?"

Everyone agreed we should get Capps a Mac prototype right away. I accompanied Bruce Daniels back to the Lisa building (where the rules required that non-Lisa employees be escorted by a Lisa team member), and I finally got to meet Steve Capps, who seemed easygoing and friendly, with a self-deprecating sense of humor. Later that afternoon, he visited Texaco Towers, and I gave him the prototype and answered a few questions about the screen address and the development environment. He assured me Alice wouldn't take long to port.

Two days later, Capps came over to present us with a floppy disk containing the newly ported Alice game, now running on the Macintosh. It ran even better on the Mac than the Lisa because the Mac's faster processor enabled smoother animation. Pretty soon almost everybody on the software team was playing Alice for hours at a time.

I must have played hundreds of games of Alice over the next couple of weeks, but the most prolific and accomplished player was Joanna Hoffman, the Mac's first marketing person. Joanna liked to come over to the software area toward the end of the day to see what was new, and she usually ended up playing Alice, for longer and longer periods. She had a natural talent for the game and enjoyed relieving work-related stress by knocking out the rival chess pieces. She complained about the game being too easy, so Capps obliged her by tweaking various parameters to keep it challenging for her, which was probably a mistake because the game became too hard for average players.

Steve Jobs didn't play Alice very much, but he was duly impressed by the obvious programming skill it took to create it. "Who is this Capps guy? Why is he working on the Lisa?" he said as soon as he saw the program, mentioning Lisa with a hint of disdain. "We've got to get him onto the Mac team!"

But the Lisa was still months away from shipping and Capps was needed to finish the printing software, so Steve wasn't able to finalize the transfer. One weekend Capps ran into Steve Jobs in Los Gatos and was told, "Don't worry, the Mac team is going to nab you!" Finally, a compromise was reached that allowed Capps to transfer over in January 1983 after the first release of the Lisa was completed.

Capps quickly became a crucial member of the Mac team, adding fresh energy and talent as we entered the home stretch, helping to finish the Toolbox and the Finder, as well as working on other stuff like Guided Tour diskette. But he also found time to embellish Alice with more cool features.

One day he showed me Alice's hidden Cheshire Cat menu, which allowed players to adjust various preferences. Alice didn't have a menu bar, so it was part of the game to figure out how to invoke the preferences. It was accomplished by clicking on the score at the top of the screen, which caused a detailed, John Tenniel–inspired Cheshire Cat bitmap to slowly come into view. Clicking on different parts of the cat set various preferences. Capps also created an exquisite, tiny rendering of the Cheshire Cat to serve as Alice's icon.

Over time, he added some interesting variations on the preferences, invoked by clicking on various parts of the Cheshire Cat. For example, one variation made some of the squares of the chessboard disappear at random, causing unlucky pieces to fall into oblivion. He also added a feature Woz suggested: as the cursor moved to the back of the board, its image got correspondingly smaller, adding to the illusion of depth.

By the fall of 1983, Capps started thinking about the best way to get Alice to market. One possibility was publishing it through Electronic Arts, which was founded a year earlier by Trip Hawkins, Lisa's former marketing manager. But Steve Jobs thought the game at least partially belonged to Apple, and insisted that Apple be the publisher. He negotiated a modest deal with Capps, promising him Apple would do a deluxe job with the packaging and marketing.

Alice was announced at the launch and featured in the original brochure, but it didn't become available until a couple of months later. True to Steve's word, the packaging was beautiful. The game disk was enclosed in a small cardboard box designed to look like a finely printed, old-fashioned book, complete with an elaborate woodcut on the cover that contained a hidden Dead Kennedy's logo, in tribute to one of Capp's favorite bands. Since Alice didn't take up the whole disk, Capps included a few other goodies with it, including a font and "Amazing," a fascinating maze generating program he wrote.

When I saw the completed packaging, I was surprised to discover the game wasn't called "Alice" anymore. Apparently that name was already trademarked for a database program. It was rechristened "Through The Looking Glass" for its commercial release.

Unfortunately, Apple never put the promised marketing effort into Alice. They were in a quandary because the market didn't understand the graphical user interface as a productivity enhancement yet. Graphics meant games, so the Mac had to live down an initial reputation as being unsuitable for business tasks. Apple didn't exactly want to promote a game for the Mac at the time, no matter how sensational, so Alice never reached as wide an audience as it deserved.

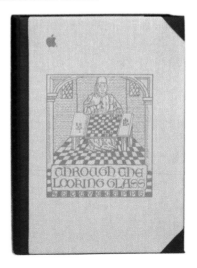

Do It   June 1982

User testing sometimes has surprising results

Many of the academic types involved in creating the earliest implementations of the graphical user interface at Xerox PARC and various universities sneered at the first generation of personal computers when they appeared in the mid-70s because they were much less powerful than the machines they were used to programming. There wasn't that much you could do with only four kilobytes of memory and no disk drive.

But Larry Tesler, who was a key member of the Smalltalk team in the Learning Research Group at Xerox PARC, felt differently. He was really excited by the potential of personal computers and bought a Commodore PET as soon as one became available in 1977. He was one of the demonstrators at Apple's famous Xerox PARC visit in December 1979, and he was so impressed by the Apple visitors that he quit PARC and started working at Apple on July 17, 1980, as the manager of the Lisa Applications team.

Larry championed consistency between applications, and made many contributions to what eventually became the Macintosh User Interface. He was also the leading advocate and implementer at Apple of user testing, of actually trying our software out on real users to see what happened. Starting in the summer of 1981, Larry organized a series of user tests of the nascent Lisa software by recruiting friends and family to try out new software while being observed by the Apple designers who recorded their reactions.

The user tests were conducted in a specially constructed room featuring a one-way mirror so observers could watch the tests without being intrusive. A moderator conducted the tests and made sure users felt comfortable and knew the basics of using a mouse. Then, with no further instruction, users were asked to perform specific tasks, without help from the moderator, such as editing and saving text. The moderator encouraged each user to mumble under their breath while doing the tasks, revealing their current thinking as much as possible. Each session was audio- or videotaped for later analysis.

When the software required confirmation from the user, it displayed a small dialog box that contained a question, followed by two buttons for positive or negative confirmation. The buttons were labeled Do It and Cancel. The designers observed that a few users seemed to stumble at the point the dialog was displayed and clicked Cancel when they should have clicked Do It, but it wasn't clear what they were having trouble with.

Finally, the team noticed one user was particularly flummoxed by the dialog box and seemed to be getting a bit angry. The moderator interrupted the test and asked him what the problem was. He replied, "I'm not a dolt. Why is the software calling me a dolt?"

It turns out he wasn't noticing the space between the "o" and the "I" in "Do It" (In the sans-serif system font we were using, a capital "I" looked very much like a lower case "l") so he was reading "Do It" as "Dolt" and was offended.

After a bit of consideration, we switched the positive confirmation button label to "OK"— which was initially avoided because we thought it was too colloquial—and from that point on people had fewer problems.

Inside Macintosh   June 1982
Developer documentation was crucial to our success

One of the main differences between the Lisa and Macintosh projects was the way they viewed third-party developers. The Lisa team was writing an integrated suite of seven office-oriented applications internally and didn't see a need to support third-party developers at first, although they planned to eventually.

The Macintosh, inspired by the Apple II, took a different approach. The Apple II's sales had increased more than ten-fold after a tiny company named Software Arts released the first spreadsheet, VisiCalc, which initially ran only on the Apple II. We wanted all the people who resonated with our Macintosh dream to be able to extend it with their own creativity, so having first-class support for third-party developers was considered a must from the very beginning.

But that was easier said than done. The Lisa team's stance was quite reasonable because consistency between applications was very important to Apple. There were virtually no third-party developers who were familiar with a graphical user interface, so we had to educate them about a whole new approach to programming. In those days, every application provided its own unique user interface, and we weren't sure it was even possible to coordinate independent developers to conform to our ideas about a consistent user interface.

In fact, in early 1982 our user interface was still evolving, and the team didn't necessarily agree on the best way to do things, especially as new issues arose. It seemed as though the next logical step was to formally document and codify our user interface, to identify and resolve open issues, and communicate it to third-party developers.

One reason to move quickly on this was a looming meeting with our initial third-party developer, Microsoft (see "Shut Up!" on page 52), who was coming to pick up their first Macintosh prototypes and developer documentation around the end of January. We held a series of intense, all-day meetings in the second week of January 1982 to thrash out disagreements and formulate a shared view of the UI, metaphorically locking ourselves in a room until we came to consensus. The meetings were attended by Steve Jobs, Bill Atkinson, Joanna Hoffman, Chris Espinosa, Randy Wigginton (who had left Apple in September 1981, but agreed to write MacWrite for us as a semi-independent developer), and me.

The Lisa User Interface was our obvious starting point, but we had a desire to simplify things, and we tried to strip out anything that seemed too complex. Triple-click was easy to get rid of, for example, but it was hard to agree on the details of scroll bars. After two-and-a-half days, we thought we were more or less in agreement and decided Joanna should write up the current state of the design. She wrote the first draft of the *Macintosh User Interface Guidelines* in time for the Microsoft meeting the following week, where we presented it for the very first time. Eventually, Chris Espinosa took over authorship of the guidelines, augmenting and amending them as necessary as development proceeded.

By April 1982, the first implementation of the User Interface Toolbox, which contained the code that implemented UI objects like windows, menus, buttons and scrollbars, was ready for the initial release to developers. Since most developers had never programmed a graphical user interface, it was very important to write high-quality developer documentation to explain the ins and outs of using the toolbox. Chris Espinosa had already written some excellent documentation for using QuickDraw, so we were off to a good start.

I met with Chris about the toolbox documentation and we decided to tackle the Window Manager first. He assigned a recently hired technical writer, a women in her mid-20s who will remain mercifully nameless in this story, to work with me to document the Window Manager API.

One afternoon, I sat down with the writer for a few hours with some printouts of the source code, and went over the Window Manager API with her in fine detail. I was a bit worried because I did most of the talking, and she didn't ask any questions, but she promised to show me her first draft in just a few days.

A few days later, Chris Espinosa handed me a few pages of Window Manager documentation, with the caveat that it was a very early draft and I shouldn't expect too much. But my heart sank as I began to read it. The actual Window

The initial "phone book" cover of Inside Macintosh

Manager calls were accurately reproduced, as were the comments from the header file, but the descriptions of each call made no sense; it was clear she didn't understand many of the underlying QuickDraw and Memory Manager concepts. Instead of asking for an explanation, she just made up whatever popped into her head.

I had a panicky meeting with Chris, but he was able to calm me down and convince me to give the writer another chance. I met with both of them, explaining the problems I had with what she had done so far. She was amazingly blithe and cheerful about it, saying she knew she didn't understand everything, but figured I would correct anything that was wrong. We had another, longer meeting, where I did my best to explain the underlying concepts like handles and regions, and went over the Window Manager API again, this time asking her if she had any questions at the end of each routine. It still seemed to me she was having trouble understanding things, no matter how carefully I tried to explain, but she didn't seem worried about it at all.

The next draft was just as bad as the previous one, and I felt even worse given all the effort I put into it. Chris was defensive and I began to despair of ever getting decent documentation for the toolbox. So I was surprised when he entered my cubicle a couple of days later with a smile on his face.

Caroline Rose in 1982

"We've just made an offer to a new writer," he said, "someone who I think will do a much better job on the technical side of things since she used to be a programmer. Her name is Caroline Rose. I'm going to assign her to the window manager documentation and see what you think."

The next week I sat down with Caroline for the first time and she couldn't have been more different than the previous writer. As soon as I started to explain the first routine, she bombarded me with questions. She didn't mind admitting it when she didn't understand something, and she wouldn't stop badgering me until she comprehended every nuance. She asked me questions I didn't know the answers to, like what happened when certain parameters were invalid. I had to keep the source code open on the screen of my Lisa when I met with her so I could figure out the answers to her questions while she was there.

Before long I figured out that if Caroline had trouble understanding something, it probably meant the design was flawed. On a number of occasions, I told her to come back after she asked a penetrating question, and I revised the API to fix the flaw she had pointed out. I began to imagine her questions when I was coding something new, which made me work harder to get things clearer before I went over them with her.

We initially distributed the raw documentation to developers piecemeal, as it was written, but eventually we wanted to collect it into one definitive reference called *Inside Macintosh*. It was almost 1,000 pages, spread across 3 volumes, mostly written by Caroline with help from Bob Anders, Brad Hacker, Steve Chernicoff, and a few others. Steve Jobs naturally insisted on very high production standards for the first edition, and we used only the best binding and paper available. But high-quality printing takes time, and the evangelists were impatient to get the definitive documentation out to developers as soon as possible.

I'm not sure whose idea it was, but a compromise was finally reached. Apple would publish a free, softbound, "promotional" edition of *Inside Macintosh* on low-quality paper as soon as possible, and send a copy to every developer. It was about as thick and flimsy as the Yellow Pages, so it became known as the "phone book" edition. Most developers still bought the high-quality, beautiful, hardback edition when it came out a few months later.

Creative Think

Think July 1982

A seminar with Alan Kay

In July of 1982, while I was in the midst of writing the Control Manager part of the Macintosh toolbox, my friend Bill Budge invited me to a computer industry seminar called Creative Think, where interesting people gave purportedly inspiring talks. It was organized by Roger von Oech, a consultant who had written a book about creativity entitled *A Whack On The Side Of The Head*. I usually avoided both creativity seminars and industry schmooze-fests, but my friend Bill had somehow finagled free tickets and I thought it would be worth it just to hang out with him.

Carver Mead gave an interesting talk on newly emerging VLSI technology, and some old chip-industry veterans recounted amusing war stories, but the last talk of the day was the one that mattered to me. It was given by Alan Kay, the inventor of Smalltalk and the Alto, and the driving force behind Xerox PARC. I had read about Alan, and been inspired by his article about Smalltalk in the September 1977 issue of *Scientific American*, but I had never seen him before in person or heard much about him.

Alan's speech was revelatory and was perhaps the most inspiring talk I ever attended. I grew increasingly excited as he made one brilliant, insightful remark after another, and took out my notebook to write as much of it down as I could. Alan articulated the values behind the work that I was doing in a way that really resonated with me. After I got back to my office in Cupertino, I transcribed my notes onto a single page and made copies for the rest of team.

I still have those notes, so I thought it would be interesting to reproduce them here as an example of some of the thinking that inspired our efforts.

Alan Kay's talk at "Creative Think" seminar 7/20/82

Outline of Talk: the real software issues
- Metaphors
- Magnetic Fields
- Snobbery
- Slogans

The best way to predict the future is to invent it

Humans like fantasy + sharing
- Fantasy fulfils need for a simpler, more controllable world
- Sharing - we're all communication junkies - we have an incredible disparity of bandwidth (easy to take in, hard to give out)

Metaphors:
- Computer as medium (clay, paint)
- Computer as vehicle
- Computer as musical instrument

Magnetic Fields - find a central metaphor so good that everything aligns to it. Design meetings not necessary. Should be crisp and fun.

SmallTalk is object-oriented but should have been message-oriented

Snobbery - turn up nose at good ideas
- must work on great ideas, not good ones

Appreciate mundanity - a pencil is high technology

One goal: disappear the computer into the environment

The computer shouldn't act like it knows everything
The whole notion of "programming languages" is wrong

Slogans:
- best is the enemy of better
- relative judgements have no place in art
- systems programmers are high priests of a low cult
- good ideas don't often scale

It's all software - it just depends on when you crystallize it

People really serious about software should build their own hardware

Final advice: Content over form, go for fun

Resource
Manager
Countdown August 1982

Bob gives Bruce thirty days to finish the Resource Manager

The Resource Manager was one of the cornerstones of the Macintosh Toolbox. It provided a way to manage chunks of data so they could be easily accessed by the code but be stored and edited independently from it. This was the basis of our localization, since text strings could be stored as resources and translated without having to change the code and rebuild the entire application.

Resources were conceived and implemented by Bruce Horn. They came a little late in the design cycle, and we had to rewrite some other parts of the toolbox to take advantage of them, although that wasn't clear initially. But in the summer of 1982, they were definitely one of the riskier parts of the design.

Bob Belleville, our new software manager, assessed the situation and decided that the Resource Manager was too big a risk and tried to convince us to drop it from the design. Bruce went apoplectic, and Bob eventually compromised on giving Bruce 30 days to implement the resource manager. Bruce agreed that if it wasn't ready within 30 days, it would be dropped from the project.

The next day, Bruce came to work with a few pads of yellow sticky notes. He tore off one note at a time, wrote a number on it, and then stuck it on the wall of the double-sized cubicle that I shared with him. Soon the cubicle was encircled with little yellow notes, each with a number from 1 to 30.

"This shows me how many days I have left," Bruce explained. "I'll tear one down each day, and it will remind me of how much time is remaining."

For the next month, the first thing Bruce did every morning was dramatically tear off the note with the lowest remaining number. As the days passed, he was making good progress, but it wasn't at all clear he was going to make it.

When there were only three notes left, I began to wonder what was going to happen if Bruce missed the deadline. The Resource Manager was mostly working now, but Bruce continued to refine the design and didn't seem to be on a path to closure.

Finally, there was only one note left on the wall. But when Bruce came in that morning, he had a new pad of yellow notes, and instead of taking the last one down, he wrote another ten numbers and posted them up. I started to laugh.

"It's overtime," he explained. "I swear I'll really be done in 10 more days."

I was waiting for Bob Belleville to confront Bruce and tell him he missed the deadline, but Bob wisely saw that the Resource Manager was far enough along that it could stay. And Bruce really did finish in the next 10 days (kind of).

You Guys Are in Big Trouble

August 1982

We receive Steve's permission to dismantle the onerous burglar alarm

The Mac team was growing so rapidly in the spring of 1982 that we had to move from Texaco Towers back to the main part of the Apple campus on Bandley Drive. We moved into Bandley 4, a medium-sized building across the street from Apple's main office.

One of the things I liked about Bandley 4 was that the software team was in the very back of the building, near the parking lot, so we could go out the back door to our cars or to play basketball, without having to walk all the way around the building. This worked out well for a couple of months, but eventually the facilities group decided to put an alarm on the back door and we couldn't go in and out freely. They didn't arm the alarm until 5:30 P.M., but that didn't help me because I usually didn't go out to dinner until after 7 P.M., and then often returned to work another couple of hours. The alarm became a major annoyance because it made me walk significantly out of my way a few times every day.

Every once in a while someone forgot that the alarm was there and would walk out the door anyway. The alarm produced a head-splitting wail, destroying any chance of concentration until a security guard arrived to disarm it, which sometimes took more than 10 minutes.

I complained about the alarm every way I knew how, but to no avail. About one quarter of the software team worked late, and the alarm was unnecessary while we were there, so I begged the facilities supervisor not to turn it on until after midnight. I even suggested we arm it ourselves when the last person left. But my pleas fell on deaf ears.

Every couple of months, Bud Tribble came down from Seattle and visited us. We'd show him the latest work we were doing so he could make his great suggestions. Late one afternoon he showed up in the software area, and the team (including Bill Atkinson and Steve Jobs) gathered around to demo new software for him.

Bill had done some neat hi-resolution scans with an improved dithering algorithm, and he wanted to show them to Bud. They were on his hard disk in the Lisa building, so he ran out the back door to get it. It was after 5:30 P.M., so the alarm went off, and a horrible, loud, pulsating noise filled the room.

It went on for at least three minutes before Steve yelled out, "Can't someone figure out how to stop that thing?"

I saw a chance to vanquish my nemesis. "Are we allowed to damage it to get it to stop?" I asked him.

"Yes, do anything you want. I don't care if you break it," he replied, holding his hands over his ears. "Just get the damn thing to stop!"

Bruce Horn and I ran over to the nearby hardware lab and picked up every tool we could find. I got a hammer and screwdriver and proceeded to pound the screwdriver into the center of the alarm, driving a stake through the demon's heart. The screwdriver went all the way through to the other side, but the alarm kept sounding.

Finally, Bruce took over and gave the screwdriver a mighty twist, and the whole thing flew apart into a half-dozen pieces and fell to the ground. The horrible noise finally stopped.

At that very moment, a grizzled security guard entered the back door just in time to see us cheering as the wrecked alarm finally gave up the ghost. He looked at us, our tools of destruction still in our guilty hands, and said, "You guys are in big trouble!!! Who's in charge here? You better show me your badge."

Steve stepped forward and handed the guard his badge. "I'll take responsibility for this," he told him.

The guard scrutinized Steve's badge. He looked at Steve, then back at the badge a few times. Finally, he shrugged his shoulders, picked up the pieces of the broken alarm, and walked away without saying another word.

We were gleeful the alarm was gone, but exactly one week later, a new one was put in its place—and it stayed there until we moved to Bandley 3 a few months later. I'm not sure why, but not even Steve could get them to set it for a later time.

"Can't someone figure out how to stop that thing?"

Five Different Macintoshes
Burrell actually designed five different Macintoshes

The awesomely creative design of the Macintosh digital board was always the seed crystal of brilliance at the core of the project, but there wasn't just one design. Burrell redesigned the digital board four different times during development and finally arrived at the shipping design in the fall of 1982.

The first Macintosh digital board, designed in late 1979, was based on Jef Raskin's specifications: it had a Motorola 6809E microprocessor, 64K of memory, and a 256 × 256 black-and-white, bitmapped graphics display. Even in this first design, Burrell was using his trademark "PAL" chips, which were small, programmable logic arrays, to provide all the system glue and give the system a very low chip count.

The first Macintosh was a cute little computer, but it was fundamentally limited by the 16 bits of address space on the 6809 microprocessor. In the meantime, Bill Atkinson was doing incredible work on the Lisa project using Motorola's 68000 microprocessor, with its capacious 32-bit registers and 24-bit address space. Bud Tribble, the Mac's only software person, was living at Bill's house and watching the extraordinary progress on Lisa's graphics package. He began to wonder if it was possible for the Macintosh to use the 68000 so it could run Bill's graphics routines.

Bud began asking Burrell if it was feasible to include the 68000 in a low-cost design. The 68000 was expensive enough on its own, but its 16-bit memory bus required twice as many RAM chips as the 6809, so the overall cost was significantly higher. But Burrell thought about the problem and came up with a characteristically brilliant idea for his second Macintosh design.

The idea was what Burrell called a "bus transformer" circuit, built out of PAL chips, which adapted the 68000 to an 8-bit memory bus by exploiting the fast "page mode" access mode of the RAMs. The new Macintosh, designed over the Christmas break at the end of 1980, featured an 8-MHz 68000, 64K of RAM, and a 384 × 256 bitmapped display. It was 60 percent faster than the Lisa (which used a 5-MHz 68000) but was a lot less expensive.

When Steve Jobs caught wind of what Burrell had come up with—an Apple II–priced machine that blew away the Lisa, he became really excited. He immediately saw that

Burrell's machine could become the future of Apple. Steve's attention was, however, the beginning of the end for Jef. Jef despised parts of Steve's personality and couldn't put up with Steve's courting of Burrell and Bud. Steve took over the project in January 1981, and the Macintosh entered the post-Jef era. It was now on track to becoming a real product.

Burrell came up with a third Macintosh design in June 1981. The main reason for a new design was that he had fallen in love with a communications chip called the SCC. The SCC could support a built-in local area network, making AppleTalk possible with no additional hardware, as well as providing nice buffered serial ports with interrupts and other hardware features. At this point it was becoming obvious we needed at least 128K of memory to support the user interface, so he also added a second row of RAM chips.

Around the end of 1981, Burrell met some engineers who were doing custom LSI chips. LSI chips were very flexible and powerful, but time consuming to design, because the software tools for chip design were still in their infancy. Burrell decided he wanted to take a shot at building the Macintosh around a single custom chip and convinced Steve he could pull it off. Instead of sitting around doing nothing while the software team finished the product, he would work with a couple of experienced LSI designers and redesign the Mac around what he called the "Integrated Burrell Machine."

It was so named because earlier in the year, Wendell Sander, the designer of the Apple III and one of Apple's best engineers, put together a small custom chip that crammed all the functionality of Woz's disk controller into a single chip. It was called the "IWM" chip, which stood for the "Integrated Woz Machine" or the "Integrated Wendell Machine." Burrell relished the potential confusion his new "Integrated Burrell Machine" might cause.

The original 68000 design was more than a year old by the beginning of 1982. The software was still nowhere near finished and Burrell was afraid some of the trade-offs of the original design were no longer current. He used the expansive canvas of a custom chip, where additional logic was almost free, to update the architecture. The most important decision was admitting that the software would never fit into 64K of memory, utilizing a full 16-bit memory bus, and requiring 16 RAM chips instead of 8. The extra memory bandwidth allowed him to double the display resolution from 384 × 256 to 512 × 342. He also added bells and whistles, such as a fancy DMA-fed sound generator with four independent voices. This was the fourth version of the Macintosh design.

But Burrell had never worked on a custom chip before. He was counting on experts like Doug Fairbairn and Martin Haeberli, who had successfully created a custom chip for an optical mouse, working with our partner VLSI Design. But they had never really worked against commercial deadlines, and a lot of tension began to build as the schedule started to slip.

Eventually, after the first silicon from an early version didn't work as expected, Burrell became frustrated and decided it was too risky to continue. He realized he could do a design with PALs that achieved most of the gains from the Integrated Burrell Machine without needing the custom chip. So, in August 1982, he quickly designed the fifth iteration of the Macintosh that adapted his earlier PAL-based design to one that had a 16-bit memory bus with a 512 × 342 display and some other features invented for the custom chip, such as sophisticated sound generation.

The August 1982 design was essentially the same as the one that finally shipped in January 1984, after one more minor revision in May 1983 when another PAL was added to support the disk drive. Burrell's digital board iterations are analogous to the sequence of Polaroids in "Busy Being Born," illustrating how the shipping product is only the tip of the iceberg of design effort required to create a breakthrough product such as the original Macintosh.

Boot Beep   September 1982
How the boot sound evolved

When you powered up an Apple II, it made a short beep sound to let you know it was alive. We thought the Mac should do something similar, sort of like an infant's first cry, to let the world know it actually made it.

The 1981 Macintosh only had a square wave sound generator, and the software controlled the frequency by loading a value into the VIA's timer. (The VIA was an I/O chip on the digital board; VIA stood for "Versatile Interface Adapter.") I wrote a boot sound routine that gradually incremented the frequency at an accelerating pace so it had a whooping quality that was almost humorous. People generally liked it, but we knew we'd have to do something better for the real product.

In August 1982, the Mac was redesigned with much better sound quality, so we had the possibility of a better boot sound, since we now had 8-bit samples to play with. I started experimenting to see if I could come up with something better.

 Around this time, Charlie Kellner decided to transfer to the Mac group from the Apple II group. Charlie was a brilliant Apple II programmer as well as a multitalented, meticulous perfectionist who wrote a classic hi-res bowling game for the Apple II before he started work at Apple. As a side project, he designed a music synthesizer for the Apple II called the AlphaSyntauri that was the basis for a small startup company. For some reason he grew bored with the Apple II and wanted to try working with the Mac team.

Charlie saw me messing around with sounds for the new boot beep and said he knew of a simple algorithm that might work pretty well. He asked me to fill the sound buffer with a simple square wave, but then make successive passes on it, averaging adjacent samples until everything reached the same level.

I coded it up and we tried it. Sure enough it had a pleasant, distinctive chiming quality. With a little bit of tweaking, it became the famous sound the Mac made when it powered up and lasted until the Mac II, which had even better sound capability, in 1987.

Charlie was pleased he was able to make a significant contribution in his first week on the project. Inspired, he asked if he could take a prototype home over the weekend for testing. The next Monday he came into work very excited.

 "I knew something wasn't right!" he exclaimed. "The sound is being completely muffled by the case! But I know how to fix it."

He had done a series of experiments with the Mac he had taken home over the weekend and found that the Macintosh's case was baffling and distorting the sound. He even printed out graphics showing the results of his measurements. Then, after analyzing the data, he drilled a hole about the size of a dime in a strategic place, which caused the measurements to improve dramatically.

He started demoing his modified prototype, showing how the hole improved the sound quality. The difference didn't sound that significant to me, but it definitely was an improvement. He showed it to Terry Oyama, who designed the case, and asked him if he could add the hole.

The next day, Steve Jobs came by in the afternoon and asked to hear Charlie's demo. He listened to the two Macs and decreed, "There's not enough improvement! There's no way we're going to put an ugly hole in the case! Just forget about it!"

Charlie was pretty disappointed and never got very enthusiastic about the Mac after that. He transferred back to the Apple II group a couple weeks later, leaving the boot beep as his only legacy.

Sound by Monday

When Burrell redesigned the Macintosh digital board in August 1982 after the Integrated Burrell Machine effort fell apart, one of the most significant improvements involved the sound generation capability. The extra logic available in the IBM chip allowed Burrell to implement four simultaneous channels of sound, each using a custom wavetable. That required too much silicon to keep without the custom chip, but he was able to maintain the fundamental capability, which was DMA-fetched sound using 8-bits per sample and a clever, pulse width–modulated digital to analog converter.

Burrell figured out the Mac could still have the four simultaneous voices he had envisioned for the Integrated Burrell Machine, only now most of the work would be done in software instead of hardware. Burrell promised Steve the redesign would feature great sound, including a four-voice synthesizer. Steve approved spending an extra dollar on an improved amplifier in order to better match the improved sound generation capability.

But there were an enormous number of different projects to complete in the summer of 1982, including getting the Mac Toolbox into good enough shape for developers to start writing applications. Burrell bugged me about writing a sound driver, including his cherished "four-voice engine," but I wasn't able to get around to it right away.

Steve Jobs grew impatient to hear our new sound capability for himself. Finally, he pulled Burrell and myself aside late on a Friday afternoon.

"You told me the new sound capability would be really great, right?" he asked Burrell. "Well, if I don't hear great sound coming out of that prototype by Monday morning, we're going to remove the amplifier. "

Then he looked at me. "You've had long enough to get the sound going. I want to hear great sound on Monday, or else." Then he stormed off, leaving Burrell and me to figure out what to do.

"I think he's bluffing," I told Burrell. "But what if he's not?"

Burrell didn't seem very upset. In fact, he seemed kind of excited. I think he was pleased Steve was on our case about the sound, especially since he really wanted me to write the sound routines as soon as possible anyway. He promised to buy me meals all weekend while we stayed at Apple to get the sound going.

"You've had long enough to get the sound going.

I had already written a basic diagnostic that generated a simple square wave. It certainly didn't meet anyone's criteria for great sound, but at least it told us the hardware was working and that we'd worked out the basic details of controlling the hardware. Burrell wanted me to get to work right away on the four-voice synthesizer because he wasn't sure we could actually make it work.

As usual, Burrell's new design was very clever. The Macintosh was already continuously fetching data from memory to drive the video display, interleaving memory bandwidth between the display and processor in a similar fashion to the Apple II. But every 44 microseconds there was a "horizontal blanking interval" where no video data was needed. Burrell used that time to fetch data for the sound. That gave us a sample rate of 22 kHz, which would allow us to do frequencies up to 11 kHz, which wasn't too bad.

The sound driver worked at the interrupt level, so sound generation could proceed in the background while the driver performed some other task. The driver arranged to receive control at the beginning of the vertical blanking interval, which occurred every 16 milliseconds. It needed to generate all the sound data for the next 16 milliseconds, which worked out to 44 microseconds for every successive sample. If our calculation took 22 microseconds per sample, for example, the sound generation would soak up half of the available processor cycles.

It only took a few hours to write a driver with a simple sound generation loop. It could do two voices well, but it didn't run nearly fast enough to do four. It took too long to generate each sample, which caused audible glitches and made everything else run like molasses. Burrell took a look at my code and saw that I was using some memory locations during the sound calculation.

"Memory? Are you kidding? You can't hit main memory. You'll never make it that way. You've got to do everything in the registers!"

"Registers" are special locations that are part of the processor chip itself and are where the action really happens. In the Macintosh's 68000 chip, they could be accessed four times faster than the bulk of memory, which was in separate memory chips. The problem was that there were only 16 registers. For each voice of sound, we needed a frequency, a waveform

I want to hear great sound on Monday, or else."

pointer, a position within the waveform, and amplitude, plus some housekeeping data. There weren't enough registers to do four voices.

I was able to rewrite the routine without touching main memory, but I was only able to get three voices since I ran out of registers. But that wasn't good enough for Burrell. By now it was late on Saturday evening and I wanted to go home, but he felt we had to get the fourth voice done before "head hits pillow," as he liked to say, or we'll never get the fourth voice.

Finally, I was able to leverage the fact that the registers were 32 bits long. We were only doing 16-bit calculations in some of them in order to hold two different values. Each sample took about 22 microseconds to calculate, so we were using roughly half of the CPU to get the four voices at the maximum sample rate. The basic four-voice capability was implemented, but we still needed an impressive demo to show it off. We went home to sleep at around midnight, after agreeing to come back around noon to work on the demo.

The next day, we decided to write a demo called "SoundLab" that would let the user control the pitch and waveform of the four independent voices. You could specify or edit a waveform by drawing it with the mouse, and control the frequency of each voice with a scroll bar. The results didn't sound like music because there was no envelope shaping, but you could make very eerie noises, which we deemed impressive enough. And it was fun to be able to hook an oscilloscope up to the sound output, draw a waveform with the mouse, and then see it on the scope.

When Steve came in on Monday, he was pleased we could demonstrate the four-voice capability, and impressed he could edit a waveform with the mouse and see it on the scope. But I don't think he was satisfied because he wanted high-quality music. There was a lot of potential in the Mac sound capability, but it would still take years and the efforts of many third-party developers to fully exploit it.

The Little Kingdom

Steve Jobs was almost 1982's Man of the Year

The cover of the February 15th, 1982 edition of *Time* magazine featured none other than Steve Jobs, appearing in an article entitled "Striking It Rich: America's Risk Takers." Steve was depicted in a drawing with a red apple balanced on his head that was pierced by a zigzag bolt of lightning emanating from an Apple II.

The article inside focused on a number of high tech startups, but there was a long sidebar by a young business reporter named Mike Moritz that told the story of Apple's meteoric rise. It was a bit critical in places ("As an executive, Jobs has sometimes been petulant and harsh on subordinates"), but it was generally positive about the company and its prospects.

Macintosh development was shrouded in secrecy, even within Apple, so we were surprised one day a few months later when Steve appeared in the software area of Bandley 4 accompanied by the Time reporter, Mike Moritz. Steve requested I give him a demo of the Macintosh and answer all of his questions. Apparently, Mike wanted to write a book about Apple and managed to convince Steve to give him total access to the company, including the Macintosh team.

"Mike's going to be our historian," Steve informed us, "so you can tell him everything. Treat him like he's a member of the team because he's going to write our story for us." The previous year, a development team at Data General was immortalized by Tracy Kidder's best-selling book, *The Soul of a New Machine*, about the ups and downs of developing a new minicomputer. Now it seemed that Mike Moritz was going to do something similar for the Mac team.

Mike Moritz, Apple historian

Over the next few months, Mike spent lots of time hanging around the Mac team, attending various meetings and conducting interviews over lunch or dinner, to learn our individual stories. Mike had grown up in South Wales and attended Oxford before moving to the U.S. for grad school and obtaining an MBA from Wharton. He was in his mid-20s, about the same age as most of us, and was very smart. With a sharp, cynical sense of humor, he fit right in, and he seemed to understand what we were trying to accomplish.

In December 1982, word somehow got around that *Time* magazine was considering awarding Steve Jobs its prestigious "Man of the Year" designation for 1982. Mike Moritz, who was by now *Time*'s San Francisco Bureau Chief, came down to Apple for another round of interviews to gather background for the lengthy "Man of the Year" story. But we were in for a surprise when the award was announced the last week of the year.

Instead of crowning Steve Jobs as the Man of the Year, *Time*'s editorial staff declared 1982 to be the "year of the computer" and explained "it would have been possible to single out as Man of the Year one of the engineers or entrepreneurs who masterminded this technological revolution, but no one person has clearly dominated those turbulent events. More important, such a selection would obscure the main point. TIME's Man of the Year for 1982, the greatest influence for good or evil, is not a man at all. It is a machine: the computer."

The cover story did include another profile of Steve Jobs, which contained some comments that were less than complimentary. One unspecified friend was quoted saying, "something is happening to Steve that's sad and not pretty." But the best quote was attributed to Jef Raskin: "He would have made an excellent King of France."

Steve became quite upset when he read an advance copy of the piece and even called up Dan Kottke and Jef Raskin early on New Year's Day to complain about it. Soon, Mike Moritz was no longer welcome on the Apple campus. In fact, Steve told the software team, "If any one of you ever talk to him again, you'll be fired on the spot!"

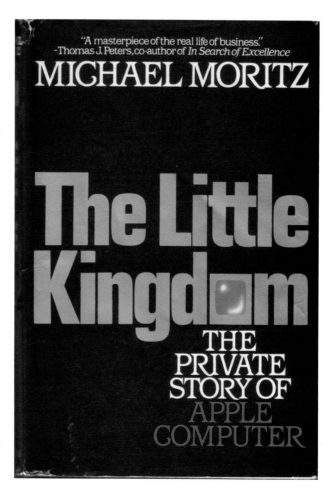

But some of us talked with Mike again surreptitiously as he was putting the finishing touches on his book, around the time of the Mac introduction. The book, entitled *The Little Kingdom: The Private Story of Apple Computer*, was published in fall of 1984; twenty years later it remains one of the best books about Apple ever written.

Perhaps inspired by the example of Steve Jobs and Apple, in 1986 Mike Moritz switched careers and became a venture capitalist. He went to work for Don Valentine at Sequoia, one of the original investors in Apple. Mike became the original investor in Yahoo! in April of 1995, convincing Jerry Yang and David Filo to commercialize their web directory, and today is one of the most respected VCs in the industry.

"TIME's Man of the Year for 1982, the greatest influence for good or evil, is not a man at all. It is a machine: the computer."

"He would have made an excellent King of France." Jef Raskin

What's a Megaflop? January 1983

We visit my alma mater to try to sell them Macs

Apple always had a natural affinity for education, and, almost from its inception, the Apple II was very successful in the K-12 education market. In the late 1970s, Steve Jobs initiated a marketing program called "Kids Can't Wait" and personally paced the halls of Congress in Washington for three weeks, lobbying for legislation granting tax breaks for donating computers to schools. Even though the national legislation was stymied by politics (it got blocked by Bob Dole), California eventually passed a similar bill and Apple soon donated almost 9,000 computers, one to every school in California.

In early 1982, Joanna Hoffman was still the only marketing person on the Mac team, and she was thinking about which market segments were likely to be early adopters of the Macintosh. She realized that the Mac was almost perfect for college students, and thought it would be worthwhile to put together a plan for selling Macs to higher education.

A few months later, after conferring with a number of consultants who understood the college market, a plan began to emerge. One of the words the consultants reiterated was "consortium"; it seemed as though colleges loved to band together into various consortiums. We knew that the paucity of software at launch would be a barrier to initial acceptance, but maybe not if we could get the colleges to form a Macintosh consortium whose members received steeply discounted Macs for students and faculty. All we had to do was sign up a few of the most prestigious schools and, we figured, many others would follow.

Mike Murray (who was now the permanent interim Macintosh marketing manager) and Joanna realized they needed a superb salesperson to take charge of recruiting customers for our consortium-to-be. The best salesperson Joanna knew on the Lisa team was Dan'l Lewin, a handsome, personable, ivy-educated ex-competitive swimmer who was frustrated with his current job of selling the Lisa to corporations. Dan'l was intrigued, and, after some negotiation, was soon barnstorming around the country visiting the leading universities, with Mike Boich in tow to run the demo and answer technical questions, trying to convince universities to sign up with Apple and buy discounted Macs by the thousands.

Some of the universities, like Drexel University in Philadelphia, were easy sells because they were already thinking about buying a computer for each freshman, and the Macintosh consortium was the answer to their prayers. But others weren't as enthusiastic and required lots of handholding to coax them into the fold. But slowly Dan'l was able to build up a fairly impressive roster.

Toward the end of January 1983, I was asked to accompany Dan'l and Mike on one of the more unusual sales calls, to Brown University in Providence, Rhode Island, because Brown was my alma mater. I hadn't been back there since I graduated in 1975. Brown had a strong computer science program, especially in computer graphics, and was considered to be rather influential with the other universities. They had recently splurged, buying dozens of powerful Apollo workstations, costing tens of thousands of dollars apiece, so we were afraid they'd think the Mac was underpowered. Convincing Brown to sign on was thought to be so important that even Steve Jobs agreed to come along on the sales call.

The most influential decision maker on the Brown faculty was a computer science professor named Andy van Dam. I was one his teaching assistants during my senior year, so I got to know him pretty well. He was high strung and hard driving, and a little bit like Steve in his tendency to think that the universe revolved around him. I thought it would be interesting to see how they interacted.

Introductions were exchanged, and we were taken for a tour of the Brown Computing Lab where they proudly showed off their brand new Apollo workstations. Then we were ushered into a conference room where Dan'l talked about the consortium while we set up the Mac. We put it through its paces for the benefit of a half-dozen faculty members and grad students, with Steve doing most of the talking, eliciting oohs and ahhs in all the right places. Finally, the demo was over and Steve asked them what they thought.

Andy van Dam cleared his throat and looked right at Steve. "Well, its really impressive, Steve, and of course we'll want to join your program. But it's not exactly what we've been waiting for."

Steve looked a little angry. "You're going to have to wait a long time to find something better than the Mac!"

"Well, 128K isn't nearly enough memory to do what we want, not even close, and the screen is just too small. We're waiting for a 3M machine, and most of the other colleges are, too."

"A what?"

"A 3M machine. There was a recently published paper that coined the term. You know, a workstation with at least a megabyte of memory, a million-pixel display, and a megaflop of computational horsepower. We believe that's what we need for an effective educational workstation."

A megaflop was the ability to execute one million floating-point operations per second. The Mac didn't have any floating-point hardware, so it was off by an order of magnitude. In fact, we were off by around a factor of 10 in each of the 3 dimensions.

"Oh, we believe in that, too," Steve shot back, without skipping a beat. "Apple will have an affordable 3M machine before anyone else. I only have one question. What's a megaflop?"

Credit Where Due January 1983
Why the Mac design team got credit for their work

Every six months or so starting in January 1982, the Macintosh team held a series of off-site retreats. A retreat usually lasted two full days, including an overnight stay. We'd travel by bus to a naturally beautiful resort within an hour or two of Apple's offices in Cupertino. Every employee on the team would be invited, as were folks from other parts of the company who were contributing to the project. The retreats were a mixture of a divisional communications meeting, an inspirational pep talk, and a company party, featuring chats with industry legends like Robert Noyce (inventor of the integrated circuit) or Ben Rosen (the VC who funded Compaq and Lotus), and entertainment from Wyndham Hill artists such as Liz Story.

The third retreat was scheduled for January 27th and 28th, 1983, at the La Playa Hotel in Carmel, and it came at a pivotal time for the project. The Lisa was just introduced the previous week, after four years of development, on January 19th (although it wouldn't actually ship for another five months), and it was becoming increasingly clear that it was time for the Mac team to shift gears, buckle down, and change our focus to doing whatever it took to finish up and ship.

After the two-hour bus ride from Cupertino, we gathered in a large meeting room to hear Steve Jobs's opening remarks, which set the agenda for the retreat. Steve was fond of summarizing the themes of the day into a few succinct aphorisms, which he called "Quotations from Chairman Jobs." The sayings from the previous retreat, held in September 1982, were "It's Not Done Until It Ships," "Don't Compromise!" and "The Journey Is The Reward." This time, they were "Real Artists Ship," "It's Better To Be A Pirate Than Join The Navy," (see "Pirate Flag" on page 166) and "Mac in a Book by 1986."

The first day of the retreat was focused on engineering, and it went by quickly, as each member of the engineering team gave a short talk about their recent and upcoming work in the form of panel discussions, moderated by engineering manager Bob Belleville. At 4 P.M., the formal part of the meeting ended for the day, and we had a couple of hours of free time to enjoy before dinner. I was about to join a group going for a walk on the nearby beach when I was pulled aside by Bill Atkinson. It was obvious that something was bothering him.

Even though he was technically a member of the Lisa team, Bill attended the Macintosh retreats. Actually, now that the Lisa was finally completed, he planned to shift to working full-time on the Mac, to create a killer graphics application to be bundled with every machine (see "MacPaint Evolution" on page 171). He was going to start working on it soon, and we were all excited to see what he would come up with.

"Do you have a minute?" Bill asked me urgently, looking kind of somber. "I want to show you something privately." We picked one of the small conference rooms, went inside, and closed the door.

Bill was carrying three magazines, which he laid out in front of me on the table. Two of them were very recent issues of personal computer magazines, such as *Byte* and *Popular Computing*, while the third was more business-oriented. They all contained articles about the recently introduced Lisa. He opened one of them and showed me an article, with a sidebar entitled "An Interview with Lisa's Designers."

"Hey, that's cool," I told Bill, "You made it into *Byte*!"

"Look closer," Bill told me, with a pained expression on his face.

I started to browse the article and noticed it interviewed engineering manager Wayne Rosing, software manager Bruce Daniels, and applications group manager Larry Tesler. I finally saw why Bill looked so upset; he wasn't included as one of Lisa's designers, which was absurd, since he did more of the design than everyone else combined.

All three magazine articles featured quotes from Wayne, Bruce, and Larry, as well as Steve Jobs and John Couch, the top Lisa executive, but apparently no one thought to include Bill, possibly because he wasn't a manager. He was very disheartened, especially because something like this had happened to him once before.

Bill told me that he was haunted by a similar incident that had occurred six or seven years earlier. He had done some groundbreaking work to create a detailed 3D animation of the human brain. He'd scanned a series of brain slices, and then written software to reconstitute them in an animated sequence, rendering them frame by frame to produce a spectacular movie depicting important brain structures in stunning detail. The movie won various awards, and a frame from it had graced the cover of the October 1978 issue of *Scientific American*, but one of the professors he was working for received most of the credit, acknowledging Bill as only a minor collaborator in the published papers. Now it seemed to be happening all over again.

I tried to cheer him up, telling him the press was usually wrong about everything anyway, and that everyone at Apple understood his leading role in both the Lisa and Macintosh projects. I said there would be plenty of opportunities to talk with the press in the future. He told me that he was so upset he was thinking about quitting unless Apple rectified the situation somehow. We both knew he needed to talk with Steve Jobs about it, but he was nervous about bringing it up. I told him I thought he was completely justified, and that Apple ought to try to make it up to him.

Quotations from Chairman Jobs

"IT'S NOT DONE UNTIL IT SHIPS"

"DON'T COMPROMISE!"

"THE JOURNEY IS THE REWARD"

A few hours later, after dinner, Bill told me he had arranged to meet with Steve in private early the next morning, before the day's meetings commenced. He then surprised me by asking me to accompany him. I told him it wasn't my business and that I felt it was inappropriate for me to attend, but Bill insisted, telling me he needed my support, if only to have someone else present to help ground Steve's infamous reality distortion field (see "Reality Distortion Field" on page 24). Even though I knew it would be awkward, I told him I'd do it.

We were both nervous as Bill knocked on the door of the small office Steve was using during the retreat. Steve opened the door, looking angry when he noticed I was present.

"What is he doing here?" he asked Bill, before turning to face me. "Go away. This isn't any of your business!"

"No, I need Andy here," Bill intervened. "He didn't want to come, but I asked him to be here to support me."

Steve shrugged and decided to continue as if I weren't there. "Okay, let's hear it. And you need to be quick, because we have to start the meeting soon. What's the big problem?"

Bill explained how upset he was that he hadn't gotten any recognition for his work on Lisa. His voice was hesitant at first but picked up conviction as he started to get emotional. He told Steve that he was thinking about leaving Apple, because he was treated so unfairly.

"REAL ARTISTS SHIP"

"IT'S BETTER TO BE A PIRATE THAN JOIN THE NAVY"

"MAC IN BOOK BY 1986"

Even though Steve had enormous respect for Bill, he began to get annoyed, although you could tell he was trying not to.

"Hey, listen, I'm sorry. But you're over-reacting and blowing things out of proportion," Steve replied in a dismissive tone. "Who cares about a couple of magazines? You should have been included, but you weren't. Someone made a mistake. It's not such a big deal."

"That's easy for you to say," Bill retorted, upset at the lack of sympathy. He raised his voice, which was by now full of emotion. "I'm serious. I'm not going to work here anymore if you don't appreciate what I've done and treat me fairly."

Steve took a step toward the door. He seemed impatient. "I don't have time to deal with this now. We'll straighten it out when we get back. I have 60 other people out there who are pouring their hearts into the Macintosh, and they're waiting for me to start the meeting." He opened the door and left the room without saying another word.

Bill and I remained behind, unable to speak. I think we were both emotionally exhausted from the intense encounter. After a few minutes, we heard a loud cheer coming from the main meeting hall as Steve made a number of announcements to kick off the second day of the retreat. Bill sighed, and we left to join the others.

The following week, Steve arranged for Bill to meet with Apple's HR team to discuss what was bothering him. Bill reiterated that his main complaint was not getting recognition for his work. After more discussions with Steve, they came up with a solution that was mutually acceptable to everyone.

The company appointed Bill as an Apple Fellow in recognition for his work on the Lisa. Apple Fellow was the most prestigious technical position at Apple and had only been awarded to two other employees: Steve Wozniak and Rod Holt. There would now be two more, Bill Atkinson and Rich Page, for their seminal contributions to Lisa. A fringe benefit of being appointed an Apple Fellow was a fresh pile of stock options, which could be quite valuable if Apple's stock price continued to rise.

But most importantly of all, Steve promised Bill he would receive public recognition for his work on the Macintosh. Mac programs had an "About Box," a descriptive dialog box invoked by the first command in the leftmost menu, which would display Bill's name. Furthermore, Bill could display his name in the title bar of the main window each time his graphics application was launched. Finally, Steve promised that the Macintosh introduction would acknowledge the folks who actually created the design, rather than the managers who supervised them.

Steve was true to his word, and the seven people he designated as the "design team" were featured in various ways during the Macintosh launch. Our advertising firm, Chiat-Day, even filmed us for a series of television commercials, but those never aired because they were deemed too self-congratulatory. It was fun to get our pictures in the national press (see "Can We Keep The Skies Safe?" on page 226), but it was also problematic, because there wasn't a fair way to draw the line. At least a dozen individuals made crucial contributions to the design, so there were some hard feelings from the people who didn't make the cut.

In fact, Steve eventually decided that giving recognition to the designers was a bad idea. Nowadays, Apple has abolished programmer names in the "About Box," and closely guards the names of their designers, allowing only a select few employees to interact with the press.

Too Big for My Britches   February 1983
My belated performance review is delivered verbally

It was Apple's HR policy that every employee should receive a performance review every six months. These reviews, conducted by departmental managers, would then be used to help determine salary increases or the award of additional stock options. But as the end of 1982 approached, I hadn't received a review for more than eight months.

This wasn't too surprising, since my boss, Bob Belleville, was not getting along very well with the software team. He thought some of us were intrinsically unmanageable and that we didn't sufficiently respect him. Bob had replaced Rod Holt as the overall engineering manager in August. He was responsible for both hardware and software and had just hired a new software manager, Jerome Coonen (who was slated to begin in January) so Bob could further distance himself from the software team. But he still had to deal with us directly one last time to write our reviews for 1982.

By the end of January, everyone on the team had received a review—except for me. Others mentioned that Bob had acted somewhat strangely during their reviews, making cryptic remarks they didn't understand, so I wasn't particularly looking forward to mine. I occasionally had to interact with Bob, but he was reticent around me, not saying much, seemingly hiding behind his enigmatic, tight-lipped smile. Finally, in mid-February, Bob's secretary called me to arrange an appointment, presumably for my belated review.

The meeting was scheduled for 5 P.M. on a Thursday afternoon. Bob was waiting for me when I entered his corner cubicle. I asked him what was up. He said he didn't want to get into it in the office and suggested we take a walk around the block. Everyone knew that walks around the block were usually reserved for firing or demoting someone, or to talk someone into staying after they had quit. I was even more apprehensive than before.

Bob waited until we were a full block away from Bandley 4 before starting to speak. "Well, Andy, you're not going to like hearing this, but you're a big problem on the software team and I'm giving you a negative review for the last six months of 1982."

I knew Bob disliked me, but I was nevertheless shocked. All my previous reviews from Apple had been extremely positive, including the last one from Bob, so this was new to me. I had been working my heart out seven days a week for more than two years, devoting my life to the Macintosh, holding the project together after Bud returned to medical school.

The problem is with your attitude, and your relationship with management. You are consistently insubordinate, and you don't have any respect for lines of authority. I think you are undermining everybody else on the software team. You are too big for your britches."

I was really doing the equivalent of two full-time jobs, writing the Mac Toolbox in assembly language by night and helping everybody else by doing whatever was necessary each day.

"How can you say that?" I responded. "I accomplished everything I was supposed to, and a lot more besides."

Bob unfurled his mirthless grin. "Oh, don't get me wrong. I think your technical work has been perfectly adequate during the review period, and I don't have a single criticism of it. That's not your problem area." He paused for a moment to take a deep breath, and then continued. "The problem is with your attitude, and your relationship with management. You are consistently insubordinate, and you don't have any respect for lines of authority. I think you are undermining everybody else on the software team. You are too big for your britches."

At this point, I broke down into tears. The Macintosh was at the center of my life, but I couldn't work for somebody who was saying this, no matter how much the project mattered to me. It was suddenly clear that I was going to have to quit.

Perhaps a bit taken aback by my tears, Bob tried to soften things a bit. "Listen, this could be a very expensive conversation. It could turn out to be either very good or very bad for both of us. I'm trying to get you to see how, if you listen to me, things could turn out very good for both of us."

I had no idea what he was talking about, or how a bad review could possibly be good for me. "What do you mean, undermining the team?" I managed to choke out, "I'm always trying to help everybody else on the team. Give me one example of someone who I've undermined."

"Larry Kenyon," Bob replied. "You're stifling Larry Kenyon. Now he is someone with a good attitude, and you're keeping him from realizing his potential."

I'd always thought I'd gotten along really well with Larry. I had recruited him to the Mac team after working with him on Apple II peripheral cards in 1980, and then handed off the low-level OS stuff to him while I worked on the Toolbox. I thought Larry was a terrific programmer and a great person. I treated him with the highest respect and always enjoyed working together. The only thing I could think of was that I had reacted poorly a few months earlier when Bob appointed Larry as temporary manager when he was away on a short trip. I thought he'd done it just to irk me.

By this point I was crying even harder, and it looked as if Bob might start crying at any moment, too. We were pretty far from Bandley 4 by now, and it was starting to get dark. The tone of the conversation seemed to shift as we both realized that we should start heading back.

"This doesn't have to be that bad," Bob said as we turned around. "All you have to do is listen to me and things will work out fine."

"What do you mean?" I asked.

"You need to show more respect to authority. It's not just me. Jerome is still new, but he's your boss now, and you need to show him respect and let him do his job. But that's not the main problem. What you really have to do is stop talking to Steve Jobs." Bob paused and flinched slightly, as if just mentioning Steve was difficult for him.

"Whenever there's something you don't like, even little things, you go running straight to Steve, and he interferes. I don't have any authority with the software team because they always hear everything from Steve before I do, and he always hears everything about the software straight from you. It's making it so I can't do my job. You should communicate through the proper channels. I can't tell Steve what to do, but you work for me, so I can tell you."

I did respect Jerome, and I was trying to make an extra effort to support him as our manager because I knew we really needed him. Jerome was a very smart guy and a passionate genius when it came to numerical software; I loved to hear him elucidate the intricacies of his beloved floating-point routines. But I did consider him to be more of a partner than a boss, just as I did everyone else on the team, and I didn't think that he had a problem with that. Apparently Bob did.

But the Steve issue was different. From the earliest days of the project, Steve would usually show up at the Mac building in the late afternoon, or sometimes after dinner, and ask us about the happenings of the day. We would demo the latest stuff to him, or he'd complain about something, or sometimes we'd just exchange the latest gossip. After Bud went back to medical school, Burrell and I were the only ones who would regularly stay late. But after a while more of the team began to hang out with us. It wasn't unusual for six or eight of us to go out for a late dinner and then return and keep working. By early 1983, most of the software team was staying late, and even some marketing and finance people would join us. But Bob Belleville never did because he had to get home to his wife and two young daughters.

"I can't stop Steve from coming around," I told Bob. "If you don't want me to talk with Steve, you're going to have to tell him about it. I like Jerome, and I have no problem working with him, but now it looks as though I have a problem working with you. If you think I'm undermining the team, I'm out of here tomorrow."

Bob looked at me intently. "I don't have the power to fire you," he said. "You're going to give me power that I don't have if you quit. Do you really want to do that?"

It was completely dark as we approached the Apple parking lot. We stopped in front of Bob's car.

"This could be a really expensive conversation for both of us," Bob muttered cryptically. "It's entirely up to you." With that, he got into his car and drove off, and I wandered back into Bandley 4, feeling stunned and drained. I got back to my cubicle, put my head down on the desk, and started crying again.

By this time it was around 6:30 P.M. and most of the software team was still around. Capps saw that I was upset and asked me what was wrong. He began to get angry when I told him and a few others what had just happened. He made me promise not to overreact until he had a chance to find out what was going on.

Larry Kenyon was still in his cubicle, and I went over and told him what Bob had said. I asked him to be honest and tell me if he thought I was stifling him in any way.

"You've got to be kidding!" Larry exclaimed. "I think it's really great working with you. That's the reason I'm on this team. I think it's an honor to work with you." With that, I burst into tears again.

I was exhausted and confused. I decided to head home to get some sleep and think about what I should do next. When I came in earlier than usual the next morning, there was a message on my desk to call Pat Sharp, Steve's secretary. When I reached her, she told me to come to Steve's office right away.

"I can't believe Bob gave you that review," Steve started talking even before I stepped into his office. "He showed it to me a week ago, but I refused to approve it, and I told him to write something more positive. Do you have a copy of it?"

I told Steve that Bob hadn't given me a copy; he'd just delivered the news verbally. I then explained that I didn't feel I could work for someone who felt that way about me and had no alternative but to quit.

"It's good that you don't have a copy, because that review is rescinded. It doesn't officially exist. I just got done talking with Bob, and after I chewed him out, he also quit because he said that he can't manage the software team. And Capps came in here and told me the rest of the software team is so upset that they're thinking about quitting, too. What a mess! You and Bob don't have to love each other to work together. We're going to sit down this afternoon and talk this thing out until it's resolved."

So, at 4 P.M. on Friday afternoon, as soon as Steve was available, the entire software team, plus Burrell, filed into one of the conference rooms. We all sat in a semi-circle of chairs on the right side of the room, waiting apprehensively. Steve finally strode in with his characteristic bouncy stride, trailed by a despondent-looking Bob Belleville, who took a seat on the left side of the room facing the software team.

Steve started talking first. He said that tensions had been building up for a while and it was time to clear the air so we could all pull together down the home stretch. All the while Bob was staring at the floor, unwilling to make eye contact with anyone else, controlling his emotions behind a tight-lipped expression, halfway between grin and grimace.

"Okay, who's going to go first? What's the problem, and how do we fix it?" Steve asked.

Capps spoke up, explaining how painful and unmotivating it was to see me broken up about an obviously unjustified review. He wanted to know how things could have gotten so screwed up.

Steve nodded to Bob, encouraging him to speak up. Bob spoke in a monotone. "I didn't give Andy a bad review. I told him that his work was fine."

I was flabbergasted. "You said I was undermining the team and stifling Larry," I blurted out.

Bob looked me in the eye for the first time. He spoke in a mild, low emotionless monotone. "I didn't say any of those things. Why are you claiming that I did?"

I was utterly shocked. Bob was denying everything he'd said the day before. Furthermore, he genuinely seemed to believe what he was saying. He looked to be in a kind of trance, both depressed and confused. I didn't know how to proceed. If he wasn't going to acknowledge what he had said, there was certainly no way to resolve it. I said nothing.

A few more people spoke up, addressing other grievances, but Bob's trance-like manner persisted and eventually the meeting broke up without anyone being satisfied. Steve tried to declare victory at the end, but no one was buying it.

I thought about things over the weekend and realized I cared too much about the Macintosh to quit before it was finished, managerial adversity notwithstanding. The situation that I feared when Bud left had actually occurred, in spades, and I wasn't confident Steve would live up to his promise to protect me. I wasn't sure what was going to happen, but I knew that my blissful days at Apple were over. Things were clearly going to be different from now on.

Steve Icon   February 1983
Having your own icon becomes a status symbol

In February 1983, I started working on an icon editor that Susan Kare could use to create icons for the Finder. Inspired by the "Fat Bits" pixel editing mode that Bill Atkinson had recently added to MacPaint, it had a large window with a 32 × 32 grid, displaying each pixel 8 times its natural size, as well as a small window that showed the icon at its actual size. Clicking on a pixel inverted it, and subsequent dragging propagated the change to the dragged over pixels.

Susan started working on icons for the Finder, but she also used my editor to draw many other practice images and to create fun icons that often reflected her whimsical sense of humor. One day, I went by her cubicle and was surprised to see her laboring over a tiny icon portrait of Steve Jobs.

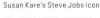
Susan Kare's Steve Jobs icon

Icons were only 32 × 32 black or white pixels, 1024 dots in total, and I didn't think it was possible to do a very good portrait in such a tiny space. But somehow, Susan had succeeded in crafting an instantly recognizable likeness with a mischievous grin that captured a lot of Steve's personality. Everyone she showed it to liked it, even Steve himself.

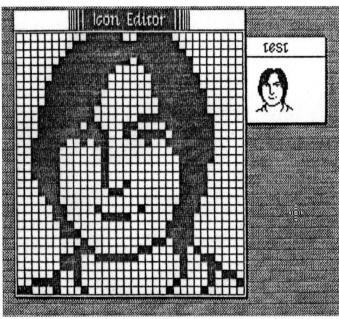

Bill Atkinson was so impressed with the Steve icon that he asked Susan to draw one of him so he could use it in the MacPaint About box. He sat in Susan's cubicle for an hour or so, chatting with her while she crafted his icon. I don't think it turned out quite as nice as the Steve icon, but it certainly was an unmistakable likeness, and it did become part of MacPaint.

At that point, it became something of a Mac team status symbol to be iconified by

Susan. As soon as he saw Bill's icon, Burrell Smith started begging Susan for one, even though he had no specific use for it. He lobbied Susan for a few days, making his standard offer of best friendship (see "I'll Be Your Best Friend" on page 5), before she gave in and had him pose.

Susan did a few more portraits for various members of the team who desired to be immortalized in a thousand dots. She usually worked on them in the late afternoon, chatting with the subjects as they posed, while other team members listened in. I got to know a few of my teammates a lot better from these sessions.

Bouncing Pepsis

March 1983
We cook up a special demo for John Sculley

The Window Manager was the one of the most important parts of the User Interface Toolbox. Its job was to calculate various regions for windows as they were created, moved, and resized, so the graphics drawn inside could be automatically clipped as necessary. It was the ultimate showcase for QuickDraw's "region clipping" technology.

The Macintosh Window Manager was based on a design Bill Atkinson wrote in Pascal for the Lisa; my job was to rewrite it in 68000 assembly language and adapt it to the Macintosh environment. The first step was to port Bill's Pascal version. I wrote a little program to test the port, which I called "Window Manager Demo," to generate some windows and put the window manager through its paces. A year earlier, I had written a fast "ball bouncing" routine using custom, 16 × 16 pixel graphics routines, that could animate hundreds of balls simultaneously. It was a fun way to show off the Mac's raw graphical horsepower (see "Early Demos" on page 34). Using QuickDraw, I decided to animate a few dozen balls in each

window of the Window Manager demo because their continuous movement would eventually cover all the bases inside a window and expose any flaws in the underlying clipping. After Susan Kare joined the Mac team in January 1983, I asked her to draw some tiny 16 × 16 bitmaps to use in the Window Manager demo instead of the by now monotonous ball shapes. We soon had a variety of little objects bouncing around the various windows, including tiny little Macintoshes, apples, insects, and alligators. At this point, I thought the Window Manager Demo was finished—but I was wrong.

Bouncing Pepsi caps in the Window Manager demo

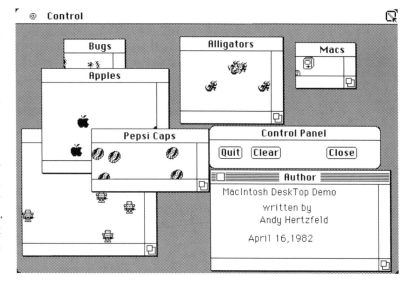

Steve Jobs, John Sculley, and Steve Wozniak at the Apple IIc introduction in April 1984

Steve Jobs came by the software area one evening a couple of months later, excited about someone he had recently met in New York City. "Hey, I want you to do a demo next week for this guy I met yesterday, John Sculley. He's the president of Pepsi," he said. "You wouldn't believe how smart he is. If we impress him, we can get Pepsi to buy thousands of Macs. Maybe even five thousand. Why don't you try to come up with something special to show him?"

It sounded a little bit fishy to me; we hardly ever demoed to potential customers at that point. But I asked Susan to draw some Pepsi imagery, and she came up with tiny little Pepsi caps, as well as Pepsi cans, in John's honor, and I put them into the Window Manager demo.

The next week, Mike Murray led John Sculley around the engineering area since Steve was out of town. He brought him by my cubicle to see the modified Window Manager demo. I opened the windows one at a time, saving the Pepsi caps and cans for last. He seemed genuinely excited to see the Pepsi stuff, but oddly cold for most of the demo. He asked a few questions, but he didn't seem all that interested in the answers.

A few weeks later, we found out the real story. The purpose of John's visit was to interview for CEO of Apple, and he took the job after being convinced by Steve's famous line, "Would you rather sell sugar water to kids for the rest of your life, or would you like a chance to change the world?"

Would you rather sell **sugar water** to kids for the rest of your life or would you like a chance to **change the world?**

Swedish Campground   August 1983
We find an unusual symbol to use for the menu command key

Early on in the development of the Macintosh, we decided it was important for the user to be able to invoke every menu command directly from the keyboard, like the Mac's predecessor, Lisa, so we added a special key for this purpose. We called it the "Apple key" and when pressed in combination with another key, it selected the corresponding menu command. We displayed a little Apple logo on the right side of every menu item with a keyboard command to associate the key with the command.

One day, late in the afternoon, Steve Jobs burst into the software fishbowl area in Bandley III, upset about something. This was not unusual. I think he had just seen MacDraw for the first time, which had longer menus than our other applications.

"There are too many Apples on the screen! It's ridiculous! We're taking the Apple logo in vain! We've got to stop doing that!"

After we told him we had to display the command key symbol with each item that had one, he told us we had better find a new symbol to use instead of the Apple logo, and, because our decision would affect both the manuals and the keyboard hardware, we had only a few days to come up with it.

It's difficult to come up with a small icon meaning "command," and we couldn't think of anything initially. Our bitmap artist, Susan Kare, had a comprehensive international symbol dictionary and she leafed through it, looking for an appropriate symbol that was distinctive, attractive, and had at least something to do with the concept of a menu command.

Finally she came across a floral symbol used on Swedish maps to indicate an interesting feature or attraction in a historical site or campground. She rendered a 16 × 16 bitmap of the little symbol and showed it to the rest of the team. Everybody liked it, and 20 years later—even in OS X—the Macintosh still has a little bit of a Swedish campground in it.

"There are too many Apples on the screen!... We're taking the Apple logo in vain!"

busy being born, part 2

Here are a few seminal Macintosh screenshots, à la the Lisa Polaroids

Bill Atkinson had the foresight to document the creation of the Lisa User Interface by keeping a Polaroid camera near his computer and taking a snapshot of each significant milestone (see "Busy Being Born" on page 89). Although we didn't systematically save pictures of key Mac milestones, I've managed to cobble together a few seminal Macintosh screenshots to present here in a similar fashion.

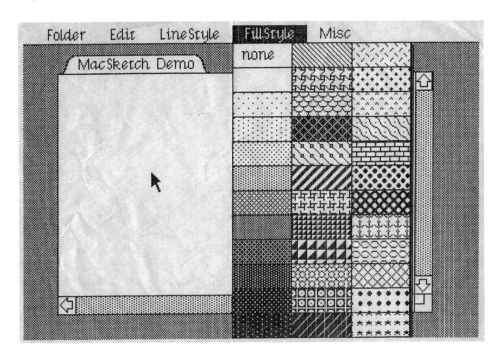

The first Mac-like demo in May 1981

Bud Tribble had a tendency to work late at night. I usually came to work at Texaco Towers around 10:30 A.M., so if Bud was there when I arrived, it usually meant he had spent all night there. One morning in the middle of May 1981, I arrived at my usual time and found Bud anxious to show me something before I could even take off my backpack.

I knew Bud had been working on the initial porting of QuickDraw to the Macintosh, but I thought he was at least a week away from getting it running. At this point, we had some cursor routines going. We also had a way to download and execute Pascal programs that were compiled on a Lisa by attaching them to the Mac by a serial cable. But we didn't have a memory manager yet, or an event manager or a filesystem, so Bud had to build scaffolding in various places to overcome these limitations. He had compiled a bitmap drawing program that Bill wrote in Pascal for the Lisa, however, and he linked it with LisaGraf and other library routines so he could debug it and fix each problem as it manifested.

Bud had made a huge amount of progress the previous evening and had the demo running pretty well. It was incredibly exciting to see Mac-like software running on the Mac for the very first time. The demo featured working pull-down menus, complete with a nicer style of drop shadow than the Lisa was using, and an elaborate, graphical pattern menu, which is illustrated in the screenshot above.

Xerox aficionados will note the use of Cream 12 as our first system font, which was the default font used by Smalltalk that Bill had converted to the LisaGraf font format. The window title bar was a folder tab because we were still confused about the difference between folders and documents. The demo already had scroll bars and a grow box that was pretty similar to what we ended up shipping, although you couldn't interact with them yet. In fact, the only part of the program that actually did something was the Quit command.

In April, I had written some screen-printing code that dumped whatever was on the display out the serial port to a dot matrix printer. Since the Mac screen was rather small, I added a feature to print it at double size, so it mostly filled a page. I used that to print the display of Bud's demo, with the impressive graphical pattern menu pulled down on the same day Bud got it working, and that's what is reproduced here.

· · · · · · · · · · · ·

Bruce Horn joined the Mac team in late 1981, with the charter to write a graphical shell we were calling the "Finder," since it helped the user find applications and documents to launch. We were influenced by ideas from the Architecture Machine group at M.I.T. (a predecessor to the better known Media Lab), as portrayed in a program called "Dataland" that allowed users to manipulate graphical objects in spatial arrangements. Bruce was excited about spatial data management, and his first assignment was to write a prototype to explore how it could work on the Mac.

Bruce came up with the idea of representing files as small tabs superimposed on an image of a floppy disk. He wrote a prototype he called the "micro-finder," which is pictured above. I started helping him implement various parts of it, and pretty soon it was actually useful. You could drag the file tabs to position them, and click on the large buttons on the right to launch programs or rename and delete files. We used the micro-finder through most of 1982 for demoing the Mac, until the real Finder started becoming usable around the end of the year.

After the micro-finder, Bruce also worked on another prototype that included folders in a two-pane view. Meanwhile, Bill Atkinson was crafting an icon-based file manager prototype for Lisa (see "Rosing's Rascals" on page 74), and we eventually decided to follow that direction for the Macintosh.

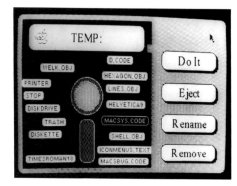

An alternate approach to the Finder in March 1982

. . . .

The following screenshot is a very early version of MacPaint, probably from March 1983, after Bill had been working on it for around one month. Notice that it wasn't called "MacPaint" yet; it still bore its original name, "MacSketch," inherited from its predecessor, LisaSketch.

This early version uses icons designed by Bill himself. Susan Kare tweaked them later. Some of the most important MacPaint tools like the paint bucket and the lasso were still months away from being implemented.

MacPaint contained a menu of miscellaneous tools, like Fat Bits, originally called the "Aids" menu, as you can see in the screenshot. But in

An early screenshot of a half-implemented MacPaint

the summer of 1983, with public awareness of the AIDS epidemic beginning to swell, Bill rechristened it the "Goodies" menu.

It's interesting to note the window-highlighting decorations, which are quite different than what we ended up with. We must have tried dozens of different ways to highlight windows before arriving at the horizontal lines in August 1983.

The featured MacPaint document was drawn late one night by Steve Capps to celebrate one of our ROM releases; he also saved and scanned the document for inclusion here.

. . . .

In early 1983, I wrote an icon editor based on Bill Atkinson's Fat Bits pixel-editing techniques that Susan Kare used to craft most of the early Mac icons. The icon editor displayed both a large and actual size representation of the icon, and allowed editing of multiple icons at once (See "Steve Icon" on page 147). I needed a way to incorporate the icons into the ROM, so I added a feature called the "Hex Window," which displayed the representation of the current icon in hexadecimal. That allowed me to add the icons to the Mac ROM source code. The screen dumps on the right are the actual ones used to enter some famous Mac icons into ROM, such as the bomb and the happy Mac.

Note that the name on the window containing the bomb icon is "Deep." That's the first word of the original, and obscene, name of the code that displayed the dreaded bomb icon on the screen. The system calls that displayed the bomb icon were all prefixed with "DS," the initials of the obscene name, which Apple understandably didn't want to use. Jerome came up with various euphemisms, such as the "Deep Sauce" manager, which evolved into the "Dire Straights" manager. We eventually settled on the more prosaic "System Error" manager.

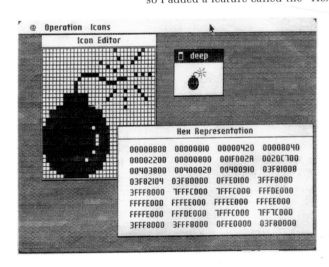

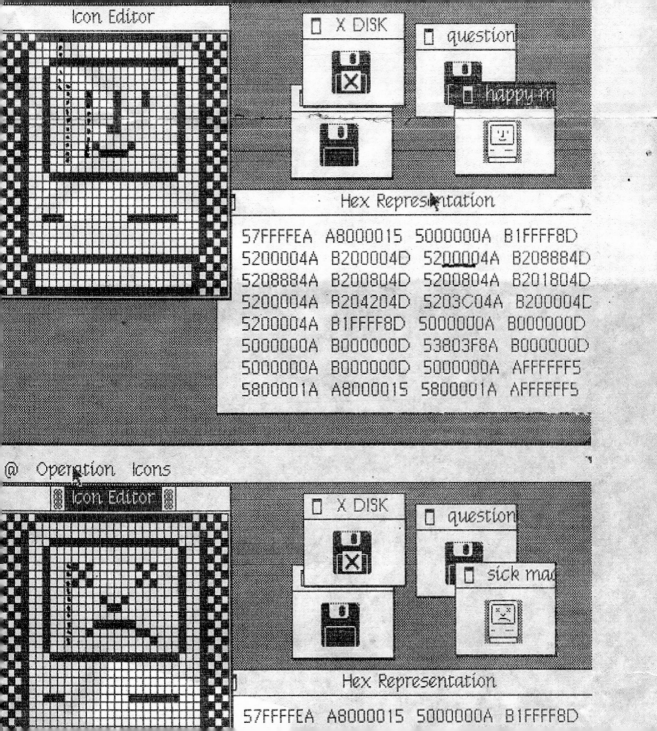

Icon Editor

X DISK

question

happy m

Hex Representation

```
57FFFFEA  A8000015  5000000A  B1FFFF8D
5200004A  B200004D  5200004A  B208884D
5208884A  B200804D  5200804A  B201804D
5200004A  B204204D  5203C04A  B200004C
5200004A  B1FFFF8D  5000000A  B000000D
5000000A  B000000D  53803F8A  B000000D
5000000A  B000000D  5000000A  AFFFFFF5
5800001A  A8000015  5800001A  AFFFFFF5
```

@ Operation Icons

Icon Editor

X DISK

question

sick mac

Hex Representation

```
57FFFFEA  A8000015  5000000A  B1FFFF8D
```

Quick, Hide in This Closet!

August 1983

Steve forbids us from working with Sony

In 1980, Apple reorganized yet again, splitting off a new "Disk Division" headed by John Vennard, who was responsible for developing a hard disk codenamed "Pippin," as well as for a next-generation floppy disk codenamed "Twiggy." Both were to be used first by the Lisa project, and then across Apple's entire product line. At Rod Holt's request, I had written some early diagnostics for Twiggy using an Apple II, but I was happy when they asked Rich Williams to transfer to the disk division as their software guy, since focusing exclusively on disks seemed pretty limiting to me.

Woz's Apple II floppy disk design was way ahead of the rest of the industry, and Apple felt confident it could continue to innovate to extend its lead. Twiggy was a fairly ambitious project that strove to more than quadruple the capacity of standard floppy disks by doubling the data rate (which required higher density media) and employing other innovative tricks like motor speed control, which slowed down the disk rotation speed on the outer tracks to cram more data on them.

The Lisa was designed to include two built-in Twiggy drives, so it made sense for the Macintosh to use Twiggy as well. But the Lisa team began to encounter unexpected difficulties in getting the drive to work properly. Soon, the optional external hard drive became mandatory, increasing the minimum price of a Lisa by more than $1,000.

Lisa was announced with great fanfare in January of 1983, but it still wasn't ready to ship. There were problems in a number of areas, but the biggest one was the low yield of the Twiggy drives, whose high error rate greatly limited production. Finally, Lisas were shipped to customers in June 1983, even though production and reliability problems with the disk drives continued.

Meanwhile, the Mac team was beginning to panic. We were using a single Twiggy drive as our floppy disk, and we didn't have a hard disk to fall back on. It looked as though the Twiggy drive was never going to be reliable enough or cost effective for the Macintosh, but we were stuck without an alternative. If we couldn't find a suitable replacement quickly enough, we'd have to slip the entire project indefinitely.

Fortunately, we were aware of Sony's new 3.5" drive that had started shipping in the spring of 1983 through Hewlett-Packard, their development partner. George Crow, the analog engineer who designed the Mac's analog board, had come from HP prior to working at Apple and was sold on the superiority of the Sony drives. He procured a drive from his friends at HP and proposed to Bob Belleville that we figure out how to interface it to the Mac as soon as possible while negotiating a deal with Sony.

The Sony drive looked really sweet, especially when compared to the Twiggy. It used the same data rate as Twiggy, but on smaller disks that could fit in a shirt pocket. Best of all, the media was encased in a hard plastic shell, making it much less fragile and more convenient to handle.

Steve Jobs was finally ready to acknowledge reality and give up on the Twiggy drive. When he saw the Sony drive he loved it, and immediately wanted to adapt it for the Mac. But instead of doing the obvious thing and striking a deal with Sony, Steve decided that Apple should take what we learned from Twiggy and engineer our own version of a 3.5" drive, working with our Japanese manufacturing partner Alps Electronics, who manufactured the Apple II floppy drives at a very low cost.

This seemed like suicide to George Crow and Bob Belleville. The Mac was supposed to ship in less than seven months, and it was preposterous to think we could get a 3.5" drive into production by then, given the disk division's dismal track record. But Steve was convinced we should do our own drive and told Bob to cease all work on the Sony drive. He instructed Rod Holt, Bob, and George to fly to Japan to meet with Alps to initiate a crash project to develop a workable 3.5" drive.

Bob and George grudgingly went along with the Alps program, but they were certain the team would discover we couldn't pull it off in the allotted time frame. They hatched an alternative plan to continue working with Sony surreptitiously, against Steve's wishes. Larry Kenyon was given a Sony drive to interface to the Mac, but he was told to keep it hidden, especially from Steve. Bob and George also arranged meetings with Sony to discuss the customizations Apple desired and to hammer out the beginnings of a business deal.

This dual strategy entailed frequent meetings with both Alps and Sony, with the added burden of keeping the Sony meetings secret from Steve. It wasn't difficult to do in Japan since Steve didn't attend those meetings, but it got a little awkward when Sony employees visited us in Cupertino. Sony sent a young engineer named Hide Kamoto to work with Larry Kenyon to spec out the modifications we required. He was sitting in Larry's cubicle

"...American business practices, they are very strange. Very strange."

with George Crow when we suddenly heard Steve Jobs's voice as he unexpectedly strode into the software area.

George knew Steve would wonder who Kamoto-san was if he saw him. Thinking quickly, he immediately tapped Kamoto-san on his shoulder, and spoke hurriedly while pointing at the nearby janitorial closet. "Dozo, quick, hide in this closet. Please! Now!"

Kamoto-san looked confused but he got up from his seat and hurried into the dark janitorial closet. He had to stay there for five minutes or so until Steve departed and the coast was clear.

George and Larry apologized to Kamoto-san for their unusual request. "No problem," he replied. "But American business practices, they are very strange. Very strange."

As predicted, a few weeks later the Alps team came back with an 18-month estimate for getting their drive into production, and we had to abandon the project. When Bob Belleville revealed that he and George had kept the Sony alternative alive, Steve swallowed his pride and thanked them for disobeying him and doing the right thing. The Sony drives eventually worked out great, and it's hard to imagine what the Mac would have been like without them.

Saving Lives   August 1983
Steve wants us to make the Macintosh boot faster

We always thought of the Macintosh as a fast computer. Its 68000 microprocessor was effectively 10 times faster than an Apple II, but our Achilles heel was the floppy disk. We had limited memory, so it was often necessary to load data from the floppy, but there we were no faster than an Apple II. Once we had some real applications going, it was clear the floppy disk was going to be a significant bottleneck.

One of the things that bothered Steve Jobs the most was the time that it took to boot up when the Mac was first powered on. It could take a couple of minutes or more, to test memory, initialize the operating system, and load the Finder. One afternoon, Steve came up with an original way to motivate us to make it faster. Larry Kenyon was the engineer working on the disk driver and filesystem, and one day Steve went into his cubicle and started to exhort him. "The Macintosh boots too slowly. You've got to make it faster!"

Larry started to explain about some of the places where he thought he could improve things, but Steve wasn't interested. He continued, "You know, I've been thinking about it. How many people are going to be using the Macintosh? A million? No, more than that. In a few years, I bet 5 million people will be booting up their Macintoshes at least once a day.

"Well, let's say you can shave 10 seconds off the boot time. Multiply that by 5 million users and that's 50 million seconds every single day. Over a year, that's probably dozens of lifetimes. Just think about it. If you could make it boot 10 seconds faster, you'll save a dozen lives. That's really worth it, don't you think?"

We were already pretty motivated to make the software go as fast as we could, so I don't think his pitch had much effect, but we all thought it was pretty humorous. And while I'm not sure we saved any lives, we did manage to shave more than 10 seconds off the boot time over the next couple of months.

Stolen from Apple   August 1983
We put a hidden icon in the ROM

In 1980, a company called Franklin Computer produced a clone of the Apple II called the Franklin Ace, designed to run the same software. They copied almost every detail of the Apple II, including all of its ROM-based software and all the documentation, and sold it at a lower price than Apple. We even found a place in the manual where they forgot to change "Apple" to "Ace." Apple was infuriated and sued Franklin. They eventually won and forced Franklin to withdraw the Ace from the market, but that victory certainly wasn't a foregone conclusion.

Franklin argued they had a right to copy the Apple II ROMs because it was just a "functional mechanism" necessary for software compatibility. We anticipated someone might try a similar trick with the Macintosh someday. If they were clever enough (which Franklin wasn't), they could disguise the code so it wouldn't look that similar at the binary level. We thought we'd better take some precautions.

Steve Jobs had the idea that a large "Stolen from Apple" icon should be embedded in the ROM and somehow be triggered to appear on the screen of any infringing machine. The routines and data required to accomplish this would have to be incorporated into our ROM in a stealthy fashion, so the cloners wouldn't know how to find or remove it.

It was tricky enough to be a fun project. Susan designed a nice "Stolen from Apple" icon that featured prison bars. Steve Capps had recently come up with a simple scheme for compressing ROM-based icons to save space, so we compressed the icon using his technique. This not only reduced the overhead but also made it much harder to detect the icon. Finally, we wrote a tiny routine to decompress the icon, scale it up, and display it on the screen. We hid it in the middle of some data tables so it would be hard to spot when disassembling the ROM.

All you had to do to invoke it is enter the debugger and type a 6-digit hexadecimal address followed by a "G," which meant execute the routine at that address. We demoed it for Steve and he liked it.

Must give appl info about ornaments like memory expense —
can force them in sys heap, too

Along with "paranoia bit" in parameter memory, we need a
"patience bit" to indicate user is ~~patient~~ patient + wants to see whizzy
things that may be time-consuming, impatient means cut the frills
Use for boot screen, at least

The thief trap →

    plot compressed icon in upper left
    4X magnify it in lower right with copyBits

Trigger:
    ~~Observe~~ trap, with #$4!48 in D0
    unimplemented

✓ ~~INC Screen for self-loop at CntCtr~~

Cutting + pasting between applications

    Instead of a single scrap, have a gallery. One gallery entry is the scrap
where most cuts + pastes go, but you can connect to other pictures
in the gallery.
    This way, you can xfer n things between apps, only switching once.

We were kind of hoping someone would copy the ROM just so we could show off our foresight, but as far as I know, no one ever did. We let it slip that there was a "Stolen from Apple" icon hidden in there somewhere, partially to deter people from copying the ROM. At least one hacker became moderately obsessed with trying to find it.

Steve Jasik was the author of the MacNosy disassembler/debugger, which could be used to create pseudo-source for the ROM. He found out about the "Stolen from Apple" icon pretty early on, and he became determined to isolate it. Because he lived in Palo Alto, I would occasionally bump into him and he'd ask me for hints or tell me his latest theory about how it was concealed. He was invariably wrong.

After two or three years of this he finally cracked it. I ran into him and he told me about the compressed icon and the address of the display routine. I congratulated him, but I was never sure if he figured it out himself or if someone with access to the source code told him where the icon was tucked away.

World Class Cities
How we named our fonts

August 1983

One memorable job I had as a bitmap graphic designer in the Macintosh group was designing the screen fonts. It was especially enjoyable because the Macintosh was able to display proportional typefaces, leaving behind the tyranny of monospace alphabets with their narrow m's and wide i's.

The first Macintosh font was a bold system font with no jagged diagonals called "Elefont." There were going to be lots of fonts included with the Mac, so we were looking for a set of attractive, related names. Andy Hertzfeld and I had met in high school in suburban Philadelphia, so we started naming the other fonts after stops on the Paoli Local commuter train: Overbrook, Merion, Ardmore, and Rosemont. (Ransom was the only one that broke this convention; it was a font of mismatched letters intended to evoke messages from kidnapers made from cutout letters.)

One afternoon Steve Jobs stopped by the software group, as he often did at the end of the day. He frowned as he looked at the font names on a menu. "What are those names?" he asked, and we responded by explaining the Paoli Local.

"Well," he said, "Cities are OK, but not little cities that nobody's ever heard of. They ought to be world class cities!"

And that is how Chicago (Elefont), New York, Geneva, London, San Francisco (Ransom), Toronto, and Venice (Bill Atkinson's script font) got their names.

contributed by
Susan Kare

Pirate Flag

August 1983
The Mac Team hoists a pirate flag

In January 1983, just after the Lisa introduction, the Mac team held another off-site retreat in Carmel (see "Credit Where Due" on page 135). Steve Jobs opened the retreat with three of his now-famous "Sayings from Chairman Jobs."

1. Real artists ship.
2. It's better to be a pirate than join the navy.
3. Mac in a book by 1986.

I think the "pirates" remark addressed the feeling among some of the earlier team members that the Mac group was getting too large and bureaucratic. We had started out as a rebellious skunkworks, much like Apple itself, and Steve wanted us to preserve our original spirit even as we were growing more like the Navy every day.

In fact, we were growing so fast that we needed to move again. So, in August of 1983, we moved across the street to a larger building that was unimaginatively designated "Bandley 3." I had worked there before, in 1980, when Apple had initially built it to house the original engineering organization. But now it was to be the new home of the newly christened "Macintosh Division," over 80 employees strong.

The building looked pretty much like every other Apple building, so we wanted to do something to make it look like we belonged there. Steve Capps, the heroic programmer who had switched over from the Lisa team just in time for the January retreat, had a flash of inspiration: if the Mac team was a band of pirates, the building should fly a pirate flag.

A few days before we moved into the new building, Capps bought some black cloth and sewed it into a flag. He asked Susan Kare to paint a big skull and crossbones in white at the center. The final touch was the requisite eye-patch, rendered by a large, rainbow-colored Apple logo decal. We wanted to have the flag flying over the building early Monday morning, the first day of occupancy, so the plan was to install it late Sunday evening.

Capps had already made a few exploratory forays onto the roof during the weekend while a few of us looked out for guards on the ground. At first, he thought he could just drape the flag on the roof, but that proved impractical, as it was too hard to see, especially when the wind curled it up. After a bit of searching, he found a thin metal pole among the remaining construction materials still scattered inside the building, which served as a suitable flagpole.

Finally, on Sunday night around 10 P.M., it was time to hoist the Jolly Roger. Capps climbed onto the roof while we stood guard below. He wasn't sure how he would attach the flag and didn't have many tools with him. He scoured the surface of the roof and found three or four long, rusty nails, which he was able to use to secure the flagpole to a groove in the roof, ready to greet the Mac team members as they entered the new building the next morning.

We weren't sure how people would react to the flag, especially Steve Jobs, but Steve and almost everyone else loved it, so it stayed. It made me smile whenever I caught a glimpse of it.

The flag waved proudly over Bandley 3 for about a month or two, but one morning in late September or early October, I noticed it was gone. It turned out the Lisa team, with whom we had a mostly friendly rivalry, had decided it would be fun to steal the flag for themselves. I think they even sent us a ransom note. A few of us stormed over to the Lisa building to retrieve it, and Capps had to wrestle it from the grasp of one of the secretaries, who was hiding it in her desk.

The flag continued to fly over Bandley 3 for more than a year. It was even photographed for a magazine or two during the Mac introduction. But suddenly one day it was missing again. We never did figure out what happened to it.

contributed by
Donn Denman

Make a Mess, Clean It Up! September 1983
Burrell's unique approach to playing Defender

Facing page:
a screenshot of Defender,
Burrell's favorite game

Working 90 hours a week requires frequent and highly effective work breaks. In the center of the Macintosh work area in Bandley 3 we had a ping-pong table, a stereo system, and a Defender video game machine. We found that competitive play gave us a jolt of adrenaline and a refreshed mindset when we resumed work. We also learned a lot about our co-workers during competition. While playing Defender one day, I got a great insight into how Burrell's mind worked.

Andy, Burrell, and I had an ongoing competition playing Defender. We'd challenge each other in two or three player competitions. Because we had to take turns playing, we could watch how the other player was doing. This gave us opportunities to refine our skills, learn the other guy's technique, and show off our prowess.

The goal of Defender was to defend humans from abduction by aliens. The evil green aliens dropped down from the top of the screen, randomly picked up the humans, and tried to bring them back up to the top of the screen. You controlled a ship and had to shoot the aliens, either before they grabbed a human or during their rise up to the top of the screen. If an alien made it to the top with a human, the alien consumed the human and became a vicious mutant that attacked very aggressively. You started the game with 10 humans. If they all died, the aliens became mutants and swarmed your ship from all sides.

After a while, surviving the first few game levels was pretty easy, unless you had been up all night programming. The Defender machine was probably a pretty good objective measure of current mental capacity. "Gee, I can't even get through level 2! I guess it's time to get some sleep." Better to put in a bad performance on Defender than mess up the current programming task, or start down the wrong path on some hardware design.

One day Burrell started doing something radical. Andy came by my cube and said, "You've got to come see what Burrell's doing with Defender. He's innovating."

"How can you innovate with a video game?" I wondered. I'd seen Burrell and Andy innovate on all kinds of things, but I couldn't image how Burrell could step outside the box of a video game where the machine controlled the flow and dictated the goals. How could you gain some control in that environment?

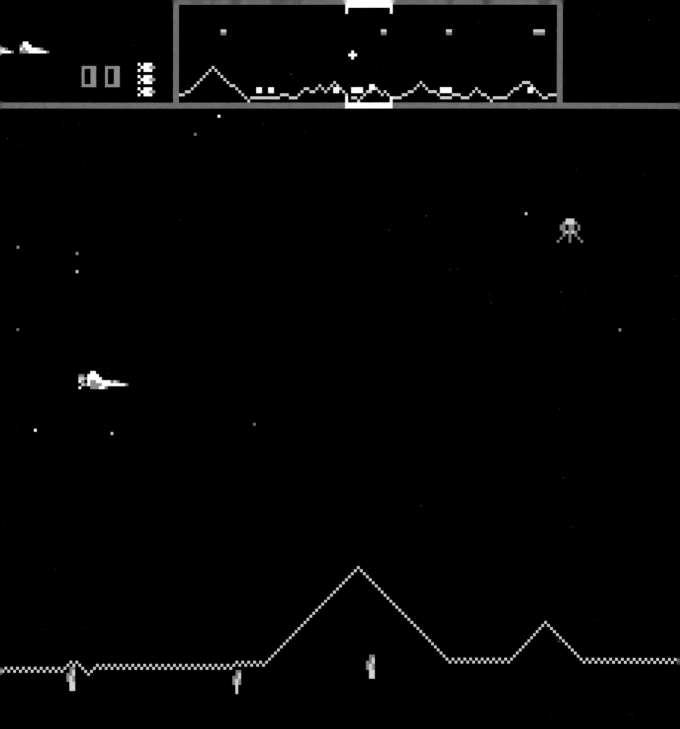

From Andy:

The first Defender machine that got us playing regularly was at Cicero's Pizza, directly across the street from Texaco Towers. We used to go there every afternoon around 4 P.M., for increasingly longer periods as Burrell's skills improved. Shortly after moving into Bandley 3, we got the opportunity to buy a Defender machine for $300, so I paid for it myself and donated it to the Bandley 3 lobby. Randy Wigginton purchased a Joust machine at the same time, so we had two video games, side by side in the lobby. The only other thing to say about Defender is that Steve Wozniak is probably the best player I've ever seen. He is the only one who could ever beat Burrell. What does it mean that that the two best computer designers also rule at Defender?

We started up a new competition and Burrell did something that stunned me. He immediately shot all his humans! This was completely against the goal of the game! He didn't even go after the aliens, and when he shot the last human, they all turned to mutants and attacked him from all sides. He glanced in my direction with a grin on his face and said "Make a mess, clean it up!"

He then proceeded to dodge the swarm of angry mutants noisily chasing after him. "Burrell's not going to win this competition," I said to myself. "He's not going to last long with a screen full of mutants!"

Often a single mutant was enough to kill you. Mutants moved so quickly over small distances that they seemed to just jump on top of your ship. Your ship was faster, though, so you had to outrun them and establish a gap. Only then could you have enough room to safely turn and fire at them.

Burrell, however, had developed a technique for dealing with a whole mass of mutants. He circled around them again and again and gathered them into a densely clumped swarm. Then, while circling, he fired a burst pattern across the whole swarm, not needing to aim at individuals. He was doing really well, cutting through the swarm like the Grim Reaper's scythe. Burrell was no longer attacking individual mutants; he was treating the whole swarm as one big target.

Burrell may have lost that game and the next few, but it wasn't long before he was mastering the machine. Instead of avoiding the tough situations, he'd immediately create them, and then start learning how to handle the worst situation imaginable. Before long, he could handle anything the machine could throw at him.

I was beginning to see how Burrell was so successful with everything he did. Like many high achievers, Burrell enjoyed challenges so much that he actually sought them out or consciously created them. He seemed to aggressively set up challenging situations throughout his life.

Why intentionally "make a mess?" So you can get really good at "cleaning up!"

MacPaint Evolution

June 1983

Bill decides to leave out a very impressive feature

While Bill Atkinson was developing LisaGraf, the crucial, lightning-fast graphics package that was the foundation of both the Lisa and Macintosh user interface (it was renamed QuickDraw for the Mac), he was also working sporadically on a simple bitmap-based drawing program for the Lisa called SketchPad. SketchPad enabled mouse-based drawing with a selection of paintbrushes and patterns, and gave Bill a quick way to test out and show off new features or improvements as they were added to LisaGraf.

Soon after the Lisa was announced at the 1983 annual shareholders meeting, Bill switched from working on Lisa system software to writing a killer graphics application for the Macintosh. Steve Jobs thought he should work on a structured drawing program, something like Mark Cutter's LisaDraw, but Bill thought structured drawing was too complex and wanted to create something that was simple, elegant, and fun to use.

He began by dusting off his old SketchPad code and got it running on the Mac as MacSketch. SketchPad used menus to select patterns and styles to draw with, but Bill replaced them with permanent palettes at the bottom of the screen and added another large, prominent palette on the left that contained a variety of drawing tools. More tools would be added over time, but the basic structure of MacPaint was there from its earliest stages.

One of the problems with early graphics programs was that as you dragged a shape or image across the screen, it had to be erased from its old position before being drawn in the new one, which caused a distracting flicker. Bill completely eliminated this flicker by composing everything in an offscreen memory buffer, which was transferred to the screen in one fell swoop, so the interim states were never visible.

In fact, despite the Macintosh's limited memory, he used two offscreen buffers, each the size of the document window, with one containing the current pixels of the document, and the other containing the pixels of its previous state, before the most recent operation. This made it very easy to implement Undo by just copying the old buffer to the new. It also enabled fast drawing because it was very easy to access the original state of the document in the second buffer as an object was being modified.

After getting basic updating working well, Bill started adding more tools to the palette. He added a rectangular selection tool that allowed the user to perform operations on a subset of the document. The selection rectangle was depicted by inverting the pixels

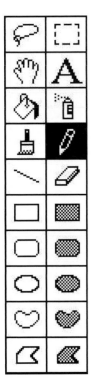

beneath it. It worked well enough over solid areas, but was confusing and hard to see when the underlying image was complex, such as a digitized picture. Bill knew he had to find a better way to do it.

He was thinking about the selection problem one evening when he went to dinner at an old beer and hamburger joint in Los Gatos, the kind of place where decades worth of initials are carved into the wooden tables. He ordered a beer, looked around the bar, and noticed a Hamm's beer sign. The sign featured an impressive animated waterfall, with the water seeming to flow down the waterfall into the lake. Bill figured out the animation was accomplished by a mask layer moving beneath the surface of the sign that varied which portion of the image was visible below it.

He suddenly realized that an animated border—animated with a technique similar to the waterfall—could solve the graphical selection problem because it would always be easy to spot no matter what the background. He raced back home and implemented the animation by using an alternating sequence of patterns that produced the illusion of continuous motion, just like the beer sign. It looked great, but he didn't know how to refer to it. A couple of days later, he showed it to Rod Perkins on the Lisa applications team, who told Bill the effect resembled "marching ants." Bill liked this name, so that's what he called it.

Around April 1983, Bill changed the name of the program from MacSketch to MacPaint. He began to hit his stride and started adding new features to MacPaint on a daily basis. One of the most important was "Fat Bits," a mode that magnified a small section of the document by a factor of 8, allowing the user to easily manipulate individual pixels. It was implemented by scaling the offscreen buffer as it was transferred to the screen, so all of the other tools and effects kept working in Fat Bits mode.

Another key improvement came when Bill implemented the Paint Bucket tool, which allowed the user to simply click once to fill an entire area of the screen with the selected pattern. It used a "seed fill" algorithm to find all the neighboring pixels of the matching color, which was difficult to implement because of our stringent memory constraints. Bill ended up implementing a few different seed fill algorithms before he settled on one that was both fast and memory efficient enough. The seed fill routine eventually migrated from MacPaint into QuickDraw as part of the 128K ROM.

Rectangular selection was useful, but users also needed a way to manipulate an arbitrarily shaped area of an image. To solve this Bill, came up with another selection tool he called the "Lasso" because it contracted around its target. It was hard to control the mouse with pixel-level precision, so the Lasso tool allowed you to roughly outline the area of interest. When you let go of the mouse button, it would automatically tighten, skipping white pixels to cinch tightly around the target. The Lasso feature sort of fell out of creating the Paint Bucket, since the seed fill routine was exactly what was needed to cinch the Lasso properly.

The Lasso allowed an arbitrary area of pixels to be selected, so it required a third offscreen buffer the size of the document window that contained a mask to indicate which pixels were part of the selection. The mask buffer allowed fast graphical operations on large, irregular areas, such as dragging an image around the screen or making the Lasso selection shimmer with the marching ants effect. The first two offscreen buffers were allocated statically, but the mask buffer needed to be de-allocated when it wasn't being used so its memory could be employed for other purposes. MacPaint was good at drawing text and allowed the user to specify characters at any position, with any font, size, or style. But once the text was instantiated, it just became pixels like everything else; you couldn't go back and edit it as text. In June 1983, Bill thought he could do something about that.

Bill decided to try to turn pixels back into characters when you selected them with the Text tool. He wrote a lot of elaborate code, probably as much as for any other MacPaint feature. First, he wrote assembly language routines to isolate the bounding box of each character in the selected range. Then he computed a checksum of the pixels within each bounding box and compared them to a pre-computed table that was made for each known font. It only had to perform the full, detailed comparison if the checksum matched.

Bill got his character recognition routines working well. Compared to the earlier MacPaint, it seemed like magic to recover and edit previously placed text. It wasn't perfect, because it would fail to recognize a character if a single dot was out of place, but it was still very useful. Everyone loved the feature and congratulated Bill for pulling off another miracle.

I was surprised a few days later when Bill told me he decided to remove the character recognition feature from MacPaint. He was afraid that if he left it in, people would actually use it a lot, and MacPaint would be regarded as an inadequate word processor instead of a great drawing program. It was probably the right decision, although I didn't think so at the time. I was amazed Bill was able to detach himself from all the effort he'd put into creating the discarded feature; I know I probably wouldn't have been able to do the same.

MacPaint was essentially finished by October 1983, long before our other key applications. The last part of finishing MacPaint involved dealing with out of memory problems, since it was really pushing the limits of the 128K Macintosh by using the three large offscreen buffers. In the worst case, there were only about 100 bytes free in MacPaint's heap. Most of the bugs we encountered when running MacPaint turned out to be bugs in the underlying system, which were exposed by running so close to the edge of available memory.

It's interesting to note that MacPaint was a rather small program by today's standards, but it had to be to run in the Mac's one eighth of a megabyte of memory. The finished MacPaint consisted of 5,804 lines of Pascal code, augmented by another 2,738 lines of assembly language, which compiled into less than .05 megabytes of executable code.

Facing page:
Bill Atkinson in 1987

part four

He can who thinks he can,
and he can't who thinks he can't.

This is an inexorable, indisputable law. Pablo Picasso

Steve Wozniak University

September 1983

Burrell's educational credentials

After numerous delays, the launch of the Macintosh was finally scheduled for January 24, 1984, so we had to start doing publicity for it in the fall of 1983. Steve decided to anoint some of the engineers plus a few others as the official "Macintosh Design Team," which meant we had to prepare to be interviewed by the press. Because some magazines have lead times of more than three months, interviews were scheduled as early as October.

As part of the preparations, our publicity gurus, the Regis McKenna press liaisons (known as the Rejettes), asked each of us to fill out a questionnaire. The standard questions were asked, such as date and place of birth, degrees, etc. Our answers would be used as the basis for a fact sheet that would be handed out to the press.

Burrell, who never attended college, didn't know how to answer the "College Attended" question. But, true to form, it took him only a moment to come up with the perfect answer: "Steve Wozniak University." I think you could say that, in some fashion, we were all graduates of Steve Wozniak University.

The official Macintosh design team. Left to right: George Crow, Joanna Hoffman, Burrell Smith, Andy Hertzfeld, Bill Atkinson, and Jerry Manock.

The Mythical Man-Year October 1983

Steve estimates the effort that went into QuickDraw

In October of 1983, we had our first encounter with the press, in the form of a group interview with *Byte* magazine. The article was set to run concurrently with the launch of the Mac in January of 1984.

Byte was one of the first PC hobbyist magazines, written for a fairly technical audience of computer enthusiasts. Two *Byte* editors were quizzing five or six of us, including Steve Jobs, when one of them asked how long the Mac's graphical user interface software had taken to develop.

"How many man-years did it take to write QuickDraw?" the reporter asked Steve. QuickDraw, the amazing graphics package written entirely by Bill Atkinson, was at the heart of both Lisa and Macintosh.

Steve turned to look at Bill. "Bill, how long did you spend writing QuickDraw?"

"Well, I worked on it on and off for four years," Bill replied.

Steve paused for a beat and then turned back to the reporter. "Twenty-four man-years. We invested twenty-four man-years in QuickDraw."

Obviously, to Steve, one Atkinson year equaled six man-years. I think that was a modest estimate.

September 1983
The famous **1984** commercial is nearly canceled

The folks at Apple always had a flair for marketing. Mike Markkula, Apple's third co-founder and a former Intel marketing executive, believed that a fledgling venture needed to act like a successful company if it wanted to become one, at least in terms of external perception, and Steve Jobs always insisted on the highest possible production values, even while Apple was still in the garage. The Apple II was featured in an expensive, 2-page spread in the September 1977 issue of *Scientific American*, for example, even though Apple had less than 20 employees and minimal sales at the time.

Apple's advertising agency was Chiat-Day, founded by Jay Chiat in 1968. Jay was compulsively innovative, brash, and irreverent, much like an older version of Steve Jobs, and the two hit it off really well when they were introduced in 1981, just before Chiat-Day acquired Regis McKenna's advertising operations. Jay and his talented team, featuring Creative Director Lee Clow and star copywriter Steve Hayden, crafted Apple's first TV commercials, recruiting talk show host Dick Cavett as a spokesperson, and created the campaign that launched the Lisa, including a TV commercial that starred a then-unknown Kevin Costner.

Toward the end of 1982, Chiat-Day's art director Brent Thomas, along with Steve Hayden, came up with the idea of doing an ad campaign based on the timely tagline "Why 1984 won't be like 1984." Chiat-Day shopped it around to a number of clients, including Apple, where it was proposed for a print ad in the *Wall Street Journal* promoting the Apple II. But Apple didn't go for it, and the idea was filed away until the spring of 1983, when they met with the Mac marketing team to start working on the launch, which was scheduled for January 1984.

Steve Jobs wanted to launch the Macintosh with an inspiring commercial that was as revolutionary as the product itself. He loved the Orwellian tagline when it was presented, and he encouraged the Chiat-Day team to pursue it. Steve Hayden and Brent Thomas put together an intriguing storyboard, envisioning a visually striking, highly symbolic, miniature science fiction epic featuring a young female athlete who liberates the subjugated masses from totalitarian domination by throwing a sledgehammer and smashing a huge screen displaying Big Brother.

Macintosh marketing manager Mike Murray and Steve Jobs loved it, but they needed to get new CEO John Sculley's approval for such a large expenditure. Sculley was a bit apprehensive (after all, the commercial hardly mentioned the Macintosh), but he gave his OK for an unprecedented production budget of over $750,000 to make the one-minute commercial.

Chiat-Day hired Ridley Scott, the best science fiction–oriented director they could find, whose previous movie, *Blade Runner*, possessed the visionary dystopian feel for which they were striving. Ridley was based in London, so they decided to shoot it there, at Shepperton Studios. Several Apple and Chiat-Day executives, as well as Mike Murray and Steve Jobs, traveled to London for the week of filming.

Ridley's team had assembled a cast of almost 200 by the time the Apple folks arrived. To play the oppressed, downtrodden workers, his people recruited dozens of authentic British skinheads, paying them $125 dollars a day to participate. It was harder to cast the young heroine because most of the models who tried out had trouble spinning with the heavy sledgehammer. Luckily, a model named Anya Major was an accomplished discus thrower; she could do it faultlessly, so got the part.

When he arrived at the studio, Mike Murray went looking for Jay Chiat. He found him lurking off to one side behind some scenery. Apparently, some of the skinheads were in a nasty mood, and they were looking for trouble during breaks in the filming. Jay thought it was prudent to make sure he stayed out of their way.

While everyone was off in London, I got a call from someone at Chiat-Day asking if I could write an Apple II Basic program to flash impressive looking numbers and graphs on the screen. They wanted to overlay these on the image of Big Brother. I spent an afternoon cooking something up and sent it off to them, although I was never sure if it was used.

Lee Clow and Steve Hayden presented a rough cut of the commercial to the Apple team a few weeks later, and everyone was ecstatic. The commercial was classy, suspenseful, and enigmatic, and seemed certain to garner lots of attention. It was shown for the first time at Apple's October 1983 annual sales conference in Honolulu. Steve preceded the showing with a clever talk positioning Apple as the industry's last alternative to IBM (see "The Times They Are A-Changin'" on page 217). The commercial got a rapturous reception. In fact the response was so great that Apple booked two expensive slots, for 60 seconds and 30 seconds, costing over a million dollars, to show it during Super Bowl XVIII, which was just two days before the Mac introduction.

Mike Murray and Steve Jobs screened the commercial for Apple's board of directors in December to get final approval for the huge Superbowl expenditure. To their surprise, every

On January 24th,
Apple Computer will introduce
Macintosh.
And you'll see why 1984
won't be like "1984"

outside board member seemed to despise the commercial. Mike Markkula even suggested that Apple begin a hunt for a new ad agency. One board member remarked it was the worst commercial he had ever seen. Steve and Mike were devastated.

The chilling reception from the board compelled John Sculley to ask Chiat-Day to sell back both of the time slots they had purchased. But Jay Chiat was true to form and sold off only the 30-second slot, telling Apple that he wasn't able to get rid of the longer one at so late a date. Apple considered using the slot for a more conventional commercial, but in the end decided to take a chance and air the 1984 spot.

We were told the commercial would air early in the third quarter, at the first commercial break after the second-half kickoff. Burrell and I wanted to see a real audience's reaction to the commercial more than the commercial itself (since we had already seen it plenty of times), so we watched the Superbowl at a sports bar near Stanford called the Oasis, with some other Mac team friends. The game was boring, but the bar was packed, and the commercial looked great. We thought we heard a small murmur in the bar after the commercial aired, but it was hard to tell if it was really related.

That evening, the commercial ran again on all the evening news shows. Apparently, because it had made such a splash and rumor already had it that it would only air once, the ad became a news item itself. Of course this just increased expectations for the upcoming launch. Ironically, it ran dozens of times on news shows in the next couple of days, gathering Apple over five million dollars worth of free publicity.

A week after the Macintosh launch, Apple held its January board meeting. The Macintosh executive staff was invited to attend but didn't know what to expect. When the Mac people entered the room, everyone on the board rose and gave them a standing ovation, acknowledging they had been wrong about the commercial and congratulating the team for pulling off a fantastic launch.

Chiat-Day wanted the commercial to qualify for upcoming advertising awards, so they ran it once at 1 A.M. at KMVT, a small television station in Twin Falls, Idaho, on December 15, 1983. And sure enough, it won just about every possible award, including best commercial of the decade. Twenty years later it's still considered one of the most memorable television commercials ever made.

Monkey Lives

October 1983

The very first location in low memory

The original Macintosh had only 128K bytes of RAM (that's one eighth of a megabyte), so dealing with memory management was usually the hardest part of writing both the system and applications. We allocated around 16K bytes for system use, and another 22K bytes for the 512 × 342 black-and-white screen, leaving applications with only 90K bytes or so. The bigger ones like MacWrite or MacPaint were bursting at the seams.

By the fall of 1983, MacWrite and MacPaint were pretty much feature-complete but still needed a lot of testing, especially in low-memory conditions. MacPaint needed to allocate three offscreen buffers, each the size of the entire screen. This meant it was always on the verge of running out of memory, especially when you brought up a desk accessory, but the specific sequences that led to crashes were difficult to reproduce.

Steve Capps had been working on a "journaling" feature for the "Guided Tour" tutorial disc that would allow the Macintosh to demo itself by replaying back events that were recorded in a prior session. He realized the so-called "journaling hooks" that were used to feed prerecorded events to the system could also be the basis of a testing tool he called "The Monkey."

The Monkey was a small desk accessory that used the journaling hooks to feed random events to the current application, giving the impression that the Macintosh was being operated by an incredibly fast, somewhat angry monkey who was busy banging away at the mouse and keyboard, generating clicks and drags at random positions with wild abandon. It had great potential as a testing tool, so Capps refined it to generate more semantically rich events, with a certain percentage of the events as menu commands, a certain percentage as window drags, etc.

The Monkey proved to be an excellent testing tool, and a great amusement as well. Its manic activity was sort of hypnotic, and it was interesting to see what kind of MacPaint pictures the Monkey could draw, or if it would ever produce something intelligible in MacWrite. At first it crashed the system fairly easily, but soon we fixed the most obvious bugs. We thought it would be a good test to see if an application could survive the monkey all night, but they usually couldn't run for more than 20 minutes. At that point, even if it didn't crash, the Monkey would invariably select the Quit command.

Bill Atkinson came up with the idea of defining a system flag called "MonkeyLives" (pronounced with a short "i" but often mispronounced with a long one). The flag would indicate when the Monkey was running and allow other applications to test for the presence of the Monkey. If the application found the Monkey running, it could disable the Quit command, as well as other commands it wanted the Monkey to avoid. This allowed the Monkey to run all night, or even longer, driving the application through every possible situation.

We kept our system flags in an area of very low memory reserved for the system globals, starting at address 256 ($100 in hexadecimal), since the first 256 bytes were used as a scratch area. The very first slot in the system globals area, address 256, had just been freed up, so that's where we put the MonkeyLives boolean. The Monkey itself eventually faded into relative obscurity as the 512K Macintosh eased the memory pressure, but it was memorialized by the curious name of the very first value defined in the system globals area.

The Monkey was a small desk accessory that used the journaling

hooks to feed random events to the current application, giving the

impression that the Macintosh was being operated by an incredibly

fast, somewhat angry monkey...

September 1983
The Puzzle desk accessory becomes controversial

The original Macintosh could run only one real application at a time, but it could also concurrently run little programs called "desk accessories" that shared memory with the main application. Like the system itself, most of the desk accessories were written in 68000 assembly language. But in the fall of 1982 I decided to write a small adaptor that allowed desk accessories to be written in Pascal, both as a proof of concept and as a way to show developers how to do it.

Desk accessories like the calculator or the alarm clock were usually utilities, but I thought we should also have a game or two to show that the Macintosh was fun as well. I decided to write a puzzle that had 15 numbered tiles in a 4 × 4 space. The object of the game was to arrange the numbers in sequential order. If you clicked on a tile next to the empty space, it slid into that space. It was a fun way to waste time and build up mouse coordination.

Since the number puzzle was written in Pascal, it had to link with the Pascal runtime, which dragged in lots of extra code that wasn't used. This made the Puzzle desk accessory over 6K bytes, although most of its bulk was just the runtime.

By the fall of 1983, it was time to make decisions about what software to include in the shipping product. We had shown the Mac to a number of industry analysts and, while most were enthusiastic, some didn't really get the graphical user interface and thought it was "game-like" and not suitable for serious computing. This made some of the Macintosh marketing folks a bit leery about the more whimsical aspects of the design, and the puzzle, being an actual game, became somewhat controversial.

Jerome Coonen, the software manager, came by my cubicle one morning to tell me that they had decided to not ship Puzzle, partially because of the game-like perception, but mostly because it was just too big. Applications were very tight on RAM, and Puzzle was one of the biggest desk accessories because it was written in Pascal. At over 6 Kbytes, it also ate into the available disk space.

I liked Puzzle and didn't want to capitulate to the buttoned-down, all-business view of the customer, so I told Jerome, "You know, Puzzle doesn't have to be so big. I bet I could rewrite it and get it to take up less than 1K bytes. Would you keep it if I got it that small, or is it really the other issue?"

Jerome thought about it, and then told me if I could get it down to 600 bytes or so it would be in the release. The only problem was I had to get it done over the weekend, because the documentation group had to send the manuals out to the printer. Besides, there was plenty of other stuff for me to work on.

Of course, I couldn't resist a challenge like that. It took only a few hours on Saturday to recode the puzzle in assembly language and, because it no longer had to link with the bulky Pascal code, get it down to the required 600 bytes. I proudly showed it off to everyone on Monday, and it did make it into the first Mac release and remained as part of the standard system for many years.

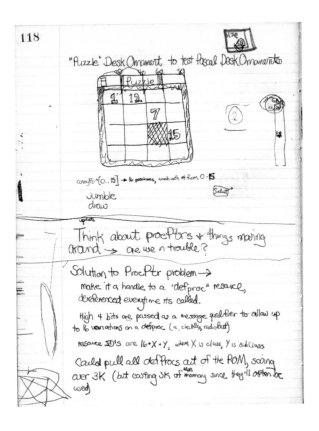

We're Not Hackers! September 1983

We were always dealing with memory limitations

From the beginning, the Macintosh was conceived as a very low-cost, high-volume personal computer. It was important for the design team to keep manufacturing costs as low as possible. Since memory was relatively expensive, we were always dealing with memory limitations.

One of the most clever parts of Burrell Smith's original, 68000-based digital board was the "bus transformer" logic that multiplexed the data bus, allowing him to hook up the 68000—which demanded a 16-bit data bus—to only 8 memory chips. He also included a single, byte-wide 64 kbit ROM chip, so that the first Macintosh, circa January 1981, had a total of 64K bytes of RAM and 8K bytes of ROM.

But as we started to get software running on the prototype, it became increasingly clear that we didn't have enough RAM for the kind of graphic intensive applications we wanted to build; after all, just the frame buffer for the bitmap display took up almost one third of the available memory. And furthermore, Bill Atkinson's graphics routines had recently exceeded the size of the 8K ROM. So, when the digital board was redesigned to incorporate the SCC chip in June 1981, Burrell added another row of 8 memory chips, doubling the RAM size to 128K, and then added another ROM chip as well, doubling the ROM size to 16K. We vowed we would fight hard to make this the last increase (in contrast with the Lisa, whose memory requirements were growing considerably faster than Moore's Law).

Even though the ROM size doubled to 16K, it was barely enough to contain our prototype environment if we included the graphics routines. Burrell figured he could add a third ROM chip, bringing the total to 24K. Two of the ROM chips were hooked up directly to the 68000's 16-bit bus, so code could run faster, while the third chip shared the "bus transformer" circuit with the RAMs.

We built 50 Mac prototypes in the fall of 1981, each containing 24K of ROM, burned into EPROM. Although the system fit readily in 24K, we were still worried that it would soon be an unbearably tight squeeze. On top of that, Burrell never liked the inelegance of three different ROMs.

One day a few months later, Burrell returned from a meeting with a semiconductor company's sales representative. He was really excited and almost ran into my office. "OK, you say that you won't be able to fit in 24K, right? Be honest. How much will we really need?"

Hey, that's not the right way to code. What are you guys, a bunch of hackers?"

We always seemed to need just a little more ROM than was available. "I think we'd definitely make it if we had 32K," I responded.

Burrell laughed. "No, you won't. It's clear that won't be enough, since the software isn't close to being finished yet. But I just heard that the 256 Kbit ROMs are really close, and they'll be ready if we ship in early 1983. So I can use two 256 Kbit chips, connected up to the 16-bit bus, and we'll have 64K bytes of ROM. 64K! ROM is half the price per bit of RAM, so it makes sense to use as much as we can. I know you'll be asking for even more someday, but that should keep you busy for a while."

At first, 64K bytes seemed boundless. We were already trying to write the tightest code we could, and it seemed as though it would be plenty because we weren't even using 32K yet. But sure enough, as the system came together in the spring of 1983, we were beginning to strain against the new size limit.

Fortunately, we had started to use the Resource Manager to load objects such as fonts and drivers, so we had some flexibility when it came to keeping data on disk instead of the ROM. Jerome and I designed the "PACK" mechanism, which used the Resource Manager to load code for optional packages, such as the floating-point routines. But code on floppy disk is much slower to load and would reduce the effective size of each disk.

Even though we tried to make our code as small as possible initially, the lack of space in the ROM made us work even harder to reduce the footprint. We developed a number of unusual space-saving techniques, some of which were inspired by tricks Woz used in the Apple II ROM. For example, we'd often push parameters on the stack out of order, sometimes four times in a row, because we had a value in a register we would need later and that we didn't want to fetch again. We knew this made the code harder to maintain, but we thought it was worth it.

As ROM freeze-time approached, the entire team started to focus on code compression. We had a few practice sessions where everyone explained their favorite space-saving techniques, and then we all plowed through the code, saving a dozen bytes here and there. Steve Capps came up with a simple way of compressing the four or five icons that were built into the ROM, saving hundreds of precious bytes in the process.

Technical Details:

Bill didn't like how we made space on the stack for a function result. He was used to doing it with CLR.W -(SP), while Larry and I preferred SUBQ #2, SP. Bill's version required a memory access while ours didn't. Bill didn't like our technique because it essentially pushed a random, unknown value into the stack, which shouldn't have mattered, but he thought it introduced unnecessary indeterminism.

Bill Atkinson didn't participate in the marathon code-crunching and, except in a few cases, wouldn't allow QuickDraw to be subjected to it. He believed that all code should be as simple and clear as possible, and thought, probably correctly, that we'd be better off without the tricks in the long run. In September 1983, just before the ROM was frozen, he found a bug in the Memory Manager that we devised a simple fix for.

I went with Bill to Larry Kenyon's cubicle where he was maintaining the Memory Manager sources. Bill looked over our shoulders as we added a little code to correct the bug. But he objected and became upset when he noticed we used one of our coding tricks.

"Hey, that's not the right way to code. What are you guys, a bunch of hackers? I'm not sure that I want to work with a bunch of hackers."

Both Larry and I cared more about pleasing Bill than saving every possible byte or cycle, so we changed our fix to use the slower, more conservative, Bill-approved technique. We also added a comment to the instruction in the source code to remind us why we did it the slower way in this circumstance. The comment said "We're Not Hackers!"

A Rich Neighbor
Named Xerox

November 1983

Steve confronts Bill Gates about copying the Mac

When Steve Jobs recruited Microsoft to be the first third-party applications software developer for the Macintosh, he was already concerned that they might try to copy our ideas into a PC-based user interface. As a condition of getting an early start at Macintosh development, Steve made Microsoft promise not to ship any software that used a mouse until at least one year after the first shipment of the Macintosh.

Microsoft's main systems programmer assigned to the Mac project was Neil Konzen, a brilliant young Apple II hacker who had grown up in their backyard, in the suburbs of Seattle. Neil started working at Microsoft while he was still a high school student and single-handedly implemented the system software for their hit Z80 card, which allowed the Apple II to run CP/M software.

Neil loved Apple, so it was natural for Microsoft to assign him to their new, top-secret Macintosh project. He was responsible for integrating Microsoft's byte code–based interpreted environment (which was actually a copy of a system used at Xerox that favored memory efficiency over execution speed and was appropriate for the Mac's limited memory) with the rapidly evolving Macintosh OS, so he quickly became Microsoft's expert in the technical details of the Mac system.

By the middle of 1983, Microsoft was far enough along to show us working prototypes of their spreadsheet and business graphics programs, Multiplan and Chart (they were also working on a word processor, but they neglected to mention it because it would compete with MacWrite). I would usually talk with Neil on the phone a couple times a week. He would sometimes request features that I would implement for him, or he would perhaps complain about the way something was done. But most of the time I answered his various questions about the intricacies of the still evolving Application Programming Interface (API).

I gradually began to notice that Neil often asked questions about implementation details he didn't really need to know about. In particular, he was really curious about how regions were represented and implemented, and would often detail his theories about them to me, hoping for confirmation.

Aside from intellectual curiosity, there was no reason to care about the system internals unless you were trying to implement your own version of it. I told Steve that I suspected Microsoft was going to clone the Mac, but he wasn't worried because he didn't think they were capable of doing a decent implementation, even with the Mac as an example.

Then, in November 1983, Microsoft made a surprising announcement at Comdex, the industry's premier trade show, which was then held twice a year in Las Vegas. Microsoft announced a new, mouse-based system graphical user interface environment called Windows, competing directly with an earlier environment announced by Personal Software called Vision. They also announced a mouse-based option for Microsoft Word. When Steve Jobs found out about Windows, he went ballistic.

"Get Gates down here immediately," he fumed to Mike Boich, Mac's original evangelist who was in charge of our relationships with third-party developers. "He needs to explain this, and it better be good. I want him in this room by tomorrow afternoon, or else!"

To my surprise, I was invited to a meeting in that conference room the next afternoon. Bill Gates had somehow manifested, alone, surrounded by 10 Apple employees. I think Steve wanted me there because I had evidence of Neil asking about the internals. But that never came up. I was just a fascinated observer as Steve started yelling at Bill about violating their agreement.

"You're ripping us off!" Steve shouted. "I trusted you, and now you're stealing from us!"

But Bill Gates just stood there coolly, looking Steve directly in the eye, before starting to speak in his squeaky voice.

"Well, Steve, I think there's more than one way of looking at it. I think it's more like we both had this rich neighbor named Xerox and I broke into his house to steal the TV set only to find that you had already stolen it."

Unfortunately, it turned out, what we had agreed to was only that Microsoft not ship mouse-based software until a year after the Mac introduction, a date defined in the contract as September 1983. Foolishly, we hadn't allowed for a floating ship date, so Microsoft was within their rights to announce Windows when they did. And since Apple still needed Microsoft's apps for the Macintosh, Steve really couldn't cut them off.

In fact it took Microsoft two more years to ship Windows 1.0—in the fall of 1985. It was pretty crude, just as Steve had predicted, with little of the Mac's thoughtful elegance. It didn't even have overlapping windows, preferring a simpler technique called "tiling." When its utter rejection became apparent a few months later, Bill Gates fired the implementation team and started a new version from scratch, led by none other than Neil Konzen.

Neil's version of Windows, released a couple of years later, was good enough that Apple filed a monumental copyright lawsuit against Microsoft in 1988, but they eventually lost on a technicality; the judge ruled that Apple inadvertently gave Microsoft a perpetual license to the Mac user interface in November 1985.

"Well, Steve, I think there's more than one way of looking at it. I think it's more like we both had this rich neighbor named Xerox and I broke into his house to steal the TV set only to find that you had already stolen it."

PRICE FIGHT

October 1983

We feel betrayed by the unexpectedly high price

The plan had always been to have the Macintosh be a very low-cost, high-volume personal computer. We wanted to keep the price as low as possible so ordinary individuals would be able to afford them. The initial target price was $500, less than half the price of an Apple II at the time, but it quickly rose to $1000 after the design team added up the cost of various components.

In early 1981, after switching from the 6809 to the more expensive 68000 microprocessor and doubling the RAM to 128K bytes, we realized we'd have to raise the retail price to $1500 in order for Apple to make its standard profit margin. $1500 was approximately the original price of the Apple II, and that was about as high as we could go while still being affordable to individuals. We worked hard to keep the price from rising further and were able to hold it at $1500 for most of the time the product was under development.

Pricing a brand new computer is tricky because costs are highly dependent on volume: the more units of a component you are willing to order, the lower the price per unit. But how can you predict how well a new type of computer will sell? It's literally a confidence game, and we had no shortage of that. Steve Jobs *knew* we were going to sell Macintoshes by the millions, and he was good at convincing our suppliers to share some of the risk with us via lower initial prices, which would be rewarded as volumes soared in the years ahead. For example, Steve was able to get Motorola to commit to a price of $9.00 for the 68000 microprocessor, which was less than a quarter of what they were quoting at the time.

By the summer of 1983, it was becoming clear that the disk division's Twiggy floppy disk drive wasn't going to make it, and if we weren't careful, it could drag down the Macintosh with it. We had to scurry (see "Quick, Hide In This Closet!" on page 158), but we were able to replace Twiggy with the Sony 3.5" drive without slipping the schedule, which was better in every way except one: it cost us an extra $50 or so. When combined with a few other recent splurges, it pushed us over the top, so we grudgingly accepted that the Macintosh would have to debut for $1995.

Meanwhile, Apple hired a new CEO, John Sculley, in April 1983. John was the former CEO of Pepsi and a world-class marketing whiz, having invented the concept of the "Pepsi Generation" and other successful promotions. He was hired by Apple mainly to apply his marketing skills to the personal computer market, and the Macintosh in particular. But big-time marketing costs big-time money.

As plans for the Macintosh launch were being finalized in October 1983, and we were frantically trying to finish the software, Steve Jobs strode into the software area one evening. He looked angry. "You're not going to like this," he told us, "but Sculley is insisting that we charge $2495 for the Mac instead of $1995, and use the extra money for a bigger marketing budget. He figures the early adopters will buy it no matter what the price. He also wants more of a cushion to protect Apple II sales. But don't worry, I'm not going to let him get away with it!"

The design team was horrified. One of the main reasons we were so passionate about the Macintosh was that we thought we were working on something we would use ourselves, along with our friends and relatives. It was crucial that it be affordable to ordinary people. $2500 felt like a betrayal of everything we were trying to accomplish. We had worked so hard to keep the price down in every aspect of the design, and we resented the idea that it was being artificially inflated to cover a glitzy ad campaign. But we believed Steve would be able to convince John that we'd do better at the lower price.

After a week or so of wrangling, much to our surprise and dismay, Steve was the one who gave in. The Mac was launched at $2495, a thousand dollars more than our target. It sold quickly at first, but sales soon bogged down. This was partially due to the lack of available software, but also to the high price. Even after sales picked up in 1986, with the Mac Plus and the proliferation of desktop publishing, Apple continued to overcharge for the Macintosh, preferring huge profit margins to growing their market share, which eventually caused major problems when this practice caught up with them in the 90s.

One of the main reasons we were so passionate about the Macintosh was that we thought we were working on something we would use ourselves, along with our friends and relatives. It was crucial that it be affordable to ordinary people. $2500 felt like a betrayal of everything we were trying to accomplish.

90 Hours a Week and loving it

October 1983

Burrell modifies his sweatshirt

Burrell is wearing the sweatshirt in this picture taken at Larry Tesler's birthday party at Caroline Rose's house in Palo Alto in April 1983. Steve Capps is up top, left to right is Burrell Smith, Caroline Rose, Marge Boots (Capps' wife), Andy Hertzfeld, and Larry Tesler. Facing page: Burrell at home in March 1985.

Most Macintosh software team members were between 20 and 30 years old, and with few family obligations to distract us, we were used to working long hours. We were passionate about the project and willing to more or less subordinate to it the rest of our lives, at least for a while. By the fall of 1983, as pressure mounted to meet our January 1984 deadline, we began to work longer and longer hours. It wasn't unusual to find most of the software team in their cubicles on any given evening—weekday or not—still tapping away at their keyboards at 11 P.M. or even later.

The rest of the Macintosh team, which had now swelled to almost a hundred people (nearing the limit Steve Jobs swore we would never exceed), tended to work more traditional hours. But as our deadline loomed, many of them began to stay late as well to help us out. Dinner was brought in for those who stayed late, and we would all put the software through its paces, competing to see who could find the most bugs, of which there were still plenty, even as the weeks wore on.

Earlier in the year, Debi Coleman's finance team decided to commemorate the team's effort in the traditional Silicon Valley manner: they made a T-shirt. Actually, to make it a little more special, they chose a high-quality, gray hooded sweatshirt. Steve Jobs had bragged to *Time* magazine that the Macintosh team was working "90 hours a week." In honor of this exaggerated assertion, they chose the tag line, "90 Hours a Week and Loving It."

The sweatshirt featured the Macintosh name in red letters, purposefully misspelled as "Mackintosh," as it had been in the *Time* article, with a black squiggle crossing out the errant "k." The "90 Hours" tagline was emblazoned in black across the back. The software team wasn't all that pleased with the whole sweatshirt thing because while we really *were* working that hard, and most of the other sweatshirt recipients weren't even coming close to 90-hour work weeks. But it was a pretty nice sweatshirt, and lots of the engineers wore them frequently, including Burrell Smith.

When Burrell finally quit Apple in February 1985, he continued to wear the sweatshirt. But, as soon as he returned home following his resignation, he immediately took some masking tape and made a big "X" across the "9," virtually obliterating it from view. From then on, he wore it nearly every day, proudly displaying the updated motto, which reflected exactly how he felt. It now read "0 Hours A Week And Loving It."

Susan Kare

MacPaint Gallery   October 1983
A gallery of Susan Kare's MacPaint art from 1983

Bill Atkinson began writing MacPaint in February 1983, just after Susan Kare joined the Mac team to design bitmaps for fonts and icons. Susan became one of the first and most accomplished users of MacPaint, trying out new features as they were developed and using it for a wide range of practical applications.

As the Mac team struggled to finish in time for the launch, Susan kept a notebook of many of the MacPaint documents she created. They provide an interesting glimpse of the daily life of the Mac team during that period.

The image on the left is an announcement of a combined birthday party for seven Mac team members whose birthdays fell in early April, including me. I remember how terrified I was of turning 30. As a birthday gift, Susan made me a jersey with a large hexadecimal number "1E" (which is 30 in base 16) on it, so I could still say I was a teenager, at least in hexadecimal.

The image on the right is for a picnic held in July 1983 to celebrate the wedding of two members of the software team: programmer Larry Kenyon and librarian Patti King. Larry and Patti actually eloped in June; the picnic happened after they returned from their honeymoon.

During the last couple of months before shipping, we held some testing marathons where the software team enticed employees from the rest of the division to stay late and help test the software by bribing them with dinner (see "90 Hours A Week And Loving It" on page 196). The image on the right is an announcement of another bug hunt, accompanied by the bug report form that was used during the testing.

Below these is an invitation to celebrate a ROM freeze at software manager Jerome Coonen's house. This wasn't the final ROM freeze, which took place in September, but the first of a series that led up to it. We had a party celebrating the final ROM freeze at Woz's house in Scott's Valley.

Please save Thursday, December 8, 5–9 p.m. to test software.

The Mac group worked hard, but Apple would occasionally throw parties for the team, sometimes with unusual themes. The poster on the far left promoted our "Punk Party." Everyone was supposed to attend in "punk" attire and a local band, "The Medflys," was hired to play. The other poster advertised a dance that featured a DJ. Some of us were so disappointed with the music he played that we left and drove to a nearby record store to buy some better music for him to play.

Steve Jobs is very visually oriented and everyone knew he would react more favorably to material presented with nice graphics and high production values. Because of this, the Finance team recruited Susan to use MacPaint to make attractive covers for the monthly financial reports. Here are some covers she made for the June and July 1983 reports.

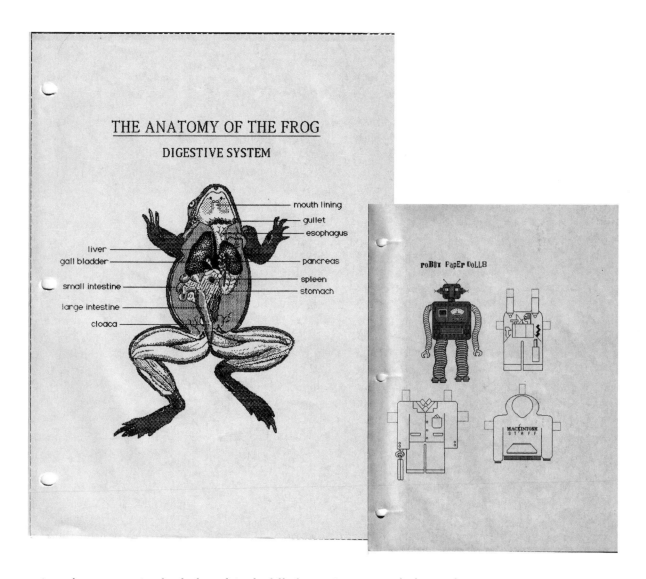

As we began preparing for the launch in the fall of 1983, Susan was asked to produce art for various marketing materials, to show off the kinds of things you could do with MacPaint. The frog on the left demonstrates how you might use MacPaint in a biology class. Susan also had a fondness for whimsical applications, as demonstrated by the picture on the right.

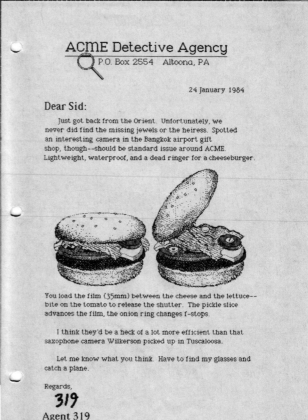

ACME Detective Agency
P.O. Box 2554 Altoona, PA

24 January 1984

Dear Sid:

Just got back from the Orient. Unfortunately, we never did find the missing jewels or the heiress. Spotted an interesting camera in the Bangkok airport gift shop, though--should be standard issue around ACME. Lightweight, waterproof, and a dead ringer for a cheeseburger.

You load the film (35mm) between the cheese and the lettuce--bite on the tomato to release the shutter. The pickle slice advances the film, the onion ring changes f-stops.

I think they'd be a heck of a lot more efficient than that saxophone camera Wilkerson picked up in Tuscaloosa.

Let me know what you think. Have to find my glasses and catch a plane.

Regards,

319

Agent 319

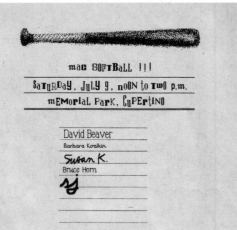

Here are some examples that Susan created for marketing. The "Japanese Lady" on the left is pretty famous because it was used in the original brochure. She started with a scan of a fine Japanese woodcut Steve had procured. I think the hilarious detective agency letter on the right was also used in an advertisement.

Sports were another outlet to blow off steam between longs hours of working. In the spring of 1983, we managed to get facilities to install a basketball hoop in the back of Bandley 4 and usually played a half-court game every afternoon. We also had co-ed softball games once per month, which could sometimes get pretty intense.

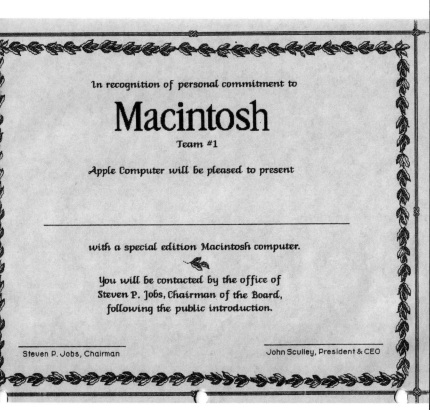

In recognition of personal commitment to

Macintosh

Team #1

Apple Computer will be pleased to present

_____

with a special edition Macintosh computer.

You will be contacted by the office of
Steven P. Jobs, Chairman of the Board,
following the public introduction.

Steven P. Jobs, Chairman   John Sculley, President & CEO

Apple gave out brand new Macintoshes to everyone on the team right after the launch (see "The Times They Are A-Changin'" on page 217). On the left is a certificate that accompanied each machine. On the right is a bottle of champagne, in honor of the launch, to complete the celebration.

Steve Capps Day   December 1983
We all dress up in honor of Steve Capps

The Macintosh software was finally coming together as the fall of 1983 wore on. The ROMs containing most of the system software were finished and were more or less holding up. Larry Kenyon devised a clever technique for fixing problems in the ROM by patching the nearest system trap to the problem. The patch code looked back on the stack for the ROM address of the caller, which allowed us to fix problems with tiny, surgical incisions, instead of replacing large chunks of the ROM with precious RAM, as we had originally envisioned.

MacPaint was already stable enough to ship by the middle of November 1983, even though it was always skirting on the edge of running out of memory if we changed something in the system. MacWrite still had lots of bugs, but its core functionality was ready as long as you weren't pushing memory limits. The only vital application that could delay our target date in mid-January was the Finder, which was the shell application responsible for launching other applications and managing files.

Bruce Horn was the only programmer working on the Finder, and he was bogged down with a variety of problems, especially involving fixing file copying in low memory conditions. The Finder was built on top of Bruce's Resource Manager using features that were barely finished before the ROM freeze. It probably should have been at least a two-man project, but Bruce was a brilliant, passionate, independent perfectionist who insisted he could get it done in time on his own.

Jerome Coonen, the Macintosh software manager, was afraid Bruce wasn't going to make it and decided to assign someone else to help. Given Bruce's perfectionism and temperament, it was going to be hard for someone else to dive in, especially this late in the game. Luckily, Steve Capps was the perfect man for the job.

Stockily built, with long brown hair and a bushy beard, Capps was an extraordinarily talented, creative, and prolific programmer. He had transferred over to the Mac team from the Lisa printing group in January 1983, giving us a new burst of energy just as we entered our sprint to the finish. Capps was one of the few people who Bruce respected enough to really listen to. And best of all, he possessed a cheerful, easygoing disposition that was the perfect complement to Bruce's high-strung intensity.

Everyone dressed up for Steve Capps day.

To minimize distractions, which were mounting as Apple's marketing machine kicked into high gear for the launch, Jerome arranged for Bruce and Capps to move into a small office a few blocks away, on Bubb Road. Capps dove in quickly and took over a bunch of tasks from Bruce. It wasn't always easy, but by the end of December it looked as though the Finder was getting more or less back on track.

Jerome thought of a unique way for the software team to show our appreciation for Capps' heroic effort. Like many hackers, Capps dressed idiosyncratically, almost always wearing a long-sleeved, white dress shirt with cut-off denim shorts, white socks, and a distinctive type of checkered sneakers called Vans. In fact, Capps had just given everybody on the team a pair of Vans as Christmas presents. Jerome had the idea to pay homage to Capps by declaring the next day "Steve Capps Day" and cooked up a scheme in which we'd all come in to work dressed exactly like Steve.

I had to go to Macy's to buy myself a white dress shirt, but I managed to come up with a reasonable facsimile of Capps' attire. It was hilarious to see everyone as we gathered in our "fishbowl" office in Bandley 3 the next morning, all dressed in our white shirts, denim shorts, and Vans. Even the French and German translators who were visiting us for the month joined in. The funniest sight, though, had to have been Patti Kenyon, who was over eight months pregnant at the time. Her extra large white shirt added just the right comic touch.

Once we had all assembled, Jerome went to get Capps and Bruce from their enclave, telling them there was an important meeting that required their attendance. We could hardly hold back the laughter as an unsuspecting Capps walked in. We all cracked up and gave him a round of applause when he realized what was going on.

A Mac for Mick

January 1984

We present a Mac to Mick Jagger

The last weeks before the Macintosh unveiling on January 24th were extremely hectic. The software still wasn't finished, and it wasn't clear if there was enough time left to get it into adequate shape. Meanwhile, the Apple PR machine was revved up to full speed, so there were also plenty of unusual diversions, such as being interviewed and photographed for the national press.

The absolute deadline for finishing the software was 6 A.M. on Monday, January 16th, eight days before the introduction. When I came into work on Friday, January 13th, I knew I would probably stay there all weekend, along with the rest of the team, working as hard as possible to shake out the remaining bugs before Monday. Steve Jobs, Mike Murray, Bob Belleville, and others were in New York City doing a press tour, so I thought we would be relatively free of distractions and able to focus on bug fixing.

I came into work later than usual, around noon, since I had been at Apple until 3 A.M. the previous evening, and I wanted to get one decent night's sleep before the final push. As I went to sit down, I noticed that a handwritten note had been placed on my chair. It was from our software librarian, Patti King, who had taken a message from Steve Jobs' secretary, Lynn Takahashi.

"Andy—Steve J. called—we can deliver a Mac to Mick Jagger tomorrow. You can fly out to meet them by tomorrow noon and bring lots of neat software. If you can come, make arrangements for the trip through Lynn. Steve will call back in a couple of hours, also, he'll be at the Carlyle Hotel tomorrow."

A chance to meet Mick Jagger was a once-in-a-lifetime opportunity, but we still had three more days before the deadline. If I flew to New York I would be absent for at least 30 hours, plus I knew I would be relatively useless from all that flying. I called Lynn to have her tell Steve I couldn't make it. But of course I was dying to know Mick's reaction, not to mention how all this had come about.

When Bill Atkinson returned from the East Coast on Sunday afternoon, he filled me in. I then got more details from Steve and Mike Murray a bit later. Apparently Steve had gone to a party on Thursday evening and was introduced to Andy Warhol. Andy got really excited about the Macintosh when Steve demoed it, and said, "You must show it to Mick." Warhol then arranged for Steve and the Apple crew to go to Mick Jagger's townhouse on Saturday afternoon to present him with a Macintosh.

Steve, Mike, and Bill then showed up at the address they were given and knocked on the door, but there was no response for several minutes. Finally, two huge guys opened it up, but they didn't seem all that impressed to be face-to-face with the co-founder of Apple Computer and his entourage.

The Apple folks were led upstairs into an elegantly furnished room to wait for Mick. Bill set up the Mac, launched MacPaint, and started to fool around with it. Then, abruptly, Mick Jagger strode into the room, dressed casually in a t-shirt and blue jeans.

Mick was polite, but he didn't seem to have heard of Apple Computer, Steve Jobs, or the Macintosh. Steve tried to strike up a conversation, but he wasn't very successful. He later told me Mick couldn't seem to put together a coherent sentence. "His speech was slurred and very slow," Steve described it later. "I think he was on drugs. Either that or he's brain-damaged." After a few minutes, it was clear Mick had absolutely no interest whatsoever in Apple or the Macintosh, and an awkward silence ensued.

Fortunately, Mick's 12-year-old daughter Jade had followed Mick into the room, and her eyes lit up when she saw MacPaint. Bill began to teach her how to use it, and pretty soon she was happily mousing away, fascinated by what she could do with MacPaint. Mick drifted off to another room, but the Apple contingent stayed with Jade for another half hour or so, showing off the Macintosh and answering her questions. They ended up leaving the machine behind. There was no way she was going to part with it.

Facing page:
Mick Jagger performing on stage at Byrne Arena during Rolling Stones concert.

Real Artists Ship

January 1984
The final push to finish the software

With the deadline for finishing the software less than a week away, it seemed obvious that there were still too many bugs to ship it. Late on Friday evening, we convinced ourselves we needed an extra week or two to fix the remaining problems. Steve Jobs was on the East Coast, along with Bob Belleville and Mike Murray, doing press for the introduction, so we arranged for a conference call early Sunday morning to tell him about the slip.

Jerome Coonen, our software manager, spoke for the team, as we sat around the speakerphone. We were exhausted and progress was slow. There were still bugs that we hadn't gotten to the bottom of yet, and it didn't seem possible that we could make it in the time remaining. Jerome proposed that we ship "demo" software to the dealers for the introduction, and update all the customers with final software a few weeks later. We thought Jerome was pretty persuasive as we held our breath waiting for Steve to respond.

"No way, there's no way we're slipping!" Steve responded. The room let out a collective gasp. "You guys have been working on this stuff for months now, another couple weeks isn't going to make that much of a difference. You may as well get it over with. Just make it as good as you can. You better get back to work!"

We did manage to wrangle an extra couple of days, by virtue of working the weekend and moving the deadline to 6 A.M. Monday morning, when the Macintosh factory (where the disks would be duplicated) opened, instead of Friday afternoon. We agreed to go home and rest before returning to work on Monday for the final push.

The final week was one of the most intense I ever experienced. Steve wanted Bill Atkinson and me to fly to New York to present a Mac to Mick Jagger, but I decided I needed to stay in Cupertino to help with the bug fixing (see "A Mac for Mick" on page 206). Some of us were pausing work to get photographed for magazines like *Newsweek* and *Rolling Stone*, which made others on the team feel terrible that they were being left out. At times, the atmosphere got pretty tense.

When Friday finally rolled around, it was clear that there were still too many bugs in both the Finder and MacWrite. Randy Wigginton brought in a gigantic bag of chocolate-covered espresso beans, which, along with medicinal quantities of caffeinated beverages, helped us forgo sleep entirely for the last couple of days. We started doing release cycles that were only a few hours apart, re-releasing every time we fixed a significant problem.

When a new release was ready, we would all grab it and start testing again. At one point, around 2 A.M. on Sunday night, I stumbled across a bug in the Clipboard code. I thought I knew what it might be, but I was too tired to deal with it. I tried to pretend I didn't see the problem, but Steve Capps was watching my expression and knew there was something wrong. He grilled me about the problem and then helped me craft a fix since I was too tired to do it on my own.

Top: Rony Sebok, Susan Kare.
Middle : Andy Hertzfeld,
Bill Atkinson, Owen Densmore.
Bottom: Jerome Coonen,
Bruce Horn, Steve Capps,
Larry Kenyon.
Front: Donn Denman,
Tracy Kenyon, Patti Kenyon.

Around 4 A.M., we had a release where everything seemed to go wrong—even MacPaint, which was usually rock solid, was crashing. But our final release around 5:30 A.M. seemed to be much better; the worst problems seemed to have receded and we thought we might actually have a decent release candidate.

That last half hour was devoted to testing the final release as much as we could. It looked pretty good, but then someone found a potential showstopper: the system seemed to hang when a blank disk was inserted while running MacWrite and the disk didn't start formatting as it should. I realized that it was probably hung up waiting for an event, so I reached out and tapped on the space bar, and formatting commenced. Jerome thought the bug was bad enough to hold up the release, but he left to drive it to the factory anyway, figuring they needed to start duplication even if it was just going to be a demo release.

The sun had already risen and the software team finally began to scatter and go home to collapse. We weren't sure if we were finished or not, and it felt really strange to have nothing to do after working so hard for so long. Instead of going home, Donn Denman and I sat on a couch in the lobby in a daze and watched the accounting and marketing people start trickling into work around 7:30 A.M. or so. We must have been quite a sight; everybody could tell we had been there all night (actually, I hadn't been home or showered for three days).

Finally, around 8:30 Steve Jobs arrived, and as soon as he saw us he asked if we had made it. I explained the formatting bug to him, and he thought it wasn't a showstopper, which meant we were actually finished. When I finally got home around 9 A.M., I collapsed on my bed, thinking I'd sleep for at least the next day or two.

Disk Swapper's Elbow January 1984
A last-minute bug causes some problems

contributed by
Steve Capps

One of the more common afflictions of early Macintosh users was the dreaded "Disk Swapper's Elbow," which was caused by a disk-copying operation run amok. Disk swapping was a necessary evil caused by having 400 KB floppy disks, 128 KB of RAM, and a single floppy drive. If a user wanted to make a backup of a disk, she had to eject the source disk, insert a blank one, format it, and then drag the source disk over the new disk. The Finder would then copy data piece by piece with the necessary swapping.

A typical application on a 128K Mac had about 85K of memory available; the rest was used by the system, mostly for the bitmap display. A simple calculation shows that copying a 400K disk should have involved about 5 or 6 swaps. Five disk swaps was barely tolerable. However, as early Finder users will remember, it would occasionally take well over 20 disk swaps.

You'd start a disk copy and hold your breath during the fifth, and hopefully, final swap. If the Mac dutifully disgorged the floppy the sixth time, you'd convince yourself you miscounted, cross your fingers, and hope for the best. By the seventh swap you started cursing because you knew you were trapped and you started wondering about investing in an external drive.

Even though the whole Finder was only 46K of code and had about 10K of overhead, the remaining 30K of memory space was too small for practical copying. So, I had to break up the code into two chunks: the bare minimum for copying and all the rest. Then, I had to carefully flush out all data that was cached in memory, preload the small disk-copying chunk of code, and coalesce the balance of RAM. Usually, the Finder ended up with 75K of free memory and things worked as planned. But, sometimes the system would mysteriously reload the larger chunk of the Finder code, fragment the free memory, and cause another case of Disk Swapper's Elbow.

It took me a long time to figure out what happened because we had rarely seen this in testing. There were a few bug reports of this problem that were never reproducible. The bug reports went like this: "Copied a disk, it took 20+ swaps! Tried a second time, it was fine." The reason this was not reproducible was because we were all expert mouse users and usually skipped the crucial misstep.

When anybody first starts using a mouse, dragging is one of the more difficult things to do. It's actually quite awkward to click down, move the mouse while holding down the button, and then release. Beginners very often accidentally release the mouse button while dragging. In the Finder, this means you could "drop" an icon you were dragging. You rarely thought about this (unless you happened to drop it over a folder and it disappeared); you'd immediately pick the icon up and continue the drag. It turned out if you dropped the disk icon during a disk copy, you'd induce the bug. Since all of the team members had been using the mouse for years by this time we rarely dropped icons, which is why we could never reproduce the problem.

To support the user's spatial memory, the Finder always remembered where icons were located on the desktop. When you dropped the icon—even for a half a second—the Finder would dutifully record its location. The routine to save the icon's location was, as you probably guessed, in the big portion of the Finder's code. When this bug occurred, the Finder would carefully massage the memory for copying and then belatedly discover the icon's location hadn't been flushed out. It would blindly call the routine to flush it and you now know what would happen....

I introduced this bug about 2 A.M. the morning we built the final disks. This bug was caused by a fix to a much more egregious bug, so it was definitely the lesser of two evils...really!

It Sure Is Great to Get Out of That Bag!

January 1984
We need a demo for the intro

It took a monumental effort, fueled by inordinate amounts of chocolate-covered espresso beans (see "Real Artists Ship" on page 208), to finally finish the first release of the Macintosh software in time for the introduction. We finished with literally no time to spare, shipping the "golden master" of the Write/Paint disk to the factory at 6 A.M. on Monday morning January 16th, just a week before the introduction. By that point, most of the software team hadn't slept for days, so we all went home to collapse.

I thought I would need to sleep for at least 24 hours, but I woke up after 6 hours with a desire to go back to Apple to see if the release held up and to see how everyone else was feeling. By 5 P.M., most of the software team had dragged themselves back for the same reason. We were lounging around in a tired daze, happy we had finally shipped the software but still not quite believing it, when Steve Jobs strode into the software area.

"Hey, pick yourselves up off the floor. You're not done yet!"

Uh-oh, I thought. Someone must have found a showstopper in the release and we're going to have to track it down. But that wasn't what he meant.

"We need a demo for the intro! The Mac deserves to have a great demo for its first public showing. I want the Mac to play the theme from *Chariots of Fire* while it's showing a slideshow of the apps. Plus lots of other cool stuff, whatever you can come up with. And it needs to be done by the weekend, to be ready for the rehearsals."

We moaned and groaned about being tired, but as we talked we realized it would be fun to cook up something impressive. We were too tired to think about it right away, but when we came back the next day, a plan started to emerge.

Capps had an idea to use a gigantic font to scroll "Macintosh" across the screen, one letter at a time, to start the demo, so he worked on that, as well as the slideshow. Bruce Horn wanted to do a starry night with twinkling stars, and a skywriter writing "Macintosh" in cursive across the night sky. Susan worked on an intro graphic of the Mac sitting in its canvas carrying bag, as well as some of the other graphics for the slideshow part. I integrated all the pieces and also signed up for the *Chariots of Fire* music part since no one else wanted to do it.

It's hard to write a music editor/player in two days. I managed to put something together that could actually play the *Chariots of Fire* theme, but it didn't sound very good, and Steve immediately rejected it and opted for using a CD of the *Chariots of Fire* song to play in the background instead.

Meanwhile, as we were working on the demo, Mike Boich came by with Mark Barton, a third-party developer who we seeded with an early Mac because he had written an impressive program for the Apple II called SAM the Software Automatic Mouth. SAM was a speech generator that converted text to speech with a distinctive, winning personality. I had helped Mark with sound driver issues as he developed it, and now it had finally made it to fruition. SAM sounded even better on the Mac because we had 8 bits per sample and a higher sampling rate.

When Steve heard SAM talk, he immediately decreed we had to incorporate SAM in the intro demo. "I want the Macintosh to be the first computer to introduce itself!" he insisted. He told Mike Boich to quickly cut a deal with Mark so Apple could bundle the speech generator (rechristened Macintalk) and use it in the intro.

Since my music generator fell through, I got to do the speech part, using Mark Barton's libraries. I knew I wasn't clever enough to be the Mac's speechwriter. I think Susan had the idea of asking Steve Hayden, Chiat-Day's head writer, to do it. Steve was the guy who conceived the 1984 commercial (see "1984" on page 180) and was as clever as they come. He was excited about helping out and got it done overnight.

Once we integrated all the pieces together, the demo didn't come close to being able to run on a standard Macintosh. Fortunately, we had a prototype of a 512K Mac in the lab, so we decided to cheat a little (there were only two in existence at the time) and use that for the demo, which made things fit.

The demo started out with Susan's graphic of the Mac hidden in its carrying bag on a curtained stage. Suddenly, the music swelled (from a CD, not generated by the Mac) and Capp's big letters scrolled nimbly across the screen, spelling out "Macintosh." Then we transitioned to Bruce's skywriter, and then to various screenshots of applications, including third-party applications like Microsoft's Multiplan and Chart. Finally, the music stopped, the screen went blank, and we waited for Steve to press the mouse button. When he did, the Mac started to speak in strange but somehow endearing tones:

"Hello, I am Macintosh. It sure is great to get out of that bag!

Unaccustomed as I am to public speaking, I'd like to share with you a maxim I thought of the first time I met an IBM mainframe: Never trust a computer that you can't lift!

Obviously, I can talk, but right now I'd like to sit back and listen. So it is with considerable pride that I introduce a man who has been like a father to me...Steve Jobs!"

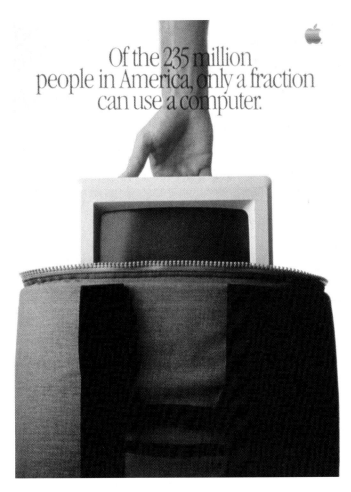

Of the 235 million people in America, only a fraction can use a computer.

"Hello, I am Macintosh. It sure is great to get out of that bag!

Unaccustomed as I am to public speaking, I'd like to share with you a maxim I thought of the first time I met an IBM mainframe: Never trust a computer that you can't lift!

Obviously, I can talk, but right now I'd like to sit back and listen. So it is with considerable pride that I introduce a man who has been like a father to me ... Steve Jobs!"

The Times
They Are A-Changin'

January 1984
The big day finally arrives

January 24, 1984—the big day had finally arrived. We had looked forward to this date for so long that it didn't seem that real to be actually experiencing the long-awaited public unveiling of the Macintosh at Apple's 1984 annual shareholder's meeting. We were excited, of course, but also nervous about our hastily contrived demo software, and still exhausted from the final push to finish the system software in time (see "Real Artists Ship" on page 208).

I had attended one of the rehearsals over the weekend, to help set up the demo, and it was fraught with problems. Apple rented a powerful video projector called a LightValve that could project the Macintosh display larger and brighter than I thought possible. The Mac had to be connected to the projector through a special board cooked up by Burrell to compensate for the Mac's unique video timings. The LightValve was quite temperamental, taking eons to warm up and then sometimes shutting down inexplicably. Plus, Steve wasn't into rehearsing very much and could barely force himself into doing a single, complete run-through.

Most of the software team usually didn't come to work until after 10 A.M., but on this morning we gathered in our fishbowl office in Bandley 3 at 7:30, so we could walk over together to the big auditorium at Flint Center, which was a half-mile away. We got to the cavernous room (which seated 2,500) early, but it was already filling up, and soon it was packed tight, with standing room only. The software team sat up close in the second row, in a section reserved for Macintosh division employees.

Finally, the lights dimmed, and Steve Jobs appeared at a podium on the left side of the stage. He was resplendent in a finely tailored black suit complete with a prominent bow tie, looking more like a Las Vegas impresario than a computer industry executive. You could tell he was nervous, too, as he quieted the rousing applause and began to speak.

"Welcome to Apple's 1984 Annual Shareholders meeting. I'd like to begin by reading part of an old poem by Dylan—that's Bob Dylan." Steve flashed a big smile as he started to recite the second verse of "The Times They Are A-Changin'," stretching an occasional vowel in a Dylanesque fashion.

Come writers and critics
Who prophesize with your pen
And keep your eyes wide,
The chance won't come again
And don't speak too soon
For the wheel's still in spin
And there's no tellin' who that it's namin'.
For the loser now
Will be later to win
For the times they are a-changin'

Steve thanked Apple's board of directors individually by name for their support in a turbulent year and then turned the meeting over to Apple's chief counsel, Al Eisenstadt, to run the formal part of the meeting. Al ran through some procedural stuff and then introduced Apple's CEO, John Sculley, who had been hired nine months earlier, for a report on the business.

John reported on Apple's latest quarter, which saw disappointing Lisa sales balanced by a fantastic Christmas for the Apple IIe, whose sales had more than doubled from the previous year. But the crowd seemed distracted, impatiently waiting for the Main Event. John sensed this and hurried through the bulk of his presentation. Finally he concluded by thanking Mike Markkula and the executive staff for supporting him during his first few months at Apple, thanking one individual in particular.

"The most important thing that has happened to me in the last nine months at Apple has been a chance to develop a friendship with Steve Jobs. Steve is a co-founder of Apple, and a product visionary for this industry, and it's my pleasure now to reintroduce Steve Jobs."

Steve reappeared on the left side of the stage as the lights dimmed again. "It is 1958," he began, speaking slowly and dramatically. "IBM passes up a chance to buy a young fledgling company that has invented a new technology called xerography. Two years later, Xerox was born, and IBM has been kicking themselves ever since." The crowd laughed, as Steve paused.

MACWORLD

Premier Issue $4.00
Canada $4.75

The Macintosh Magazine

Macintosh

**Apple's Remarkable
New Personal
Computer**

**An Exclusive
Look Inside the
Macintosh**

**Word Processing
Tips for
Mac Writers**

**MacPaint's
Amazing
Electronic
Easel**

*Steven Jobs,
Chairman of the Board,
Apple Computer*

*Investing with Multiplan
A Tour of the Mac Desktop
Programming Preview
Macintosh Art Gallery
The Making of the Macintosh*

Steve had cooked up this spiel for the sales meeting in Hawaii the previous fall to introduce the 1984 commercial. I had seen him do it a few times by now, but never with as much passion, intensity, and emotion dripping from his voice.

"It is 10 years later, the late 60s," he continued, speaking faster now. "Digital Equipment Corporation and others invent the minicomputer. IBM dismisses the minicomputer as too small to do serious computing, and therefore unimportant to their business. DEC grows to be a multi-hundred million dollar company before IBM enters the minicomputer market." Steve paused again.

"It is now 10 years later, the late 70s. In 1977, Apple Computer, a young fledgling company on the West Coast, introduces the Apple II, the first personal computer, as we know it today. IBM dismisses the personal computer as too small to do serious computing, and therefore unimportant to their business," Steve intoned sarcastically, and the crowd applauded.

"The early 1980s. 1981—Apple II has become the world's most popular computer, and Apple has grown to a 300 million dollar corporation, becoming the fastest growing company in American business history. With over 50 companies vying for a share, IBM enters the personal computer market in November of 1981, with the IBM PC." Steve spoke very quickly at this point, picking up momentum.

"1983. Apple and IBM emerge as the industry's strongest competitors, with each selling approximately one billion dollars worth of personal computers in 1983. The shakeout is in full swing. The first major personal computer firm goes bankrupt, with others teetering on the brink. Total industry losses for 1983 overshadow even the combined profits of Apple and IBM."

He slowed down, speaking emphatically. "It is now 1984. It appears that IBM wants it all. Apple is perceived to be the only hope to offer IBM a run for its money. Dealers, after initially welcoming IBM with open arms, now fear an IBM dominated and controlled future and are turning back to Apple as the only force who can ensure their future freedom."

Steve paused even longer, as the crowd's cheering swelled. He had them on the edge of their seats. "IBM wants it all and is aiming its guns at its last obstacle to industry control, Apple. Will Big Blue dominate the entire computer industry? The entire information age? Was George Orwell right?"

'IBM wants it all and is aiming its guns at its last obstacle to industry control, Apple. Will Big Blue dominate the entire computer industry? The entire information age? Was George Orwell right?"

The crowd was in a frenzy now, as the already famous 1984 commercial (see "1984" on page 180), which was shown for the first and only time during the Superbowl two days before, filled the screen, featuring a beautiful young woman athlete storming into a meeting of futuristic skinheads, throwing a sledge-hammer at Big Brother, imploding the screen in a burst of apocalyptic light. By the time the commercial finished, everyone in the auditorium was standing and cheering.

Steve then went on to describe the Macintosh as the third industry milestone product, after the Apple II and the IBM PC. "Some of us have been working on Macintosh for more than two years now, and it has turned out insanely great!"

All this time, a lone Macintosh had sat in its canvas carrying case near the center of the stage. Steve walked over to the bag and opened it up, unveiling the Mac to the world for the very first time. He pulled it out and plugged it in, inserting a floppy, and the demo began to run, flawlessly (see "It Sure Is Great to Get Out of That Bag!" on page 213). The Macintosh became the first computer to introduce itself, speaking in a tremulous voice:

> "Hello, I am Macintosh. It sure is great to get out of that bag!
>
> Unaccustomed as I am to public speaking, I'd like to share with you a maxim I thought of the first time I met an IBM mainframe: Never trust a computer that you can't lift!
>
> Obviously, I can talk, but right now I'd like to sit back and listen. So it is with considerable pride that I introduce a man who has been like a father to me... Steve Jobs!"

Pandemonium reigned. Steve had the biggest smile I'd ever seen on his face and was obviously holding back tears as he was overwhelmed by the moment. The ovation continued for at least five minutes before he quieted the crowd down.

The rest of the meeting was an anticlimactic blur as Steve ran through some marketing material and introduced new versions of the Lisa. He showed a slide-show tribute to the Mac team, with voiceovers from the most important contributors. Finally, he turned the meeting back to Al Eisenstadt to announce the shareholder tallies and complete the formal portion of the shareholders' meeting.

Every member of the audience was given a copy of the first issue of MacWorld magazine, with Steve on the cover, as they departed. Most of the Mac team hung around near the stage, congratulating each other and waiting for the crowd to disperse.

A little later, after we had returned to Bandley 3, we were surprised to see a large Apple truck pulling up in the parking lot near the back of the building. It contained 100 brand new Macintoshes, one for each member of the team, each one personalized with a little plaque on the back. Steve presented them one at a time to each team member with a handshake and a smile as the rest of us stood around cheering.

We were so keyed up it was impossible to get back to work that afternoon, but most of us didn't want to go back home, either. The Macs were supposed to go on sale that very day, immediately following the introduction. I thought it would make it more real to me if I actually could go out and buy one, so five or six of us walked to the nearest Apple dealer to see if that was possible. The first, closest dealer didn't have any units in stock and told us they weren't for sale yet, but we didn't give up. The next dealer was willing to sell me one, even though he didn't have any units in yet either.

Thanks to Scott Knaster, who had a videotape of the 1984 introduction, which allowed me to quote so much of Steve's presentation—my memory isn't that good!

part five

Every act of creation
is first of all an act of
destruction.

Pablo Picasso

Can We Keep the Skies Safe?

January 1984

Burrell and I get our pictures in Newsweek

The marketing campaign that launched the original Macintosh was almost as imaginative and innovative as the product itself. It included a carefully orchestrated press blitz, masterminded by Regis McKenna, the legendary Silicon Valley marketing guru whose business card read "Regis McKenna, Himself," and his team of bright, young female assistants, who we nicknamed the "Rejettes": Andy Cunningham, Jane Anderson, and Katie Cadigan.

The basic idea was to create a perception of the Macintosh introduction as an epochal event by garnering as much attention as we could from every possible venue, all coordinated to appear around the January 1984 launch. Because some of the monthly magazines had more than three months lead time, the press briefings and interviews began in October 1983 with *Byte* magazine (see "The Mythical Man-Year" on page 179), and became more numerous with each passing week.

One of the most sought-after goals of the press campaign was to obtain a cover story from either *Time* or *Newsweek* during launch week. Regis and his team were experts at the delicate dance of courtship that such an endeavor required, since journalistic ethics mandated that the cover could not be bought or promised ahead of time. In mid-December, after *Newsweek* interviewed Steve and some of the design team, we heard they were potentially interested in doing a cover story on the Mac.

It looked promising enough that the Rejettes arranged for Steve to make an impromptu trip to New York City to meet the top brass at *Newsweek*. Apparently, they were interested in featuring Burrell Smith and me in the article, too, so we accompanied Steve on a whirlwind three days in New York. We stayed at Steve's favorite hotel, the Carlyle, which cost over $400 per night. We got a tour of *Newsweek*'s main offices, demoed the Mac to the editorial staff, and even spent some time chatting with Katharine Graham, the long-time publisher of the *Washington Post* and *Newsweek*.

After we returned to Cupertino, we got word we had passed muster and that *Newsweek* was enthusiastic about doing a cover story about the Macintosh introduction. Burrell and I were interviewed again, this time by *Newsweek* reporter Michael Rogers—who had written a novel called *Silicon Valley* that I had read the previous year—and were scheduled to be photographed the following day.

The software still wasn't finished, even though there were only five days left to work on it, and tension around the office was high (see "Real Artists Ship" on page 208). When the *Newsweek* photographer arrived, he wanted to photograph me in my office, but I was afraid that would be too disruptive to the rest of the team. I told him I often worked at home and convinced him to do the shoot in the messy office of my Palo Alto home.

Unfortunately, the *San Jose Mercury News* somehow discovered we had been granted the *Newsweek* cover and mentioned it in their business gossip column that Friday. *Newsweek* didn't want the world to think their cover was predetermined, so at the last minute they pulled our cover and used a standby instead. The new cover asked the burning question, "Can We Keep The Skies Safe?"

While we were all really disappointed about the cover flop, it was still amazing to come into work the day before the introduction, and see the January 30, 1984 issue of *Newsweek*, opened to a four-page story about the Macintosh. The article opened with separate pictures of Burrell and me in our respective homes. Burrell was sitting on the floor playing his beloved nine-string guitar, with engineering diagrams spread out on the rug in front of him. I was sitting on a chair in the spare bedroom of my house that I used for an office, which was in its usual state: extremely cluttered.

There was a long review of the Macintosh, which was generally positive, although it said that the some users might find the graphical user interface to be "visually tiring to use." Burrell had the best quote in the entire article, which was used to end it. When asked what he wanted to do next, he responded, "I want to build the computer of the 90s. Only I want to do it tomorrow."

The week following the public launch, Steve Jobs and the Mac design team flew to Boston to recreate the Mac introduction for an East Coast audience: the Boston Computer Society. Steve Wozniak also came along and participated in a panel discussion with the design team following the intro spiel.

On the flight to Boston, Burrell and I were seated together in a row of seats near the middle of the plane. We were just settling in for the long flight when a flight attendant approached us, holding a copy of *Newsweek*, open to the page with our pictures.

The cover of January 30,
1984 edition of Newsweek
was supposed to feature the
Macintosh.

"I recognized you from your pictures," she told us.
"Can I have your autograph?"

I was flustered, because no one had ever asked me
for an autograph before. I demurred, but eventually
Burrell and I both signed our names near our
pictures, feeling slightly embarrassed.

I turned on my Walkman, pushed back my seat
and tried to relax, hoping to fall asleep, but about 20
minutes later we were approached by a different flight
attendant, also holding a copy of the *Newsweek* issue.
"Are you the guys who designed the Macintosh?" she
asked. "I'd love to get your autographs."

Wait a second, I thought, Woz is on this flight,
too. Woz was a notorious prankster. Maybe all this
attention was his doing. Sure enough, when I stood
up and turned around, Woz was also standing,
pointing at us and cracking up. He had convinced
the flight attendants to cooperate in pulling one
of his typical pranks on us. I started laughing too,
because it was a pretty good one.

Leave of Absence

March 1984

I didn't know how to deal with my bad review

I didn't know how to deal with the bad performance review I received from Bob Belleville in February 1983 (see "Too Big for My Britches" on page 140). I had always loved my job at Apple, and had been devoting myself to working on the Macintosh, which I passionately believed would change the world significantly for the better. But it was clear that Bob was out to get me for reasons that I only partially understood.

Jerome Coonen had recently started as the new software manager, so I at least didn't have to interact with Bob directly very often. In fact, Bob seemed to want to avoid me even more than I wanted to avoid him. My initial instinct was to quit, but I believed in the Macintosh too much to leave until it shipped. This was at least six months away, so I resolved to keep working hard while I thought about what I should do.

It seemed as though the main problem was that Bob and I had very different views concerning the organization. I worshiped at the altar of the Apple II and romanticized my work, seeing it more as a calling than a job. I was much more enthusiastic about the computer we were creating than the engineering organization that was creating it, and I was difficult to manage because I was self-righteous and immature (although I didn't see it that way at the time) and thoroughly disrespected organizational authority.

Bob Belleville, by contrast, saw his job as rescuing the Mac team from the chaotic development process I thrived in. He was determined to instill a modicum of order and predictability, which was necessary to scale the organization. He saw my lack of respect for lines of authority as undermining the organization, which was unacceptable to him. I think Bob intended the negative review as a wake-up call, a way to compel me to change my style to fit his vision of the organization. I know he was surprised that I took it as hard as I did.

Since he disavowed having said the critical things he did on that late afternoon walk, and since I never received a written review, there didn't seem to be any way for me to reconcile with Bob. Furthermore, I didn't think I wanted to work in the type of organization he was trying to establish anyway. And so I decided that while I still wanted to work for Apple, I didn't want to—even indirectly—work for Bob. Perhaps it was inevitable that the Macintosh team would eventually mature into a more cumbersome and top-heavy organization, but I figured Apple would always need small teams and people like me to get the ball rolling on something new.

When Bud Tribble left the Mac team to return to medical school at the end of 1981 (see "Gobble, Gobble, Gobble" on page 76), I considered leaving, too. Steve Jobs persuaded me to stay, partially by promising to protect me from authoritarian managers. But over the next few months, whenever I tried to discuss the situation with him, he tended to be dismissive, belittling the problem and telling me that I didn't have to love Bob to work for him. Sometimes, he would cryptically hint he had some solution in mind, but nothing ever materialized.

As 1983 drew to a close, I was swept up in the monumental effort to finish the software (see "Real Artists Ship" on page 208), and then the blissful joyride of the product introduction (see "The Times They Are A-Changin'" on page 217). But by the middle of February, things had calmed down and I knew it was time to make a decision about my future at Apple.

By this time my relationship with Bob Belleville had worsened, if that was possible, after he went on a tirade in his staff meeting in December 1983 when he found out I had assisted Burrell Smith and Brian Howard by writing diagnostics for the LaserWriter prototype they were working on. Everyone on the software team was exhausted from the high-pressure marathon effort to finally complete the software, and tension with Bob made it hard for me to be enthusiastic about the future.

Then in February, after laying off a quarter of the Lisa people, Apple decided to merge the Macintosh and Lisa groups together, putting the Mac people in all of the top positions. Steve had always promised us that the group would never exceed 100 people. But now, when combined with more than 200 Lisa folk, it would be over 300 employees strong.

I watched as Steve stood up in front of the assembled Lisa team and announced the merger and layoffs, telling the laid-off folks they had screwed up and were B or C players. "So, today we are releasing some of your fellow employees to give them the opportunity to work at our sister companies here in the valley," he declared in classic Steve Jobs style.

Around this time someone suggested that I consider taking a leave of absence, instead of quitting entirely. That sounded good to me. I would retain my badge and the prerogatives of an employee, plus I could more easily return if things seemed better after they settled down. I decided to take a six-month leave, starting on March 1st, 1984.

Facing page: Brian Howard, Andy Hertzfeld, and Burrell Smith promoting Radius in 1987

When I told Steve Jobs about my leave of absence plans, he said he regretted them, but he didn't offer me any alternative that was acceptable to me. Now that the division had over 300 people, I proposed we spin off another small team that could work directly for him, but he wasn't interested. With the Macintosh finally shipping and the divisions combined, Steve felt he needed managers like Bob Belleville to manage the huge battalion of employees more than he needed creative types like myself. Also, he told me he was sure I'd be so bored in a month or two that I'd come back early from my leave.

A couple of days before my leave was to start, Steve came into the software area escorting a surprise guest. They came over to my cubicle and Steve introduced me to Apple's newest employee, Alan Kay (see "Creative Think" on page 114). Alan had recently departed from Atari and had just signed on as an Apple Fellow. He was one of my heroes, and it made me even more depressed than I already was to know that leaving would mean I wouldn't get to work with him.

At the end of my last day of work, the software team held a farewell dinner for me at a small, fancy, continental restaurant called Maddalena's, which was around five blocks from my house in Palo Alto. Now that my last day had actually arrived, I was really sad about leaving all my friends at Apple. I walked over to the restaurant with Burrell Smith, who lived in the house next door to me, wondering if I would be able to survive the dinner without bursting into tears.

Most of the software team came to the dinner, as did Steve Jobs. I was in a sort of daze as the elaborate dinner was served, followed by some toasts where people said how much they liked working with me. I only had sporadic success at holding back tears. Bill Atkinson said he had no idea what I would work on next, but he knew he would be amazed by it. Steve Jobs said he would miss me and that he hoped I would hurry back from my leave. But then he made a strange comment that I didn't quite know how to read: "The thing I like best about Andy is that it's so easy to make him cry."

Finally, the dinner was over and I walked back home with Burrell, still feeling numb, as if I didn't want to think about my conflicted feelings just yet. When I awoke at my usual time the next morning, I had to fight the urge to drive down to Apple as usual. It took a week or two before it stopped feeling strange not to go into work.

Spoiled?

The Mac team's "spoiled" reputation

The Macintosh team had a reputation for being spoiled, which was certainly true by the middle of 1984, but it wasn't always the case. Steve Jobs was fond of bragging that the Mac designers were Apple's best engineers. That may have been true, but it certainly wasn't reflected in our pay.

Two weeks before I transferred to the Mac team after a shake-up in the Apple II group in February 1981 (see "Black Wednesday" on page 16), I received my regular six-month review and was slated for a nominal raise in salary, from $22,000 per year to $24,000. I thought I should still get my raise, even though I had switched groups, so after working on the Mac for a few weeks I approached Bud Tribble, my new manager, about it.

"Well, that sounds reasonable to me," Bud told me when I explained the situation to him, "but there's a problem. I'm only getting paid $20,000 a year."

I was shocked. The average manager in the Apple II group was making at least twice that much. I then asked Burrell Smith about his compensation and found out that he was getting paid even less than Bud, since he started at Apple as a lowly service technician (see "It's The Moustache That Matters" on page 13) and had hardly gotten any raises as his responsibility grew. Less than two months earlier, the Mac was an iffy research project under Jef Raskin. I guess Steve hadn't seen to it to adjust anyone's salary when he took over.

The next day, I went and talked with Steve about the pay issue. I told him about my incipient raise, and asked him why, if the work we were doing was so important, Burrell and Bud had such low salaries. Steve was uncharacteristically nonchalant, professing that he didn't know what their salaries were and that he hadn't given anyone raises because no one had asked for one. Then he quipped that we had much more important things to worry about than our salaries, but agreed to give all three of us modest raises right away. Even after the raises came through, the Mac team was still relatively underpaid compared to the rest of Apple.

Rod Holt, the designer of the Apple II power supply and the first Macintosh engineering manager, was an extraordinary, opinionated individual who could expound brilliantly on a startling range of topics. He was the unlikely combination of a committed socialist and a multimillionaire, by virtue of his being one of Apple's earliest employees. On one occasion, the Mac team hired an older analog engineer to work on the disk controller and paid him almost twice what Burrell was making, even though he was only doing a small fraction of the work. When we complained, Rod invoked his economic theories about how people should be paid according to their needs instead of their talents. We didn't necessarily buy that, but it was true that we weren't working mainly for the money, and Rod was so charmingly philosophical that we let it slide.

Our offices at Texaco Towers were also kind of quaint by Apple standards. Most of Apple's offices were outfitted with high-tech, partitioned, Herman Miller cubicles, but Texaco Towers was more old-fashioned, with funky, older desks and secondhand furniture. Steve was generally tight with money and usually turned down any extravagant requests. For example, he allowed us to buy an IBM PC to dissect for $2,000 in August 1981 (see "Donkey" on page 55), but nixed our similar request for a $20,000 Xerox Star.

Most afternoons around 4 P.M., Burrell and I used to walk down to the nearby Texaco station to get soft drinks from their vending machine. One afternoon, in the summer of 1981, Steve brought a visiting dignitary by for a demo while we were out, and, frustrated by our absence, decided to bring in a refrigerator stocked with soft drinks so we wouldn't have to miss work time to get beverages. Free sodas were the first unusual perquisite for the Mac team.

The team's lifestyle began to change as it grew throughout 1982. In mid-1982, we moved from Texaco Towers to Bandley 4. Bandley 4 was a typical, ordinary Apple building, but it was only intended to be temporary quarters for the Mac team, until the building across the street, the much larger Bandley 3, could be renovated to accommodate us. The salaries of the early team also rose, as we had to pay competitive salaries to newcomers.

The design for our new quarters in Bandley 3, which we moved into in the summer of 1983, showed the first signs of extravagance. The software team was ensconced in a large area with glass doors that we dubbed "the fishbowl," because a passerby could observe us without opening the door. The showpiece of the building was a large atrium in the lobby, with fancy skylights and some interesting furnishings.

To one side of the lobby were two video games we had the opportunity to purchase cheaply a month or so after moving in; I paid for Burrell's favorite, Defender (see "Make a Mess, Clean it Up!" on page 168), while Randy Wigginton contributed Joust. On the other side of the lobby was an expensive stereo system bought by Steve, which featured a then-very-novel compact disc player and almost 100 CDs (which was just about every one released at the time).

Bandley 3 also had a nice little kitchen, near the software area, with a much bigger refrigerator than we had in Texaco Towers. Steve decided sodas weren't very healthy and had the refrigerator stocked with expensive Odwalla fruit juices, delivered fresh every day, as well as an assortment of other beverages.

In the spring of 1984, right about the time I left Apple, the lobby began to fill up with more interesting artifacts, purchased by Steve Jobs on his various travels. There was an outrageously expensive Bosendorfer piano that was soon accompanied by a BMW motorcycle, both on display as examples of exquisite craftsmanship. It was rumored that Steve had actually purchased them to impress Hartmut Esslinger, the industrial designer he was enamored with at the time. Hartmut's firm, Frog Design, designed the case of the Apple IIc.

That was right around the time that the 100-person Macintosh Division merged with the 250-person Lisa Division, with the Mac people occupying most of the management roles. The Mac had completed its journey from a funky research project to the center of the company, but I continue to think it was a lot more fun when we had a lot fewer resources.

THUNDERSCAN June 1984

A clever device transforms a printer into a scanner

The first project I worked on for Apple after starting in August 1979 was writing low-level software for the Silentype printer—a cute, inexpensive, thermal printer for the Apple II—that was based on technology licensed from a local company named Trendcom. In typical Apple fashion, we improved on Trendcom's design by replacing their relatively expensive controller board with a much simpler one that relied on the microprocessor in the Apple II to do most of the dirty work.

The only other engineer working on the project was Victor Bull, who was the hardware designer and also the project leader. Vic was smart, taciturn, and easy to work with. I learned a lot from him about how thermal printers work, as well as how things worked at Apple. We finished the project quickly, and the Silentype shipped in November 1979, less than four months after I began working on it.

In May 1984, during my leave of absence from Apple (see "Leave of Absence" on page 229), I received a phone call from Victor Bull, who I hadn't heard from in a couple of years. He had left Apple more than a year before to work with his friend Tom Petrie at a tiny company named Thunderware that sold a single product called Thunderclock, an inexpensive calendar/clock card for the Apple II. Victor thought I might be interested in writing software for an exciting, clever, new product Thunderware was developing for the Macintosh, which he refused to describe over the phone. He invited me to come visit them and check it out.

In early June, I drove up to Thunderware's office in Orinda, which was about an hour's drive from my house in Palo Alto. After I arrived at their modest headquarters, Vic introduced me to his partner, Tom Petrie, and I signed a nondisclosure agreement before they ushered me into a back room to see their demo.

The most popular printer for both the Apple II and the Macintosh was the ImageWriter, a $500 dot-matrix printer capable of rendering bitmapped graphics. It was designed and manufactured by a Japanese company named C.Itoh Electronics and was marketed by Apple. Virtually every Macintosh owner purchased an ImageWriter because it was the only printer Apple supported. Tom's demo consisted of an ImageWriter printer hooked up to an Apple II that at first glance appeared to be busily printing away. But when I looked closer, I noticed that instead of blank paper there was a glossy photograph of a cat threaded through the printer's platen, and the printer's black plastic ribbon cartridge was missing, replaced by a makeshift contraption containing an optical-sensing device that trailed an umbilical cord back to the Apple II.

Their potential new product, Thunderscan, was a low-cost way of turning an ImageWriter printer into a high-resolution scanner by replacing the ribbon cartridge with an optical sensor and providing some clever software. Since the resolution was determined by the precision of the printer's stepper motors, Thunderscan, priced at under $200, had better resolution than flatbed scanners costing more than 10 times as much. I loved the ingenious concept and the Woz-like elegance of saving money and adding flexibility by doing everything in software, but there were also a few problems.

The biggest issue was that Thunderscan could only capture one scan line's worth of data on each pass of the print head. This made it nine times slower than regular printing because the print head could deposit nine dots at a time. This made for frustratingly slow scanning, often taking over an hour to scan a full page at the highest resolution. Thunderscan was never going to win any races.

Another apparent problem was the disappointingly low quality of the image being captured and displayed by Tom Petrie's Apple II application. Tom and Vic said their scanner was capable of capturing up to 32 different levels of light intensity, but both the Apple II (in hi-res mode) and the Macintosh only had one bit per pixel to display, so the software had to simulate grayscales using patterns of black and white dots. It looked as though Tom

Previous page: the Macintosh software team in the spring of 1985 Below: Thunderscan in action.

was using a simple threshold algorithm to do the rendering, which threw away most of the grayscale information and made the resulting image look unacceptably blotchy. It was hard to tell if the quality promised by Tom and Vic was there or not.

Tom and Vic proposed hiring me to write Macintosh software for Thunderscan. I knew that a low-cost scanner would be a great product for the image-hungry Macintosh, but only if it had sufficient quality. I told

them I'd think it over during the next few days, and, as I did, I grew more excited about the potential of Thunderscan for the Macintosh, realizing the slow speed wouldn't be an impediment if the quality and resolution were good enough. The low image quality in Tom's prototype was probably caused more by the Apple II software than by anything inherent in the scanner. The Macintosh was almost 10 times faster than the Apple II, and I figured it should be able to sample the incoming data better to obtain more horizontal resolution. Plus, I knew a much better algorithm for grayscale rendering that would be fun to try out in practice.

My friend and colleague Bill Atkinson was a talented photographer, and one of his hobbies was experimenting to find the best algorithms for rendering digitized pictures. Bill loved to explain his current work to whoever would listen to him, and I had learned a lot about rendering grayscale images simply by being around him. Over the years Bill had progressed from using an "ordered dither" algorithm, which specified varying threshold values in a sliding matrix, to his current favorite, a modified version of what was known as the "Floyd-Steinberg" algorithm, which maintained and distributed an error term proportionally to neighboring pixels.

I called Thunderware and told them I was interested in working on Macintosh software for Thunderscan in exchange for a per-unit royalty. I drove back up to Orinda, where Tom and Vic gave me lots of documentation about the scanner along with the sample code Tom had written for the Apple II. For the next couple of months, I drove up to Orinda once a week, usually on Thursday, to show Tom and Vic my progress, prioritize development issues, and discuss complications as they arose. We would also discuss business terms, but we didn't sign a formal contract until the software was almost finished, when we settled on a royalty of $7.50 per unit.

Tom and Vic had already encountered and surmounted a number of tough problems just to get scanning going at all. For example, the ImageWriter printer was not really designed to be stepped one scanline at a time. If you tried to, the paper would bunch up against the roller and cause distortion. Tom and Vic solved the problem by commanding the printer to move three steps up and then two steps back, instead of a single step up. This held the paper snugly against the roller as required. They'd also created techniques for sensing the beginning and end of the scan line, and some timings that were determined by tedious experimentation for how long it took the printer to respond to a command.

It took a week or so to get basic scanning working on the Macintosh, and then a few more days to render the grayscale data with Bill's modified Floyd-Steinberg dithering. After working out a few additional problems, involving synchronization between the printer and the software, I was impressed by the consistent high quality of the results. I went through a brief, elated phase of scanning every image in sight that would fit through the printer, just to see how it would turn out.

One important design decision that I made early on was to save the grayscale data in a file in order to allow more flexible image processing. Thunderscan documents had 5 bits per pixel before the Macintosh generally supported grayscale, and the user could manipulate the contrast and brightness of selected areas of the image by dodging and burning to reveal detail in the captured image. This also paid off in later versions when we implemented grayscale printing for Postscript printers.

My favorite feature that I came up with for Thunderscan had to do with two-dimensional scrolling. Thunderscan documents could be quite large and you could only see a portion of them in the image area of the window. You could scroll the image by dragging with a MacPaint-style "hand" scrolling tool, but you had to drag an awful lot to get to the edges of a large image. I decided to add what I called "inertial" scrolling. This allowed you to give the image a push and it kept scrolling at a variable speed in the direction of the push. I had to add some hysteresis (simulated inertia) to keep the image from moving accidentally, but I soon had it working and it felt great to be able to zip around large images by pushing them.

The hardest feature to perfect was bidirectional scanning. At first, Thunderscan scanned only from left to right, and it wasted time to return the scanner to the left after every scan line. We could almost double the speed if we scanned in both directions, but it was hard to get lines scanned in opposite directions to line up properly. Ultimately, we made bidirectional scanning an optional feature for those willing to trade a little quality for greater speed.

ThunderScan.™

The new optical scanning device that turns printed images into detailed, high-resolution MacPaint documents.

- Set up your business forms on Mac
- Create your own clip art collections
- Become an instant artist
- Insert diagrams, illustrations, maps and photos into reports, newsletters and correspondence
- Digitize mechanical drawings, modify them and print them out
- Make personalized greeting cards
- Use ThunderScan and a modem as an inexpensive Facsimile machine

The possibilities are nearly endless!

Thunderscan's application software provides a complete set of image processing tools for controlling contrast, brightness, and half-toning, as well as selecting, scrolling, drawing and erasing.

ThunderScan is a complete digitizing system for Macintosh, combining a proprietary high-resolution optical scanning technology with the precision mechanism of the Imagewriter printer. With ThunderScan you can turn any printed material, from postage stamps to full 8″ x 10″ documents into MacPaint documents (not MacWrite). Just roll your original into your Imagewriter, tell ThunderScan's application software what area you want digitized, key in the enlargement or reduction and click your mouse. ThunderScan zips back and forth, translating the printed image into an electronic image which appears on Mac's screen.

Now you can change or enhance the image with a complete set of image processing tools. You can adjust the contrast, brightness and half-toning. On all or part of the image.

ThunderScan's application software also includes many tools you've already learned to use with MacPaint. Tools for selecting, scrolling, drawing and erasing. Its EDIT menu supports CUT, COPY, PASTE, CLEAR, SELECT ALL, INVERT and FATBITS. You can use these tools on entire documents or selected parts of them. So its easy to CUT and PASTE more or less than what you see on the screen. And you can use most of these tools on any MacPaint document. Even those you've previously created and filed.

Once you've digitized an image and modified it as desired, you can save it in your own clip art file, print it out on your Imagewriter or send it via modem. Or all three. ThunderScan features two printing modes, a normal 72 dots per inch mode and our "Hi-Res" 144 dots per inch mode.

The effec observe Mexico. Ov

9-point type scanned at 350% original size.

Enlarging and reducing.

ThunderScan can enlarge images to four times their size (actually 16 times by area). And reduce them to 1/4 size (actually 1/16). When a finished enlargement is larger than Mac's screen area, the screen serves as a document window. The digitized image can be scrolled on the screen and printed out in sections on your Imagewriter. If you enlarge an 8″ x 10″ document four times, you can actually piece together a finished 32″ x 40″ document.

Locomotive scanned at original size.

Locomotive reduced to 1/2 original size.

Locomotive enlarged to 4 times original size.

Technical information

ThunderScan requires a 128K Mac and an Imagewriter printer. The addition of an external disk drive, hard disk, or 512K Mac will further enhance ThunderScan's performance. Digitizing resolution is user selectable from 18 dots per inch, up to 288 dots per inch with 32 levels of gray-scale. The largest original area ThunderScan can digitize is 8″ x 10″. Time required to digitize a document depends on the size of the area to be scanned and the enlargement/reduction factor. Scanning a full 8″ x 10″ document at 100% size takes from 10 to 14 minutes.

ThunderScan

Thunderware Inc., 19 G Orinda Way, Orinda, CA 94563
(415) 254-6581

I finished the software in November 1984, after taking a short break to work on my Switcher project (see "Switcher" on page 243). Thunderscan shipped in December 1984 and did well from the very beginning, with sales gradually rising from around 1,000 units/month to over 7,500 units/month at its peak in 1987. For a while, it was both the least expensive and highest-quality scanning option for the Macintosh, although I'm sure it frustrated a lot of users by being so slow. I did three major revisions of the software over the next few years, improving the scan quality and adding features like grayscale printing and, eventually, grayscale display for the Macintosh II.

Eventually, the flat bed scanners caught up to Thunderscan and then surpassed it in cost, quality, and convenience. Over its lifetime, Thunderscan sold approximately 100,000 units and improved countless documents by providing users with an inexpensive way to capture high-resolution graphics with their Macintoshes.

Switcher

The first commercial product I worked on after going on leave of absence from Apple (see "Leave of Absence" on page 229) was a low-cost, high-resolution scanner for the Macintosh called Thunderscan. I created Thunderscan in collaboration with a tiny company named Thunderware. I started working on it in June 1984, and by early October, it was almost complete.

Tom Petrie, one of the two principals at Thunderware (the other was Victor Bull, who I worked with on my first project for Apple, the Silentype thermal printer), arranged a few demos for various computer magazines in hopes of currying favorable reviews to promote the product. On October 11th, 1984, I drove with Tom to an office in Hillsborough, just south of San Francisco, to demonstrate Thunderscan for *Byte* magazine.

The *Byte* reviewer was John Markoff, a technology scribe for the *San Francisco Chronicle* and one of the best reporters covering the personal computer industry. Tom described Thunderscan while I set up the demo and started scanning. John asked a few questions, taking notes with his IBM PC, which was running a character-based text editor I viewed with the typical pious disdain of a Macintosh purist. As I was answering one his questions, the phone rang.

"Excuse me," he said. He then pressed a key combination on his keyboard and his monitor screen instantly changed to a different program. He talked on the phone for a minute or two, occasionally typing, before he finished the conversation and pressed a key combination to switch back to his Thunderscan notes.

"What did you just do?" I asked John, curious about the software that he was running. "How did you switch to another application so quickly?"

"Oh, I'm running Memory Shift. Haven't you seen it?" John responded. "It's a DOS utility program that keeps multiple applications resident in memory and allows you to switch between them quickly. I've been using it a lot lately." John typed the switch command a few times in rapid succession in order to show me how fast it could do its thing.

"You know, I think I could do that for the Macintosh," I suddenly blurted out, before I even thought about what I was saying.

The 512K Macintosh, with four times the memory of the original, had just started shipping a few weeks earlier. I had considered trying to run multiple applications simultaneously on the 512K Mac, but I was stymied by low memory conflicts and other potential "gotchas."

But now, as I observed Memory Shift in action on John's PC, I suddenly saw a simple way to do it.

"Yeah, that would be cool," John agreed. I continued with the Thunderscan demo, but it was hard for me to concentrate because I couldn't stop thinking about application switching. There were a few intricate problems to solve, but it seemed eminently doable, and I thought it would be incredibly useful if I got it to work.

Tom Petrie didn't fail to notice how excited I was about the new idea. As we drove home, he reminded me of my prior commitments and made me promise I would finish the alpha release of Thunderscan before daring to start something new. We agreed on a list of a dozen or so tasks, which I thought I could accomplish within two weeks. Once the alpha release was completed, he assured me, I could take a short hiatus, in order to work on application switching.

During the next two weeks, I focused on polishing Thunderscan to get it ready for the alpha release, but I also spent idle moments pondering the design of the application switcher. One fundamental decision I had to make was whether or not to load all the applications into a single heap—which would make optimal use of memory by minimizing fragmentation—or to allocate separate "heap zones" for each application. I decided to opt for separate heap zones to better isolate the applications, but I wasn't sure that was right.

There were lots of little problems to solve. The most crucial one was that the system software kept lots of application-specific global variables in low memory (see "Mea Culpa" on page 258), which needed to be swapped during context switching so each application could maintain its own set of them. The hard part was coming up with the precise list of exactly what needed to be swapped; many of the variables were obvious, but some were quite subtle and dependent on how applications were using them. I knew that my first cut wouldn't be perfect, but I was confident that I could debug the inevitable problems once I saw how the applications were actually failing.

A few days after starting the push to finish Thunderscan, I received an intriguing phone call from Jeff Harbers, the manager of Microsoft's Macintosh applications team. Jeff told me that Microsoft had a very strategic project they needed for the Macintosh, and they thought I was the ideal person to implement it. He wouldn't tell me anything else over the phone, but he offered to fly me up to Seattle to discuss it in person. Even though I was right in the middle of trying to complete Thunderscan, I was intrigued enough to accept his offer and arranged to visit with him the following Tuesday.

Jeff picked me up at the airport and we drove to Microsoft's main building where Neil Konzen, a talented 23-year-old who was Microsoft's main systems programmer on the Macintosh, joined us. I knew Neil from his days as an early Apple II hobbyist when he was only 16 years old, when we collaborated on adding features to an assembly language development system.

Jeff asked me what I was working on and I told him about Thunderscan, which he seemed to be interested in. But when I mentioned I was about to start some experiments with an application-switching utility, his jaw dropped.

"That's just what we wanted to talk with you about!" he exclaimed. "It's great that you're already working on it."

Jeff explained that Microsoft had put a lot of effort into getting their applications to run well in the tiny space available in the 128K Macintosh, which they considered to be a key competitive advantage. But as things stood, the 512K Mac would undermine their efforts because it allowed for much larger applications. Plus, Lotus had recently announced an integrated application suite for the 512K Macintosh called Jazz, which made it easy to switch quickly between different functional areas. But if the Macintosh could run multiple applications simultaneously, the small memory footprint of the Microsoft apps would continue to be advantageous, since their lower memory requirements meant more of them could run concurrently, and users could put together customized application suites on their own. The purpose of the visit was to convince me to write an applications switcher under contract to Microsoft.

Neil Konzen had contemplated a potential design, which he conveyed to me in front of a whiteboard. He decided to use the single heap approach I had rejected, along with a few interesting twists to minimize memory fragmentation. I told him about the alternate approach of using separate heap zones, and how I thought it was probably worth it to trade some memory fragmentation for greater robustness. I told him I would give his approach some more thought.

"You're a really good programmer, right? I think you must be a really good programmer...How long do you think it will take to do this project? A month or two?"

Finally, my afternoon at Microsoft culminated in a private meeting with Bill Gates. Jeff ushered me into Bill's office and reviewed the afternoon's discussions for him, before excusing himself to leave us alone to negotiate a development deal. I had met Bill a few times during the course of Macintosh development, and while I respected his understanding of technology, I was wary of his burgeoning reputation as a conniving businessman.

After we had exchanged a few pleasantries, and he told me how much the Macintosh mattered to Microsoft, he looked me in the eye and said, "You're a really good programmer, right? I think you must be a really good programmer."

"I guess so," I responded, not understanding why he was attempting to flatter me.

"Well, I think you are. How long do you think it will take to do this project? A month or two? I think a really good programmer like you could get it done in less than two months."

"I really have no idea," I replied. "I'm not far enough along to know if it's even feasible yet."

"Well, let's figure it out," he said in a slightly condescending tone. "I don't think it could be more than 10,000 lines of code, and a really good programmer like you should be able to write at least a thousand lines of code per week, so I think it will take you less than 10 weeks to write it, if you're as good as I think you are."

I didn't know how to respond, so I kept quiet and let him continue.

"And how much do you think a really good programmer should get paid? Around here we pay our best programmers around $2,000 per week. Do you think you should be paid more than that?"

"I don't know," I replied. I was finally beginning to see where he was coming from. Bill was trying to get me to brag that I could write the application switcher really quickly, so he could justify paying me a lower price for it.

"Well, I don't think you could expect to get more than $4,000 per week, tops. Actually, I think that's too much, but let's go with it. If it takes ten weeks, and you get paid $4,000 per week, you'd get paid $40,000 for writing it."

Forty thousand didn't sound like very much to me, especially if it was as strategic to Microsoft as it seemed to be. I think Bill was expecting me to make a counteroffer, but I wasn't very enthusiastic about selling the switcher to Microsoft regardless of compensation, since I thought it should eventually be part of the Mac OS.

"...A really good programmer like you should be able to write at least a thousand lines of code per week, so I think it will take you less than 10 weeks to write it, if you're as good as I think you are."

"Listen, I really want to write this completely independently from you guys, so you won't have to pay me anything to do it. I certainly don't want to negotiate a deal until I see how it turns out; there might be a showstopper and I won't be able to get it to work at all. And if I pull it off, it really should be bundled with every 512K Macintosh."

Bill shifted his tactics. "OK, I don't really care if Microsoft owns it as long as it's available to our users. I want you to commit that you'll apply your best efforts to making sure it runs well with our applications, and that you'll call Jeff if you run into any snags. We can talk again about publishing it later, if you want to, after you're further along. How does that sound?"

I told him it sounded good and promised to do my best to make it work with Microsoft's applications, which I wanted to do anyway, since the Microsoft apps were important to most users. We shook hands and I departed on a positive note.

By the time I returned home that evening, I was burning with the desire to see if I could get something going quickly. Even though I still had a few more days of work to complete the Thunderscan alpha release, I decided to see if I could write a proof of concept prototype of the application switcher first.

I would eventually have to write a user interface for selecting applications, but the proof of concept didn't have to worry about that; it was hardwired to run MacPaint, MacWrite, MacDraw, and the Finder. I worked for 20 hours straight writing the core of the program, which worked by patching traps to extend a few essential system calls, such as GetNextEvent, Launch, and ExitToShell. The hardest part was going through all of the low memory locations and determining what needed to be swapped. Even though it was crashing all the time, it was incredibly satisfying to see it begin to work and then stabilize as I tracked down various problems.

I had it working for an hour or so when I saw Bud Tribble, who lived next door to me, return home. Bud had finally finished his M.D./Ph.D. program at the University of Washington, and had even interned for a year, but he decided working on the Macintosh was more fun than being a doctor, and he had returned to Apple in his old job as software manager a few months earlier. Bud was living at Burrell Smith's house, which was next door to mine.

I dragged Bud over to my house to show him how I could rapidly switch between MacPaint, MacWrite, and MacDraw. He was impressed, but to my surprise he complained that the switching, which was almost instantaneous, was actually too fast.

"OK, I've seen enough…It's great. Apple is going to bundle it with the Mac. Congratulations."

"I think it might be confusing to switch from one application to another without any feedback," he told me. "What if someone switches accidentally? Maybe you could use animation to make a smoother transition."

That sounded like a great idea to me. We decided that one application should scroll off the screen horizontally while another was scrolling on, which gave the users a simple, concrete mental model of the applications wrapped around a kind of Lazy Susan, which they could rotate to move the desired application to the visible area. I quickly wrote some fast scrolling routines, and was blown away by how cool it looked to see the applications zip across the screen.

I started showing my proof of concept demo to my friends at Apple, as well as to a few user groups, and it was very positively received. Unfortunately, I still had to finish up the product release of Thunderscan, which I barely managed to do by the end of November as I had promised. After taking a short vacation, I got back to work on what I was now calling "Switcher" in early December, and by Christmas I had much of it implemented, including a simple UI for selecting applications, along with "Switcher Documents" for remembering sets of related applications.

In early January 1985, I got a phone call from Guy Kawasaki, one of Apple's third-party evangelists, who told me Apple was interested in buying Switcher, and that he was assigned to make that happen. The first step was arranging a demo for Steve Jobs.

I entered Steve's office with a bit of trepidation because I thought Switcher was worth at least a quarter of a million dollars to Apple, but I was sure Steve would never want to pay me that much. But I was also proud of Switcher and was interested in seeing how Steve would react to it.

I booted up my by-now standard demo of MacWrite, MacPaint, MacDraw, and the Finder, as well as a little maze-generating program written by Steve Capps. I configured Switcher with the scrolling animation initially turned off, so it would have more impact when I showed it later. I demoed cutting and pasting between MacWrite, MacPaint, and MacDraw, in seconds instead of minutes, and then I turned on the scrolling animation and started switching rapidly between them, in both directions.

But then he paused, and stared at me for a moment with an incredibly intense gaze, as if he was sizing me up or maybe just trying to scare me.

"OK, I've seen enough, " Steve interrupted me. "It's great. Apple is going to bundle it with the Mac. Congratulations."

But then he paused and stared at me for a moment with an incredibly intense gaze, as if he was sizing me up or maybe just trying to scare me.

"But I don't want you taking advantage of this situation. I'm not going to allow you to take advantage of Apple."

"What do you mean?" I asked him, genuinely puzzled.

"There's no way you could have written that program without confidential information you learned working at Apple. You don't have the right to charge whatever you like for it."

I started to get angry. "The program is only half finished, and if I don't think you're paying me fairly, I won't be motivated to finish it."

Steve gave me another intense stare as he paused for a second. Then he stated a single number, without explanation.

"One hundred thousand dollars."

"I don't know," I told him. "I think it's probably worth a lot more than that."

"Don't argue with me. One hundred thousand is fair, and you know it."

I didn't seem to have any alternative but to capitulate to Steve's price fixing, since he was difficult to argue with and I really wanted Switcher bundled with the Mac. I eventually negotiated the final agreement with Guy Kawasaki, where, in addition to the $100,000, I managed to get a 10 percent royalty of the wholesale price if Apple sold Switcher separately, which Steve swore they would never do. Eventually the royalty delivered another $50,000.

Getting Switcher going wasn't that hard, but it was a very difficult program to finish because it overturned some of the underlying assumptions the applications were making, yet it was committed to keeping everything working anyway. Much of the work in the latter stages involved testing it with every application I could get my hands on and debugging crashes. Usually I could concoct some kind of technique that would mitigate the problem without causing worse problems elsewhere.

Switcher
by Andy Hertzfeld

Version 4.4 -- August 12, 1985
© 1985 Apple Computer, Inc.

Helpful Hints:

Use ⌘[and ⌘] to rotate between applications.
Use ⌘\ to return back to the switcher.
Use the option key to transport the clipboard between applications (or not).
Use ⌘-shift-option-period as an "emergency exit" to exit hung applications.
The Finder can be run under the Switcher; open Switcher to quit from the Finder.
Click on the screen of the Mac icon to toggle saving screen bits to save 22K.

Thanks to John Markoff and Bud Tribble.

Switcher's "About" box

Predictably, the hardest part of finishing Switcher was making it work smoothly with the Microsoft applications. That was partially because Microsoft was a very early developer and took liberties with the system most developers would shy away from, but it was mostly because the instructions comprising their applications were encoded in pseudo-code to save space, in the tradition of the byte-code interpreters from Xerox, which Charles Simonyi advocated.

Unfortunately, the pseudo-code kept me from disassembling the program when it crashed, which made it more difficult to debug. I finally developed a debugging technique by single stepping through their interpreter, six instructions at a time, to get to the instructions that were doing the work, but it was pretty painful. I was determined to slog through it because of the promise I had made when I visited Microsoft.

One of the last problems I addressed before finishing the first release of Switcher in March 1985 had to do with applications hanging. If you're running multiple applications, you don't want one hanging application to take down all of them. I added a feature that allowed the user to kill the current application if it was hung up by monitoring for a specific key combination during the vertical blanking interrupt handler.

I knew I had to pick a very rare key combination, because you didn't want users killing their applications accidentally. I decided on shift-command-option-period, four keys held down at once, which I figured would be pretty hard to stumble into accidentally. I was surprised, then, when I got a call from Jeff Harbers at Microsoft.

"Hey, I like that abort feature you just added, but you're going to have to change the key combination. We're using that one in Microsoft Word," Jeff told me. Microsoft Word was very complex and it possessed an enormous range of keyboard shortcuts, way too many as far as I was concerned.

"Okay, suggest something else and I'll consider it," I told Jeff.

Jeff didn't have anything specific in mind, so he told me he'd get back to me soon. I had to laugh when he called back the next day and withdrew his request. He told me I should go ahead and keep shift-command-option-period as the abort sequence.

"OK, that sounds good to me, " I told him. "But why the change? Doesn't it still conflict with Word?"

"We'll change Word in the next release not to use it. The problem was we couldn't find a safe sequence—I guess we're already using every key combination!"

I officially released the finished version of Switcher in April 1985 and maintained it for a few versions after that. Eventually, I handed it off to Phil Goldman, a tremendous young programmer from Princeton who was recently hired at Apple, who went on to write MultiFinder (with Erich Ringewald), Switcher's eventual successor, in 1987.

Handicapped
The reason Steve parks in the handicapped space

Most of the anecdotes I've included in this book are firsthand observations, but sometimes a second- or thirdhand story is just too good to pass up. I didn't actually witness the following encounter but a book of Mac folklore would be somehow deficient without it.

Steve Jobs was not the most considerate individual at Apple, and he demonstrated that in lots of ways. One of the most obvious was his habit of parking in the handicapped spot of the parking lot—he seemed to think the blue wheelchair symbol meant the spot was reserved for the chairman.

Whenever you saw a big Mercedes parked in a handicapped space, you could be sure it was Steve's car. (Actually, it was hard to be sure otherwise because Steve had a habit of removing his license plates.) This sometimes caused him trouble, since unknown parties would occasionally retaliate by scratching the car with their keys.

Anyway, the story goes that one day Apple executive Jean-Louis Gassee, who had recently transferred to Cupertino from Paris, had just parked his car and was walking toward the entrance of the main office at Apple when Steve buzzed by him in his silver Mercedes and pulled into the handicapped space near the front of the building.

As Steve walked past him brusquely, Jean-Louis was heard to declare, to no one in particular, "Oh, I never realized those spaces were for the *emotionally* handicapped!"

Are You Gonna Do It?

February 1985
Burrell quits Apple, but fails to live up to his threat

No matter how much resolve you could muster, it was still difficult to quit Apple if Steve Jobs wanted you to stay. You'd have to sit down with him for a reality distortion session, which was often effective at getting people to change their minds. One day, a few of us were talking about strategies to overcome Steve's persuasiveness.

"I've got it!" said Burrell. "I know the perfect way to quit that will nullify the reality distortion field."

Of course we wanted to know how he could do that.

"I'll just walk into Steve's office, pull down my pants, and urinate on his desk. What could he say to that? It's guaranteed to work." We laughed, thinking not even Burrell would have the guts to do that.

A year and a half later, it finally was time for Burrell to quit, after months of scuffling with Bob Belleville and some of the other managers who wanted to cancel the "Turbo Mac" project, a redesigned, faster Mac based on a semi-custom chip with an internal hard drive, that Burrell was working on with Brian Howard and Bob Bailey.

Burrell told Bob Belleville (who was probably relieved, since he knew Burrell didn't respect him) and the Human Resources department he was quitting, and then made an appointment to see Steve that afternoon. When he walked into Steve's office, he was surprised to see Steve grinning at him.

"Are you gonna do it? Are you really gonna do it?" asked Steve. Obviously word about the urination threat had gotten back to Steve, and he was genuinely curious to see if Burrell would really go through with it.

Burrell looked Steve in the eye. "Do I have to? I'll do it if I have to."

Steve's expression gave him the answer, and, with that, Burrell turned and walked out of the office, thereby ending his career at Apple.

MacBASIC June 1985

The sad story of MacBasic

When the Apple II was first introduced in April 1977, it couldn't do very much because there were few applications written for it. We knew it was important to include some kind of programming language so users, who were mostly hobbyists, could write their own programs. BASIC, designed by two Dartmouth professors in the 1960s for teaching introductory programming, became the language of choice for early microcomputers because it was interactive and easy to use. The Apple II included a BASIC interpreter known as *Integer* BASIC that Steve Wozniak wrote from scratch. It was stored in 5K bytes of ROM on the motherboard and was almost as idiosyncratically brilliant as his hardware design. It also came with Microsoft's BASIC interpreter, dubbed Applesoft BASIC, on cassette tape. Sadly, Applesoft eventually displaced Integer BASIC in ROM in the Apple II Plus because it had the floating-point math routines Woz never got around to finishing.

Donn Denman started working at Apple around the same time I did in the summer of 1979. His job was to work with Randy Wigginton on porting Applesoft BASIC to the Apple III. They needed to rewrite parts of it to deal with the Apple III's tricky segmented memory addressing, as well as to port it to SOS, the new operating system designed for the Apple III. It was easy for me to track Donn's steady progress because he sat in the cubicle across from mine.

By the summer of 1981, the Macintosh project was beginning to hit its stride, and we started thinking about the applications we wanted to have at launch to show off the Mac's unique character. Besides a word processor and a drawing program, we thought a BASIC interpreter, like the one on the Apple II, would be important to allow users to write their own programs. We decided we should write it ourselves, instead of relying on a third party, because it was important for the BASIC programs to be able to take advantage of the Macintosh UI, and we didn't trust a third party to "get it" enough to do it right.

I still had lunch with some of my friends in the Apple II group a couple of times a week, and I started trying to convince Donn to join the Mac team to implement our BASIC. He was reluctant at first because the Mac project was still small and risky, but he was pretty much finished with Apple III BASIC and was full of ideas about how to do it better. He eventually couldn't resist and joined the Mac team in September 1981.

A BASIC interpreter consists of a text editor for inputting your program, a parser to translate it into a series of byte codes, and an interpreter to execute the byte-coded instructions. Donn wrote the interpreter first, and then hand-coded some byte codes to test it. He implemented some graphics primitives early on as well because they were nice to demo. In a few months, he had a pretty impressive demonstration program going. It showed off the interpreter's threading capabilities by drawing elaborate graphical trees recursively and in multiple windows simultaneously.

By the spring of 1982, it was apparent Donn needed some help if we wanted BASIC ready for the introduction, which at the time was scheduled for January 1983. We decided to hire Bryan Stearns, whom Donn knew from the Apple II team, to help him. All of 18 years old, Bryan was excited about the project. Donn thought they had worked well together on the Apple II project, so we gave him a chance.

But BASIC still had a hard time getting traction, especially because the system was evolving rapidly beneath it. After six months or so, I was surprised to hear that Bryan was quitting the project to work at a tiny start-up founded by Chuck Mauro, who I had helped with his 80-column card for the Apple II. I tried to talk him out of it, but he left anyway. By the spring of 1983, it was so obvious that BASIC wouldn't be ready for the introduction that the software manager, Jerome Coonen, pulled Donn off it to work on other parts of the ROM and the system. Donn worked on desk accessories and wrote the Alarm Clock and Notepad, as well as the math guts of Calculator (see "Desk Ornaments" on page 56).

After the Mac shipped in January 1984, Donn went back to work on BASIC with renewed vigor, determined to get it finished. Apple brought in some freelance writers to write books about it (including Scot Kamins, who was a co-founder of the first Apple users group in the Bay Area). But Microsoft surprised us and released a BASIC for the Macintosh that they didn't tell us they were developing. It was everything we expected and feared, since it was essentially console-based and didn't really use the Mac user interface. Donn was making good progress and we looked to be on track to ship in early 1985; we were excited to show the world what BASIC should really look like on the Macintosh.

Unfortunately, there was another problem on the horizon. Apple's original licensing deal with Microsoft for Applesoft BASIC had a term of eight years and was due to expire in September 1985. Apple still depended on the Apple II for the lion's share of its revenues, and it would be difficult to replace Microsoft BASIC without fragmenting the software base.

Bill Gates had Apple in a tight squeeze, and, in an early display of his ruthless business acumen, he exploited it to the hilt. He knew Donn's BASIC was way ahead of Microsoft's, so, as a condition for agreeing to renew Applesoft, he demanded that Apple abandon MacBASIC. He then bought it from Apple for the price of $1 and buried it.

Bill Gates had Apple in a tight squeeze, and, in an early display of his ruthless business acumen, he exploited it to the hilt. He knew Donn's BASIC was way ahead of Microsoft's, so, as a condition for agreeing to renew Applesoft, he demanded that Apple abandon MacBASIC. He then bought it from Apple for the price of $1 and buried it. He also used the renewal of Applesoft—which would be obsolete in just a year or two as the Mac displaced the Apple II—to get a perpetual license to the Macintosh user interface. This probably was the single worst deal in Apple's history, executed by John Sculley in November 1985.

Donn was heartbroken when he found out MacBASIC had been cancelled. His manager told him "it's been put on hold indefinitely" and instructed him to destroy the source code and all copies, but refused to answer Donn's questions about what was going on. Later that day Donn went for a wild ride on his motorcycle and crashed it, returning home scraped up but with no real damage, except to his already battered ego.

Bill Atkinson was outraged that Apple could treat Donn and his users so callously, and let John Sculley know how he felt. But the deal was done and couldn't be reversed.

Donn quickly filed for a leave of absence, but eventually returned to Apple to work on various projects, including AppleScript.

The Beta version of MacBASIC had been released to interested parties, including Dartmouth University, which used it in an introductory programming class. Apple tried to get back all the copies, but the Beta version was widely pirated. Two books on MacBASIC were eventually published and sold quite well for several years.

I had never programmed in BASIC but I sensed that due to books of games in BASIC, this was the right language to go with. I had never written a language, not even for a class. In fact, I'd never taken a class on interpreter or compiler writing. But back in early college days, Allen Baum did send me some Xeroxed notes from texts on such subjects and I bought books on it anyway in the colleges I'd attended. At one point I sat day after day in math classes trying to figure out how to write a FORTRAN compiler for a Data General Nova computer in assembly language. The 6502 was the "latest" microprocessor at this point in time (late 1975). I had a hunch that nobody had written a BASIC for it and I had a chance to be the first. I started by learning a little BASIC by studying HP BASIC from a manual in our (calculator division) lab. I decided to put a syntax chart right into memory and use it to scan input by the user. I started generating my syntax diagrams with full floating-point capabilities. But I had such a strong desire to be the first with a 6502 BASIC that I deleted the floating-point parts to save maybe a month. I was strong on integer operation for accuracy and speed.

Even our HP scientific calculators did the calculations with integer algorithms, even for transcendental functions. An integer language would lead to fast games and would let me run logic simulations at work. The BASIC took me 4 months to write, demonstrating it bi-weekly at the Homebrew Computer Club. It involved much more work for me than the Apple I and Apple II computer designs together. I was too shy to talk and had to do impressive things to get others to speak first, and this BASIC did help. I had much floating-point experience. In fact, my floating-point math routines were included in the Apple II ROMS, although not incorporated into the BASIC. A floating-point BASIC was listed as one of the highest priorities for the Apple II in the same meeting that listed a floppy drive as the other one. Both were important for the Checkbook program that was shipping on cassette tape with the Apple II. Randy Wigginton and I were working on defining a rather advanced BASIC with floating point, and much more, when Microsoft sent us their 6502 BASIC. There was little need to work on our own at that point.

Steve Wozniak

Mea Culpa

A confession of our worst mistakes

Almost everyone involved with the design of the original Macintosh is proud of the work that they did on the project, both individually and collectively. However, this doesn't mean we aren't also embarrassed about some of the mistakes we made. I'd like to consider, if not apologize for, the worst decisions that I was personally responsible for, as well as other major faults in the system software and product as a whole.

The worst blunder I perpetrated had to do with the memory manager. Bud Tribble adapted the Lisa intra-segment memory manager for the Macintosh (see "Hungarian" on page 61), but we needed to add a few features. One was a "locked" attribute associated with a relocatable memory block that temporarily prevented the block from being moved. Another enhancement was a "purgable" attribute that told the memory manager it could release a block if memory was getting full. The big mistake was where I chose to locate the bits that controlled the attributes.

I decided to put the bits controlling the "locked" and "purgable" attributes in the high-order bits of the master pointer (a pointer to the current address of a memory block), because they weren't being used for anything else. The 68000 had a 24-bit address bus that allowed 16 megabytes of addressable memory. The processor didn't use the high-order 8 bits of an address, making it the easiest one to test and adding yet another reason I thought it was efficient to locate the flags there.

Of course, it was foolish to count on unused address bits to stay that way for very long, and it became a problem when the Macintosh transitioned to the 68020 processor in 1987 with the introduction of the Macintosh II. The 68020 had a full 32-bit address bus, which meant the memory manager could no longer get away with using the high-order master pointer bits for flags. It wasn't that hard for Jerome Coonen to convert the memory manager to keep the flags in the block header instead of the master pointer (which was where they should have been in the first place), but the practice of manipulating them directly had crept into third-party applications, even though it wasn't supposed to. It took another year or so to identify and eradicate all the transgressions to upgrade the Macintosh software base to be "32-bit clean" so the full address space could be used.

I paid a more direct price for my second worst mistake, which was to use fixed low-memory addresses for toolbox globals. The Apple II kept important system globals in low

1

Miscellaneous ToolBox Problems/Changes + other Things to Do   1/23/83

✓ ① Command Key Dragging doesn't seem to work in 1.95

✓ ② Range checking on SetCtlMin/Max   Fix GrowBoxRoutine stuff

✓ ③ Is MenuKey broken for upper/lower case. It doesn't seem to be but... Bill A. says it is...

✓ ④ Add boundsRect to DragWindow   ✓ ㉔ Do Cheap Solution ⌐ Action Rect only

④ On the fly value for TrackControl of Thumb

✓ ⑤ Desk hook in FindWindow   ㉕ Fix SndOn reentrancy problem (?)

✓ ⑥ Enable Flag for Down sweep

✓ ⑦ Flash MBar utility   ㉖ Make TrackControl ignore mus, inactive ags   Drag

✓ ⑧ Make sound use low memory "SoundBase" for page switching

⑨ Beeper (pitch, duration, volume) Real Sound Driver

⑩ Deep Shit Manager   ㉒ Test "SetCtlTitle" (use Burch's program...)

✓ ⑪ "Memory Window" Desk ornament as debug aid   ㉓ Make DeskMgr preserve the ports

✗ ⑫ New Font Manager, integrate LisaGraf   ㉓ Add CloseWindow

⑬ Test out GetMenu, GetMBar, GetNewWindow, GetNewCntrl

⑭ Add alerts to booting   ㉑ Disk cursor doesn't take effect until mouse moves

⑮ Real BootStrap (Larry)

⑯ HyperSlide Projector   ✓ ㉒ CalcMenuSize should be saved about minus width

⑰ Control Panel   ✗ Force origin 0,0 in controls?

✓ ⑱ Change I/O calls in DeskMgr for new system

⑲ Change DeskOrn model for "heap obliterated" call   control call

✓ ⑳ FindWindow only works at Origin (0,0) → fix?   Control   9/6

memory, and the 68000 included a special "short" addressing mode that made accessing addresses in the first 32K of memory more efficient. This motivated us to use low memory for various globals. While that may have been acceptable for system globals, it was clearly a mistake for the toolbox. Because each application required its own copy of the toolbox globals, it precluded us from running more than one application at a time.

That didn't matter much at first because, with 128K of RAM, we barely had enough memory to run a single application at a time anyway. But when the 512K Macintosh was released in September 1984, it started to become an issue. In October 1984, after I left Apple to work on my own, I realized I could solve the problem by swapping all the application-dependent low memory locations when you performed a context switch. In a few days, I wrote the core of the Mac's first multitasking environment, which we called Switcher (see "Switcher" on page 243). Switcher used the low memory swapping technique that kept multiple programs resident in memory at once and switched between them with a nifty scrolling effect. Using low memory in this manner ended up making context switching a few milliseconds slower than it should have been. It also made it harder to eventually use a memory management unit, but it didn't turn out to be as devastating as I once feared.

We wanted the Macintosh to have relatively simple system architecture so it could perform well with limited hardware resources, but perhaps we went a little too far. We decided we could live without a memory management unit, which was the right decision because of the expense of the associated hardware. But we also decided to eliminate the distinction between user and system code by running everything in supervisor mode. This empowered applications and simplified the system, but it was a poor choice in the long run because it made it harder to control the software base as the system evolved.

Even Bill Atkinson made an occasional error. His worst mistake was using signed 16-bit integers as sizes in various QuickDraw data structures like regions and pictures. This limited the maximum size of a region or picture to 32 kilobytes, which became a significant limitation a few years later as memory sizes grew. Bruce Horn's resource manager suffered a similar problem by using 16-bit offsets, thus limiting the size of resource files unnecessarily.

The biggest issue with the Macintosh hardware was its limited expandability. But the problem wasn't really technical as much as philosophical: we wanted to eliminate the inevitable complexity that was a consequence of hardware expandability, both for the user and the developer, by having every Macintosh be identical. It was a valid point of view, even somewhat courageous, but not very practical; driven by the relentless tides of Moore's Law, things were still changing too fast in the computer industry for it to work. Burrell did try to sneak some expandability into the design (see "Diagnostic Port" on page 50) but was only partially successful.

Limited hardware expandability exacerbates other flaws in the design because you don't have the flexibility for yourself or third parties to easily correct them. One of the biggest mistakes we made in the first Mac was inadequate support for a hard drive. Our first filesystem used a simple data structure that didn't scale well to large drives (in fact, it was suggested to us by Bill Gates in July of 1981), and we didn't have a way to get bits in and out of the box at the rates a hard disk required. In our defense, it was hard to for us to consider adding a hard disk to the Macintosh because it was one of the last differentiators from the Lisa, which was more than three times as expensive. But the lack of hardware flexibility made it more difficult for third parties to jump into the breach. Of course, some did anyway.

From a broader perspective, I think many of our mistakes came from a lack of understanding about exactly what we were doing. We thought we were making a great product while reincarnating the Apple II for the 1980s, but we were actually creating the first in a long line of compatible computers that would persist for decades. However, the latter wouldn't have happened if we didn't succeed at the former. Perhaps our design would have given the future more priority over the present if we had understood how long it would last.

Things Are Better than Ever

September 1984

My leave of absence draws to a close

Toward the end of August 1984, my six-month leave of absence (see "Leave of Absence" on page 229) was drawing to a close, and I still hadn't decided whether I would return to Apple. I continued to feel very close to the company, so it wouldn't be easy for me to turn in my badge, but I didn't see a reasonable alternative.

Either way, I was sure I would continue to write software for the Macintosh, which was still brand new and providing many exciting opportunities for me to create innovative applications (see "Thunderscan" on page 238). I was confident I could earn more money working independently than Apple was willing to pay me, even if I counted the appreciation of stock options, but financial matters were not my paramount consideration.

The main issue was that I wanted to continue making a difference in the Mac's evolution, and I felt that no matter what I did on my own, it would have only a minor impact because, as a third-party developer, I wouldn't be able to work on the core of system. Even though things had gone relatively well so far, the Mac's long-term success was far from certain, and it was entirely dependent on the moves Apple made to evolve the platform.

Many of my closest friends were still working on the Mac team, so I heard a lot about what was going on at Apple. I usually drove down to Cupertino to visit them once every week or two, hanging out in the Bandley 3 fishbowl (see "Spoiled?" on page 233), tentatively at first, but growing more comfortable when I saw that I was still welcome there. I lived next door to Mac hardware designer Burrell Smith, so I heard about Burrell's trials and tribulations at work on a daily basis. Unfortunately, the news wasn't very encouraging.

The Mac team had merged with the Lisa team in February of 1984, a few weeks before I started my leave, creating a single large division. At the time, Steve Jobs claimed that the merger would help transform the rest of Apple into an organization that would be more like the Mac team, but to me it seemed that the opposite had occurred. The idealistic version of the Macintosh team that I yearned for had apparently vanished, subsumed by a large organization of the type that we used to make fun of, rife with bureaucratic obstacles and petty turf wars.

The core software group was still recovering from the intense effort to ship (see "Real Artists Ship" on page 208) and hadn't done very much all spring and summer, suffering from a classic case of massive postpartum depression. The LaserWriter printer was the current main focus of development, along with the AppleTalk network required to support it, and the core software team didn't have much to do either. No one had set a compelling new goal for the team, and now it was just drifting.

Burrell Smith had completed the LaserWriter digital board and moved on to work on the "Turbo Macintosh," a new Macintosh digital board featuring a custom chip that supported 4-bit/pixel grayscale graphics and a fast DMA channel to interface an internal hard drive. But Burrell frequently complained of sparring with engineering manager Bob Belleville and others on Bob's staff over trivial design decisions. He thought Bob didn't really want to add a hard drive to the Mac, favoring the development of a Xerox style "file server" instead, and was therefore trying to surreptitiously kill the Turbo project. I didn't think Burrell would put up with it much longer; as he phrased it, he was "asymptotically approaching liberation" from Apple.

The one saving grace was that Bud Tribble had finally completed his six-year M.D./Ph.D. program at the University of Washington and decided to forgo practicing medicine in favor of returning to his old job at Apple as Macintosh software manager, working for Bob Belleville. In July 1984, he moved into a spare bedroom at Burrell's house in Palo Alto, next door to mine, so I got to see him frequently. I still had the highest respect for Bud, and I loved to show him whatever I was working on because he always managed to improve it with an insightful suggestion or two.

I had mixed feelings about returning to the lumbering Macintosh division, but Bud was a strong link to the good old days, and I thought perhaps we could establish a little outpost in the large organization where the original Macintosh values could prevail. But that didn't seem possible if Bud worked for Bob Belleville, my nemesis whom I blamed for many of the problems. The only solution I could think of was for Bud to work directly for Steve Jobs instead of for Bob. Bud was all for it, but only Steve could make it happen. I called Steve's secretary Pat Sharp and arranged to have dinner with Steve and Bud to discuss my possible return to Apple.

We met in the lobby of Bandley 3 and walked to an Italian restaurant on De Anza Boulevard a few blocks away. Steve seemed a bit preoccupied, and I was nervous about how he would react to what I had to say because I had to implicitly criticize him to make my case. After we ordered dinner, I cleared my throat and tentatively plunged ahead.

"As you know, I care a lot about Apple, and I really want to return from my leave of absence. I'd love to work for Bud again, but things seem really messed up right now." I paused for a moment as I gathered my resolve. "The software team is completely demoralized and has hardly done a thing for months, and Burrell is so frustrated that he won't last to the end of the year…"

Steve cut me off abruptly with a withering stare. "You don't know what you're talking about!" he interrupted, seeming more amused than angry. "Things are better than ever. The Macintosh team is doing great, and I'm having the best time of my life right now. You're just completely out of touch."

I couldn't believe what I was hearing or tell if Steve was serious or not. I looked to Bud, who communicated his bewilderment with an apologetic shrug of his shoulders, but I could see he wasn't going to corroborate my views.

"If you really believe that, I don't think there's any way that I can come back," I replied, my hopes for returning sinking fast. "The Mac team that I want to come back to doesn't even exist anymore."

"The Mac team had to grow up, and so do you," Steve shot back. "I want you to come back, but if you don't want to, that's up to you. You don't matter as much as you think you do, anyway."

I saw that we were so far apart there was little point in continuing the conversation. We finished dinner quickly and walked back to Apple without further discussion.

Actually, quitting was easier than I thought it would be; I just called up Apple's HR department and let them know that I wouldn't be coming back. I didn't even have to sign any paperwork or turn in my badge, which I still have today, almost 20 years later. I had thought it would feel devastating to finally resign, but instead I actually felt relieved the situation was resolved, as well as optimistic about writing Macintosh software on my own.

Facing page: Andy posing for the cover of MacWorld in February 1985

The End of an Era

The original Macintosh enjoyed robust sales following its spectacular launch in January 1984 (see "The Times They Are A-Changin'" on page 217). Steve Jobs defined success as selling 50,000 units in the first 100 days, which was a high hurdle for a brand new computer with only a handful of applications available. In fact, Apple was able to sell more than 72,000 Macintoshes by the end of April, and over 60,000 units in June 1984 alone.

I traveled to the 1984 National Computer Conference show in June with the Mac team and shared a hotel room with Burrell Smith, even though I was on leave of absence (see "Leave Of Absence" on page 229). Apple had assembled over a dozen small software developers who had written cool applications for the Macintosh in order to display their wares at the trade show. Steve Jobs was ebullient, and thought that the sprouting applications and blossoming sales meant we had turned the corner. When I ran into him on the floor of the show, he put his arm around my shoulder and exclaimed, "Look at all these applications! We did it! The Macintosh has made it!"

High sales spurred even rosier predictions for the upcoming holiday season. But as summer turned into fall, Macintosh sales began to decline. For a couple of months, the University Consortium (see "What's A Megaflop?" on page 132) kept volumes high by selling tens of thousands of low-cost Macs to college students, but by Thanksgiving 1984, sales had slowed significantly. The marketing team forecast selling over 75,000 Macs per month for the important holiday season, but actually they didn't even break 20,000 per month. In December of 1984, the Apple II still accounted for about 70 percent of Apple's revenues.

As the New Year dawned, Steve Jobs seemed oblivious to the slowing sales and continued to behave as if the Macintosh was a booming, unqualified success. His lieutenants in the Macintosh division, which had swelled to more than 700 employees, had to deal with a growing reality gap, reconciling the ever-changing audacious plans for world domination emanating from their leader with the persistent bad news from the sales channels.

Meanwhile, the Macintosh engineering team had not been very productive. The Mac was crying out for an internal hard drive, as well as some kind of high-bandwidth port to attach it to, but there weren't any significant upgrades on the horizon, even though the basic hardware hadn't changed (except for additional RAM) for a year. In the fall of 1984, Steve Jobs tried to rally the remains of the original Mac team around the "Turbo Mac" project, featuring a new digital board with custom chips and fast I/O for an internal hard drive to be designed by Burrell Smith. But Burrell felt that engineering manager Bob Belleville was flinging lots of gratuitous obstacles in his path, and it eventually became so frustrating that he quit the company in February 1985 (see "Are You Gonna Do It?" on page 253).

The only new upcoming product was the LaserWriter printer, based on Canon's 300 dots-per-inch (DPI) laser-printing engine, with a digital board designed by Burrell Smith and software written by Adobe (a new company founded by Xerox alumni John Warnock and Chuck Geschke). Like the Macintosh itself, Adobe's PostScript software that was at the heart of the LaserWriter was years ahead of its time and was capable of producing exquisitely beautiful pages. Unfortunately, the LaserWriter had one major flaw: its retail price was over $7,000, which was almost triple the cost of a Macintosh.

Joanna Hoffman, the Mac team's original marketing person, transferred from international marketing back to the main product marketing group in early 1985 to help deal with the growing crisis. At the first sales meeting she attended, she was surprised to see that the sales forecasts for the upcoming quarter were unchanged from six months ago—when things were still looking good—and were almost four times what they were currently selling. Everybody was informally assuming more realistic numbers, but no one had the heart to cut the official forecast because they were afraid to tell Steve about it. To the relief of the sales and manufacturing team, Joanna immediately slashed the forecasts.

The weak sales were beginning to put pressure on the relationship between Steve Jobs and John Sculley for the very first time. They had gotten along fine when everything was going well, but hitherto they never had to deal with much adversity. Unfortunately, in early 1985 the personal computer market was descending into one of its periodic downturns, and even Apple II sales were starting to falter. Steve did not take criticism very well, and sometimes reacted to suggestions for improving Macintosh sales as if they were personal attacks. Steve and John's relationship began to sour as John put pressure on Steve to address the Macintosh's problems.

Steve Jobs had never suffered fools gladly, and as the pressure mounted, he became even more difficult to work with. Employees from every part of the company began to approach John with complaints about Steve's behavior, including some of Steve's direct reports in the Macintosh division. John felt especially strong about building more compatibility bridges with the IBM PC, an approach Steve disdained. John began to view Steve as an impediment toward fixing Apple's problems, and the board of directors was urging him to do something about it.

Steve had often professed he preferred working with small teams on new products, and that he didn't really want to run a large organization with hundreds of employees. Apple's board felt he should hand the reins of the Macintosh division over to a professional management team, and return to his core strength as a new product visionary.

Steve had recently met an interesting character named Steve Kitchen, who was introduced to him by Steve Capps. Steve Kitchen was a fast-talking, enthusiastic entrepreneur who had developed a couple of successful Atari video games. He claimed to have recently invented a revolutionary flat screen display technology that could facilitate portable computers. Steve Jobs was intrigued by the prospect of developing a lightweight portable computer years ahead of its time, and he considered having Apple buy the technology and start a research organization called "Apple Labs" to develop it. But he seemed ambivalent. Sometimes he was enthusiastic about starting Apple Labs, but other times he seemed determined to prove he could manage the large division.

The conflict came to a head at the April 10th board meeting. The board thought it could convince Steve to transition back to a product visionary role, but instead he went on the attack and lobbied for Sculley's removal. After long, wrenching discussions with both of them, and extending the meeting to the following day, the board decided in favor of John, instructing him to reorganize the Macintosh division, stripping Steve of all authority. Steve would remain the chairman of Apple, but for the time being no operating role was defined for him.

John didn't want to implement the reorganization immediately because he still thought he could reconcile with Steve and get him to buy into the changes, thereby achieving a smooth transition with his blessing. But after a brief period of depressed cooperation, Steve resumed attacking John behind the scenes in a variety of ways. I won't go into the details here, but eventually John had to remove Steve from his management role in the Macintosh division involuntarily. Apple announced Steve's removal, along with the first quarterly loss in their history and significant layoffs, on Friday, May 31, 1985—Fridays being the traditional time for companies to announce bad news. It was surely one of the lowest points of Apple history.

I was shocked when I heard the news that morning from a friend at Apple, and immediately drove down to Cupertino to see what was going on and commiserate with my friends. I was aware of the problem with Macintosh sales, but it was still inconceivable to me that the board could oust Steve Jobs, difficult as he could sometimes be, because he was clearly the heart and soul of the company. It was almost impossible to imagine the Macintosh team without him at the helm. I thought that perhaps I wasn't hearing the whole story, and that something would emerge to help it make more sense.

I arrived at the Apple campus soon after Sculley's communication meeting finished, during which he explained the nature of the reorganization and the accompanying layoffs. The way people were milling around listlessly reminded me of Black Wednesday four years earlier (see "Black Wednesday" on page 16), when Mike Scott unexpectedly purged the Apple II group. A few folks from the Apple II division—who resented Steve's superior attitude—seemed elated, and a few others saw the shakeup as an opportunity for personal advancement, but most of Apple's employees were somber, depressed, and uncertain about the future.

Many people had varying stories about what had actually happened. I thought that maybe it meant Steve had decided to pursue Apple Labs, and that maybe I could come back to Apple to work on a small team again. I was anxious to talk to Steve himself and find out his take on it. I wasn't the only one, so Bill Atkinson, Bud Tribble, Steve Capps, and I arranged to visit Steve at his house in Woodside for dinner on Sunday evening, two days after the reorganization was announced.

I had never been to Steve's house in Woodside before. It was a 14-bedroom, 17,250-square-foot Spanish colonial–style mansion built in 1926 that Steve had purchased a year before, in 1984. We knocked on the door and waited a few minutes before Steve appeared and led us inside. The massive house was almost completely unfurnished, and our footsteps echoed eerily as he led us to a large room near the kitchen with a long table, one of the few rooms that had any furniture.

We stood around the kitchen chatting as Steve prepared some food. His girlfriend Tina was there; I'd met her a few times before and was impressed by her mix of kindness and intelligence. Bill started chatting with Tina as I finally got a chance to ask Steve about the reorganization.

"So what really happened at Apple?" I asked him, even though I was scared to bring it up so directly. "Is it really as bad as it looks?"

"No, it's worse," Steve replied with a pained expression. "It's much worse than you can imagine."

Steve was adamant about blaming John Sculley for everything that had happened. He felt that John had betrayed him and he had little faith that Sculley or anyone else could manage Apple without him. He said his role as chairman was completely ceremonial, and it left him with no actual responsibilities. In fact, Apple had already moved his office from Bandley 3 to Bandley 6, a small building across the street that was almost empty. The new office was so remote from day-to-day operations that it was later nicknamed "Siberia."

We had a pleasant dinner, huddled around one end of the long table, mainly reminiscing about the good old days developing the Mac but occasionally engaging in grim speculation about Apple's future. Steve had arranged for some gourmet vegetarian food to be delivered, and we drank some excellent wine. Dessert consisted of handfuls of locally grown Olson's cherries, grabbed from a large wooden crate that Steve kept in the kitchen.

After dinner, we retired to another room that had an expensive stereo system and an elaborate model of the mostly underground house Steve planned to build to replace the one we were standing in. I had brought along a copy of Bob Dylan's new album, "Empire Burlesque," which was just released earlier that week, because I knew that Steve, like myself, was a big Bob Dylan fan, even though Steve thought Dylan hadn't done anything worthwhile since "Blood on the Tracks" a decade before. I placed the album on a hi-tech turntable that seemed to be mounted on aluminum cones and played the last song, "Dark Eyes," which was slow and mournful, with a fragile melody and lyrics that seemed relevant to the situation at Apple. But Steve didn't like the song, and wasn't interested in hearing the rest of the album, reiterating his negative opinion of recent Dylan.

Later, when it was time to leave, we lingered outside under the beautiful summer night sky. We were all pretty emotional by then, especially Steve. I tried to convince him the change wasn't necessarily so bad, and that I would be excited about returning to Apple to work with him on a small team again. But Steve was inconsolable, and more depressed than I had ever seen him before. As we left, I thought it was lucky he had Tina there to keep him company in the cavernous mansion.

It took a while for me to understand the consequences of the reorganization. The best news for me was that my nemesis Bob Belleville had resigned from Apple because he had sided with Steve during the recent infighting and burned too many bridges to continue. Most of the rest of Steve's staff stayed on to work for Jean-Louis Gassee, who replaced Steve in the reorganized division, although Mike Murray resigned soon thereafter. Steve Jobs spent most of the summer traveling, trying to figure out what to do next. He was still the chairman of Apple Computer, but he was so at odds with the rest of its leadership that it was hard to see how he could remain there much longer.

The Father of the Macintosh

Who is the father of the Macintosh?

In the early days of the personal computer industry, breakthrough products could still be created single-handedly, or by very small teams. Steve Wozniak, for example, is indisputably the father of the Apple II. He designed the entire digital board himself and wrote all of the system software, including a BASIC interpreter, most of it before Apple was even incorporated. But even Woz required help from Rod Holt for the analog electronics (the Apple II's switching power supply was almost as innovative as the digital board), and from Steve Jobs and Jerry Manock for the industrial design (ditto for the plastic case).

By the 1980s, things had become more complicated. The development of the Macintosh was more of a team effort. At least a half-dozen people made significant, invaluable contributions. Steve Jobs anointed 7 of us (not counting himself) as the official "design team," but it could just as easily have been 5 or 15. Some people felt bad they weren't included. It was obvious there was no good way to draw the line.

But if you look up the phrase "Father of the Macintosh" on Google, you get lots of links mentioning the name Jef Raskin. Jef was a former computer science and music professor at UCSD who started at Apple in January 1978 as Apple employee #31. Jef, along with his friend Brian Howard, had contracted to write Apple's manual for Basic at their consulting firm (which was named Bannister and Crun in a playful appropriation from the legendary Goon Show). Apple liked the Basic manual so much they hired Jef and Brian to be founders of their internal publications group.

In early 1979, after successfully building an outstanding pubs department, Jef turned the reins over to Phyllis Cole and started thinking about what it would take for personal computers to expand beyond the current hobbyist market. He wrote up his ideas in a series of short papers. In March, he presented his idea for an ultra low-cost, easy-to-use appliance computer to Mike Markkula, and in September got the go-ahead to hire a few people and form an official research project. Jef named it Macintosh, after his favorite apple. Most of his ideas for the new machine were collected in a set of papers he called *The Book of Macintosh*.

There's no doubt Jef was the creator of the Macintosh project at Apple. It was his articulate vision of an exceptionally easy-to-use, low-cost, high-volume appliance computer that got the ball rolling. And his vision remained near the heart of the project long after Jef left the company. He also deserves ample credit for putting together the extraordinary initial

Steve Jobs in 1989

team that created the computer, recruiting former student Bill Atkinson to Apple and then hiring amazing individuals like Burrell Smith, Bud Tribble, Joanna Hoffman, and Brian Howard for the Macintosh team. But there is also no escaping the fact that the Macintosh we know and love is very different from the computer Jef wanted to build, so much so that he is perhaps much more like an eccentric great uncle than the Macintosh's father.

Specifically, Jef did not want to incorporate what became the two most definitive aspects of Macintosh technology: the Motorola 68000 microprocessor and the mouse pointing device. Jef preferred the 6809, a cheaper but weaker processor which had only 16 bits of address space and would have been obsolete in just a year or two because it couldn't address more than 64K bytes. He was dead set against the mouse as well, preferring dedicated meta-keys to do the pointing. He became increasingly alienated from the team, eventually leaving entirely in the summer of 1981, when we were still just getting started. The final product utilized very few of the ideas in Jef's *Book of Macintosh*. In fact, if the name of the project had changed after Steve took over in January 1981, as it almost did (see "Bicycle" on page 36), there wouldn't be much reason to correlate it with Raskin's ideas at all.

So, if not Jef, does anyone else qualify as a parent of the Macintosh? Bill Atkinson is a strong candidate, since he was almost single-handedly responsible for the breakthrough user interface, graphics software, and killer application (MacPaint) that distinguished the

Mac. A case could also be made for Burrell Smith, whose wildly creative digital board was the seed crystal of brilliance everything else coalesced around. But ultimately, if any single individual deserves the honor, I would have to cast my vote for the obvious choice: Steve Jobs. The Macintosh never would have happened without him, in anything like the form it did. Other individuals are responsible for the actual creative work, but Steve's vision, passion for excellence, and sheer strength of will, not to mention his awesome powers of persuasion, drove the team to meet or exceed the impossible standards we set for ourselves. Steve already gets a lot of credit for being the driving force behind the Macintosh. In my opinion, it's very well deserved.

Facing page: Apple's
Fremont Macintosh
factory warehouse

Epilogue: The Macintosh Spirit

The attitudes and values of the team forged the spirit of the Macintosh

The original Macintosh was designed by a small team that worked long hours with a passionate, almost messianic fervor inculcated by our leader, Steve Jobs. The excitement that we felt during its creation shines through in the finished product. The attitudes, values, and personalities of the designers are reflected in the thousands of subtle choices they made in the course of their design, coalescing into a spirit or feeling imparted to its users.

We were excited because we thought we had a chance to do something extraordinary. Most technology development is incremental, but every once in a while there's an opportunity to make a quantum leap to a whole new level. A few years earlier, the Apple II and other pioneering systems made computing affordable to individuals, but they were still much too hard for most people to use. We felt that the Mac's graphical user interface had the potential to make computing enjoyable to nontechnical users for the very first time, potentially improving the lives of millions of users.

As soon as he seized the reins from Jef Raskin in January 1981, Steve Jobs galvanized the Macintosh team with an extreme sense of urgency. One of his first acts as head of the project was to bet John Couch, the executive in charge of the Lisa Division, $5000 that the Macintosh would beat the Lisa to market, despite the fact that Lisa had more than a two-year head start, and we had barely begun. The Mac team always had incredibly optimistic schedules because Steve was never satisfied with more realistic estimates (see "Reality Distortion Field" on page 24), as if he could make things happen faster through sheer force of will.

But the desire to ship quickly was counterbalanced by a demanding, comprehensive perfectionism. Most commercial projects are driven by commercial values, where the goal is to maximize profits by outperforming your competition. In contrast, the Macintosh was driven more by artistic values, oblivious to competition, where the goal was to be transcendently brilliant and insanely great. We wanted the Macintosh to be a technical and artistic tour-de-force that pushed the state of the art in every conceivable dimension. No detail was too small to matter (see "PC Board Esthetics" on page 41), and good enough wasn't good enough. If Steve could perceive it, it had to be great.

Steve encouraged the Mac designers to think of ourselves as artists. In the spring of 1982, he took the entire Mac team on a field trip to a Louis Comfort Tiffany exhibition in San Francisco because Tiffany was an artist who was able to mass-produce his work, as we aspired to do. Steve even had us individually sign the interior of the Macintosh case, like artists signing their work (see "Signing Party" on page 68), encouraging each one of us to feel personally responsible for the quality of the product.

Other groups at Apple had an elaborate formal product development process that mandated lengthy product requirement documents and engineering specifications before implementation commenced. In contrast, the Mac team favored a more creative, flexible, incremental approach of successively refining prototypes. Burrell Smith developed a unique hardware design style based on programmable array logic chips (PAL chips), which enabled him to make changes much faster than traditional techniques allowed, almost with the fluidity of software. Instead of arguing about new software ideas, we actually tried them out by writing quick prototypes, keeping the ideas that worked best and discarding the others (see "Busy Being Born" on page 89). We always had something running that represented our best thinking at the time.

You might think that impossible schedules and uncompromising perfectionism would lead to an oppressive work environment. But most of the time, the ambiance of the Mac team was spontaneous, enthusiastic, and irreverent. Jef Raskin had a playful management style, encouraging a workplace teeming with toys and semi-organized games (see "Good Earth" on page 14) that carried over to the Jobs era. Most of the early team members were around the same age, in our mid-20s, and we enjoyed each other's company. We increasingly hung out together as the project demanded ever-greater chunks of our time, abandoning the distinction between work and play. Despite the incessant pressure, we loved what we were doing.

Given Steve's autocratic tendencies, the Mac team was surprisingly egalitarian. Unlike other parts of Apple, which were becoming more conservative and bureaucratic as the company grew, the early Mac team was organized more like a startup company. We eschewed formal structure and hierarchy in favor of a flat meritocracy with minimal managerial oversight. Steve Jobs would sometimes issue an unreasonable edict or veto something that everyone else wanted, but at least he would relent when he saw he was wrong (see "Quick, Hide In This Closet!" on page 158). At our third retreat in January 1983, Steve reinforced our rebel spirit, which was waning as the team grew larger, by telling us, "it's better to be a pirate than join the navy" (see "Pirate Flag" on page 166).

Enthusiasm is contagious, and a product that is fun to create is much more likely to be fun to use. The urgency, ambition, passion for excellence, artistic pride, and irreverent humor of the original Macintosh team infused the product and energized a generation of developers and customers with the Macintosh spirit, which continues to inspire more than 20 years later.

Scanner To Do 10/18/84

1. ~~Test memory size consistently (set flags)~~
2. Estimated time feedback
3. Re-halftone off at certain scales
4. Re-halftone, focus during scan
5. ~~Keyboard screwup - sp/move e De-config VIA ??~~
6. ~~Small Image Draw → paint white in diff Rgn~~
7. ~~Print Abort, test print, hires print every 6 lines~~
8. Black Dot during save image, truncated menu?
9. Make select Rect visible in window
10. ~~Fast Scan check Box~~
11. ~~B-D at~~ 80% isn't working right
12. ~~Prairity Range Map → Light Intensity Gauge Abort → Clr Scan, reprocess rehm~~
13. Sense edge tape & default to uni if not present
14. ~~B-D in scan dialog?~~
15. ~~Different error for scan out of range, test~~
16. ~~Only 1 alert box~~

Check
SqPrint complete
enable

50K

① For "save as paint", if selection, use upper left

SaveDCE
```
        MOVE.L    A2, A1        ; remember table base
        CLR.W     (A1)          ; start with zero entries
        MOVE.L    $UnitTable(A3)
        MOVE.W    UnitCnt,D3
        MOVEQ     #0, D3
SDCELoop MOVE.L   (A3)+, D0
        BEQ.S     Next
```

easy — just do it

Cut
Copy
Copy

How the Book Came to Be

A Look into the Publishing Process at O'Reilly

When I began to write stories for the Macintosh Folklore site (http://www.folklore.org/index.py) in June 2003, I had no intention of trying to publish them in book form. I was excited by the idea of developing a website to facilitate collective historical storytelling, where a group of participants could collaborate to recollect an interesting event. I chose the format of numerous interlinked anecdotes because it seemed natural for the Web and better suited to a collaborative effort than a single, continuous narrative, allowing a tale to be elaborated indefinitely without compromising the voices of the individual authors.

After I got the initial site running in August 2003, with about 20 stories, I began to show it to various original Mac team members, and others, to gather feedback and encourage participation. When I showed the site to Tim O'Reilly, I was surprised he suggested that his company publish it as a book. At first, I thought conforming to a book format might compromise my goals for the site, but I soon realized that the site's anecdotal structure could work in book form, and I got excited about the idea. After all, I own dozens of indispensable O'Reilly books, so I was thrilled at the chance to become one of their authors. Without showing it to other publishers, I signed a contract with O'Reilly in December 2003, promising a finished draft by June 2004.

Tim introduced me to the talented team at his company, including my editor, Allen Noren, who specializes in O'Reilly's more humanistic efforts (his previous two books were Dan Gillmor's We the People and Paul Graham's Hackers and Painters). Allen guided me through the laborious process to transform the raw material of the Folklore site into a beautiful book.

After completing the writing phase in June 2004, we embarked on the editing and layout process. The first step was copyediting. All 90 or so of the stories had to be thoroughly edited, in batches of 10 at a time. Most of the changes involved fixing grammatical errors and punctuation, and removing unnecessary verbiage, chopping up my Proustian run-on sentences (like this one), but they occasionally involved additional writing to provide more explanation or clarification. My editors also wanted to delete many of the most technical passages, fearing they would alienate nontechnical readers. After editing was completed on a batch, I had to accept or reject each individual change. I accepted all the grammatically oriented ones, figuring my editors knew better than I did, but I fought to keep most of the technical detail, since I thought it was an important part of the story, although we did eliminate a few of the most technical stories entirely. Sometimes we'd argue about the merits of particular changes, but it usually wasn't that hard to reach consensus. I decided to keep the original text on the site, so you can compare it with the book if you're interested in seeing what changed.

The next step was working on the layout. We decided to maintain the basic format of the site, but we divided the stories into five parts at natural breaking points, to give the reader a chance to rest. We decided to use an unusual trim size, eight inches square, which seems simultaneously large and small at the same time. I was delighted when Allen told me they wanted to print it in full color on high quality paper without increasing the price.

Unfortunately, I discovered that it's a lot harder to publish images in a book than on the Web. On the Folklore site, I didn't have to worry too much about obtaining permissions, since if anybody ever complained, I could easily remove an offending image. But once published, a book is immutable, and my contract required that I obtain formal rights for every image in the book. Some photographs require multiple layers of permissions (from the subjects, the photographer, and the original publication); with 20-year-old photographs, it's difficult to track everything down. That kind of work is not my forte, but luckily Allen introduced me to a consultant who was willing to obtain permissions for $50 per image. To make matters worse, the printed page still has much higher resolution than a computer display, so we needed to procure higher resolution images than the ones on the site.

Before unveiling the site publicly in January 2004, I gathered up my courage and showed it to Steve Jobs. He was fairly enthusiastic about it, but as usual, he had some complaints. "I like what you've done with the site," he told me, "but the quality of some of the scans you're using is terrible! Can't you do better than that?" When I complained that it was hard to find pristine copies of decades old material, he suggested that I could probably access Apple's corporate marketing archive to find better versions of lots of the images.

I didn't even know that Apple had a marketing archive. It took a few months to track down the right people, since I didn't want to bother Steve about the details, but I eventually found Sue Runfola, who works on rights and permissions in Apple's Legal Department and who introduced me to Del Smith Penny, who maintains Apple's marketing archive as a part-time job. The archive is just a single room in a nondescript building a few blocks away from the main Apple campus, stuffed to the gills with maybe 40 long file cabinets. There were stacks of cardboard boxes on top of the cabinets that Del told me were acquired from Mike Markkula's garage, containing marketing material from Apple's first four years that no one had time to examine yet.

Some of the material in the archive was indexed in a Filemaker database running on an old Mac, but Del admitted that much of it still wasn't indexed at all, since he barely had time to keep up with the new stuff coming in. But he was willing to help me search for everything

I asked him about, and by the end of the afternoon, Del and I were able to locate a treasure trove of around 30 high-quality slides of relevant product and publicity photos, including some that were never published before. We also uncovered a rare videotape of potential TV commercials shot in October 1983 featuring the Mac design team that were never aired, but that's another story.

Allen introduced me to Michelle Weatherbee, an award-winning book designer who had just been hired to work full-time as O'Reilly's art director; my book was her first project as an O'Reilly employee. Michelle had me bring lots of my old Macintosh relics to O'Reilly headquarters in Sebastopol, including my design notebooks, which she borrowed for a few weeks to scan. I worked with Michelle and layout artist Melanie Wang to match the images to the proper stories. Michelle and a few others at O'Reilly helped choose other relevant images from commercial image clearinghouses like Corbis.

Allen told me that I needed a foreword for the book and suggested that I ask Steve Jobs to write one, but I didn't have the courage to ask him to do something like that. I suggested Apple cofounder Steve Wozniak instead, who told me that he loved the site and had even contributed a few comments to some of the stories. Woz was enthusiastic about writing the foreword, which he thought he could get done in a few weeks. We told him we needed it by the end of June.

I warned Allen that while Woz always had the best intentions, he often was a notorious procrastinator. If he didn't do something right away, it had a tendency not to get done indefinitely. Predictably, the foreword wasn't finished by the end of July and Allen began to send Woz emails to remind him about it every few weeks. Woz always replied promptly, promising to make room in his busy schedule to get it done soon.

Finally, in September, while I was meeting with Allen and the team in Sebastopol to finalize the layout, he told me that he had some bad news. He had finally given up on Woz's foreword, because Woz hadn't responded to an email Allen had sent a few days earlier informing him the final deadline was approaching. I laughed and told Allen that was actually good news, because not responding to the email meant that Woz was probably actually writing it, and sure enough I was right. A few days later, Woz sent Allen an eloquent, stirring foreword that was a perfect start for the book.

I assumed the title of the book would be Macintosh Folklore, just like the website, but while I was working with Michelle and Melanie on the layout, I noticed them referring to the book as Revolutionaries. I asked Allen what was up and he told me that the sales department didn't think my title was appealing enough, and that sales honcho Mark Brokering had renamed the book Revolutionaries in the Valley, but they were waiting to tell me until they had the cover art finished. I cringed, because I wanted to be modest and avoid hyperbole, but Allen insisted I'd love it once I saw the cover.

The next time I visited Sebastopol to work on the layout, Michelle showed me a mockup of the cover, which used a black-and-white Norman Seeff photo that was taken for Rolling Stone magazine in January 1984, the one where Norman told us not to smile. They had colorized the Macintosh and added a bright red background. I liked the photo but disliked the red color, and was surprised to learn that my opinion didn't matter all that much. The O'Reilly team was adamant, telling me that I wasn't in a good position to judge, since it was supposed to appeal to young people, a group to which I no longer belonged. Eventually they wore me down and today I even sort of like it. At least I was able to get them to change Revolutionaries to Revolution, which I thought seemed slightly more modest.

My biggest disappointment with the book has to do with the story links. We decided to keep the story links in the book, even though you can't click on them. To compensate, they were supposed to include the page number of the referenced story, but apparently that was too much for O'Reilly's layout system to cope with, given that page numbers changed frequently as edits were made. I hope we're able to improve this in subsequent printings.

Now that the book is complete, it's interesting to compare it to the website. Once I finally got a finished copy of the book in my hands, I was amazed at how much better it seemed than the website for continuous reading, in terms of ease and enjoyment, even though most of the content was crafted for the site instead of the book. Computers still have a long way to go before they match the ease of use of books. The website has some compensating strengths, though, and is better than the book for only reading stories about a particular character or topic.

But by far the main advantage of the website over the book is that it's a living document, capable of correcting itself and growing indefinitely. That might seem ironic, given the moribund state of the Folklore site since I finished writing in June 2004. But there's a (somewhat feeble) reason: I didn't want to write new stories while the book was in production, because I knew that I would want to squeeze them into the book, and I didn't want to delay it. Hopefully, this essay helped to shake off some of the rust, and I will start adding new stories soon, probably at the rate of around one per month.

Afterword for the New Edition

Andy Hertzfeld, September 5, 2011

When we were writing the stories for this book, it wasn't clear where we should stop, since the Macintosh never stopped evolving. At first I thought it should end with the catharsis of the intro at Apple's annual shareholder's meeting in January 1984, which was the emotional high point of the story. But eventually I realized that there was a lot to be learned from the denouement that unfolded in the following year and a half, as the team went their separate ways. It became clear that the natural place to break was when Steve Jobs got involuntarily separated from the team in June 1985—I called that sad story "The End of An Era."

Here, in September 2011, I'm feeling wistful because the end of another era is upon us, since Steve Jobs stepped down as CEO of Apple on August 24th. After spending more than a decade estranged from Apple, Steve returned as reluctant CEO in July 1997, and quickly resuscitated Apple's original values, which had slowly atrophied during his absence over the previous decade. Apple once again began to produce imaginative, innovative products, starting with the first iMac and its courageous, stunning industrial design.

The iPod, released in October 2001, re-imagined music players. With its elegant user interface and prodigious capacity, the iPod quickly became a beloved, colossal hit, fueled by the ground-breaking convenience of the iTunes store. But the most impressive part was how Apple developed the discipline to relentlessly improve it, year after year, making it ever more elegant and useful while pushing the previous year's model into obsolescence before the competition could even copy it.

But Apple and Steve were just getting started. In 2005, it was obvious that multi-purpose cell phones would eventually subsume music players, and that the iPod would have to evolve into a phone. Most companies would have done it by extending their popular, existing UI. Apple, however, once again re-imagined the device, ditching the scroll wheel for a large, multi-touch screen with numerous sensors and a brilliant new UI optimized for fingers. The following year, the launch of the App Store and the SDK unleashed the creativity of 3rd party developers and completely transformed the industry.

Today, Apple is by far the most successful consumer electronics company on the planet. Its products are widely imitated but rarely surpassed. The iPad is upending the traditional PC industry, by stripping away the hated complexity that was inflicted on consumers for decades, and offering a great experience for most common applications for a reasonable price. Steve is leaving the company in excellent shape, and it's likely they will prosper for the foreseeable future.

Many of the stories in this book offer illustrations of Apple's unique core values, which Steve applied relentlessly to create the foundation of their prior and current success: design featuring simplicity, elegance, artistry and extreme cleverness, combined with a strong dose of rebellion and an impatience with the status quo, harnessed to a sense of urgency and humor and an unwillingness to compromise, all in the service of making something you want for yourself more than anything else in the world. Even with Apple's immense success, these values continue to be all too rare in the corporate world. It will be interesting to see how well they flourish in the absence of their promulgator—here's to hoping they are still in full force as you're reading this.

Acknowledgments

Like the Macintosh itself, this book resulted from the efforts of many talented individuals. I'd especially like to thank my friends and original Mac team members Steve Capps, Donn Denman, Bruce Horn, and Susan Kare for contributing their stories to the book. I'd also like to thank Eric Barnes, William Donelson, Scott Knaster, Dan Kottke, Jerry Manock, David Ramsey, Caroline Rose, Paul Tavenier, and Tom Zito for contributing stories to the Folklore.org web site, where this book originated.

Thanks to original Mac team members Bill Atkinson, Steve Capps, Jerome Coonen, George Crow, Donn Denman, Joanna Hoffman, Bruce Horn, Brian Howard, Steve Jobs, Susan Kare, Larry and Patti Kenyon, Scott Knaster, Dan Kottke, Jerry Manock, Caroline Rose, and Bud Tribble for unearthing artifacts and sharing their memories from twenty years ago.

Apple Computer generously allowed me to rummage through their corporate image archive to obtain photographs for the book. Thanks to Donna Dubinsky, Nancy Heinen, Steve Jobs, Del Penny, and Sue Runfola for helping to make that happen.

The hardest part of turning the Folklore web site into *Revolution in The Valley* was obtaining permission to use dozens of photographs. Thanks to Sara Nickles, Robin Rossi, Michele Filshie, and Terry Bronson for helping to obtain image permissions, and Mike Stern for legal advice.

I showed Tim O'Reilly my Folklore web site in October 2003, and he suggested that his company publish it as a book. I'd like to thank Tim for initiating the project and introducing me to everyone at his amazing company.

My original title for the book was *Macintosh Folklore*. I'd like to thank Mark Brokering, the associate publisher at O'Reilly, for coming up with *Revolution in The Valley*.

The design and layout of the book was done by a talented team at O'Reilly, including interior designer Melanie Wang, cover designer Ellie Volckhausen, and art director Michele Wetherbee. Other folks at O'Reilly who helped include illustrator Rob Romano, photographer Derrick Story, production editor Philip Dangler, proofreaders Mary Brady and Marlowe Shaeffer, and product manager Betsy Waliszewski. A special thanks is due to my editor, Allen Noren, who shepherded this novice author through the publishing process.

Finally, I'd like to thank my wife, Joyce McClure, for reminding me in May 2003 that I wanted to pursue my Folklore project. I'd also like to thank my earliest readers, who provided me with crucial advice and encouragement: Andrew Francis, Mitch Kapor, Chao Lam, Scott Rosenberg, and Nikolas Tanaka.

Photo Credits

Cover: The Mac team. Photo by Norman Seeff, courtesy of Apple Computer, Inc.

Flap: Andy Hertzfeld. ©Elisabeth Fall

5: Andy Hertzfeld, Burrell Smith, and Brian Howard. Courtesy of San Francisco Examiner Photograher Paul Glines

15: NERF BALL®. © 2004 Hasbro, Inc. Used with permission.

27: Mac analog board. Photo courtesy of Apple Computer, Inc.

31: Macintosh photograph. Photo courtesy of Apple Computer, Inc.

37: Bicycle illustration. Photo courtesy of Apple Computer, Inc.

38: Adam Osborne. © Bettmann/CORBIS

46: Traffic signs. © Photos.com

48: Bill Budge. Photo courtesy of Bill Budge

51: Digital board photograph. © Derrick Story

53: Macintosh Software Team. Photo courtesy of Apple Computer, Inc.

54: Bill Gates. © Doug Wilson/CORBIS

60: Apple Lisa Computer. Photo courtesy of Apple Computer, Inc.

68–69: Design team signatures. Photo courtesy of Apple Computer, Inc.

72: Members of the Lisa team. © Roger Ressmeyer/CORBIS

79: Andy Hertzfeld sitting on his car. © D.W. Mellor

83: Crowd at US Festival. © Bettmann/CORBIS

85: Steve Wozniak playing air computer. © Roger Ressmeyer/CORBIS

99: Steve Jobs and Bill Atkinson. © Norman Seeff

104, 107: *Alice* packaging. Photos courtesy of Apple Computer, Inc.

128: Mike Moritz. © Matthew Naythons

150: Steve Jobs, John Sculley, and Steve Wozniak. © Bettmann/CORBIS

169: Defender® screenshot. Used with permission of Midway Games, Inc.

175: Bill Atkinson in 1987. Photo courtesy of Bill Atkinson

178: The Mac design team. © Norman Seef. Photo courtesy of Apple Computer, Inc.

180, 182, 183: 1984 commercial stills. © Apple Computer, Inc. Used with permission. All rights reserved. Apple® and the Apple logo are registered trademarks of Apple Computer, Inc.

184: Monkey graphic. © Clipart.com

197: Burrell Smith. © D.W. Mellor

198–203: MacPaint Art by Susan Kare. Photos courtesy of Apple Computer, Inc.

206: Mick Jagger. © Neal Preston/CORBIS

209: Pyramid photo. © Norman Seeff. Photo courtesy of Apple Computer, Inc.

214: Mac in a bag advertisement. Photo courtesy of Apple Computer, Inc.

249: Andy Hertzfeld and the Mac team. © Norman Seeff. Photo courtesy of Apple Computer, Inc.

224: The Mac software team. © Norman Seeff. Photo courtesy of Apple Computer, Inc.

232: Brian Howard, Andy Hertzfeld & Burrell Smith. Courtesy of *San Francisco Examiner* Photographer Paul Glines

238–239: The Macintosh software team in the spring of 1985. © D.W. Mellor

267: Andy Hertzfeld in February 1985. Photo courtesy of Apple Computer, Inc.

275: Steve Jobs. © Ed Kashi/CORBIS

277: Apple's Fremont Macintosh factory warehouse. Photo courtesy of Apple Computer, Inc.

278: Macintosh line art. Courtesy of Apple Computer, Inc.

Index

Dates

1979
  August, 5–6
  November, 7–8
1980
  February, 9–12
  September, 13
  October, 14–15
1981
  January, 26–28
  February, 16–20, 24–25
  March, 29–31
  April, 32–40
  May, 43–46
  June, 47–49
  July, 41, 50–54
  August, 55
  December, 60
1982
  January, 61–62
  February, 63–70
  March, 71–79
  April, 88, 99–100
  May, 101–103
  June, 104–113
  July, 114
  August, 116–119
  September, 80–84, 123–127
  December, 128–130
1983
  January, 132–140
  February, 140–148
  March, 149–150
  June, 171–174
  August, 152, 158–167
  September, 168–170, 178, 181–183, 186–190
  October, 179, 184–185, 194–203
  November, 191–193
  December, 204–205
1984
  January, 206–223
  March, 229–232
  April, 233–235
  June, 238–242
  September, 262–264
  October, 243–251
1985
  February, 253
  May, 266–271
  June, 254–256

Symbols

1984 commercial, 181–183
3M machine, 133
80k language card, 7–8
90 Hours a Week and Loving It, 196

A

Adler, Darin, 78
alarm, dismantling, 118–119
Alexio, Peggy, 78
Alice, 104–107
Anders, Bob, 113
Anderson, Jane, 226
Apple's first office in Cupertino, 14–15
AppleScript, xxi, 256
Applesoft BASIC, 255
Apple II, xvii–xxv

68

Fill algorithm can be improved by flattening out recursion

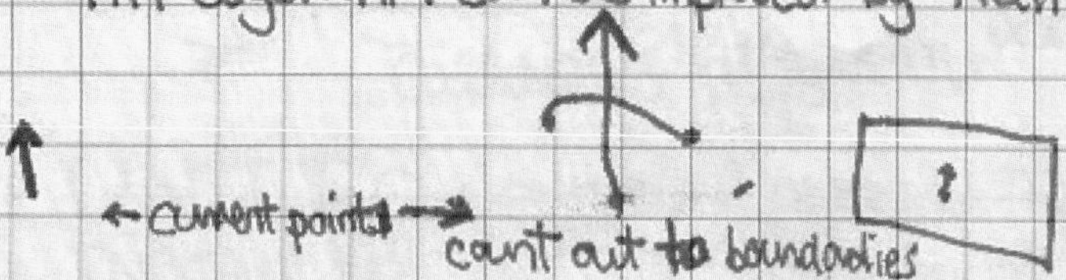

← current points →
count out to boundaries

fill can work on scan lines instead of pixels?

Funhouse Distortion

BottomPtr = 255
Top Ptr = 255

repeat until bottomptr < 0

    repcount = 1
    for i = 1 to 4

    copy

Line Draw →

easy cause always
45 degress (or - 45

Copy into page
instead of plotti

Source = 255   Start = 255 04
Dest = 255

Repeat

    SourceFill = Start   05   A4
    Dest Fill = start   D   A5
    repcount = 1
LOOP   for i = 1 to n
        for j = 1 to repcount

```
RWERR      MOVE    #$FFFF,A0     ; indicate error
           BRA     DONERWTS
```

~~~~~~~~~~~~~~~~~~~~~~~~~~~~~~~~~~

Slideshow → track1 start

```
SLIDESHOW         MOVE.B   POWERON, D1
                  MOVE.L   #$3000, D2
                  BSR      MSWAIT
                  BSR      RECAL
```

globals:
280 TRACKNUM
282 SECTNUM
284 BUFNUM

; ~~push initial parameters on stack~~

```
SLOOP1            MOVE     #9, D5        ; 10 pictures
                  MOVE     #1, TRACKNUM
                  CLR      SECTNUM

SLOOP2            MOVE     #47, D6       ; 48 sectors/pic
                  MOVE.L   #$000000, BUFNUM

SLOOP3            MOVE.L   BUFNUM, -(SP)
                  MOVE.W   SECTNUM, -(SP)
                  MOVE.W   TRACKNUM, -(SP)

                  BSR      RWTS

                  ~~MOVE.L   (SP)+, D0~~
                  ADD      #8, SP        ; pop off params

                  ADD      #1, SECTNUM
                  CMP      #16, SECTNUM
```

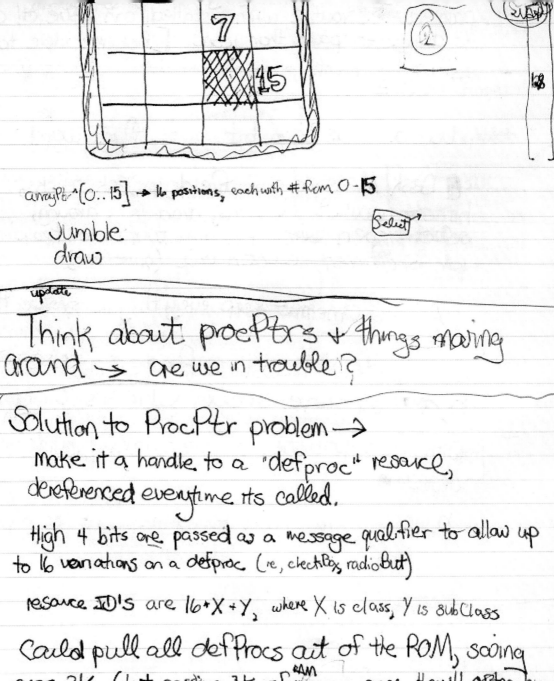

7

15

2

128

arrayPtr^[0..15] → 16 positions, each with # from 0-15

Jumble
draw

Select

update

Think about procPtrs + things moving
around → are we in trouble?

Solution to ProcPtr problem →
make it a handle to a "defproc" resource,
dereferenced everytime its called.

High 4 bits are passed as a message qualifier to allow up
to 16 variations on a defproc (ie, checkBox, radioBut)

resource ID's are 16*X+Y, where X is class, Y is subClass

Could pull all defProcs out of the ROM, saving
over 3K (but costing 3K of RAM memory since they'll often be
used)

"Gallery" desk ornament is resource based

§0 PICT + TEXT, prefers pictures

CUT, PASTE, COPY, scrolling

The Gallery

→ 5 ▯⊫

The Gallery

← → 16 items

(Cut) (Copy) (Paste)

(Name:)

(Cut)(Copy)(Paste) (Delete)

Messages:
 FeedEvent → update, mousedown
 Cursor
 No run, menu   how is order maintained?
 Edit   for (where is new one inserted?   [list][id][ids]

 open   when opened,
 Close   ⎧ makes list of IDs in handle
              ⎩ kept in DCH storage

Short Term Things to Do   10/3/83

√ ① ~~Title Bar Highlighting, clean up window deflocc~~

② ~~Gallery~~

User Interface Manager [Window Manager]

Objects Known to UI Manager:

Panes (Folders) →
Buttons (Icons)
Dials (Scroll Bars)
Menus
Events

Panes are ~~just so a rectangular~~ areas of the screen. They may overlap eachother. A folder is a special pane that has a tab, title and outline drawn. They are used mainly to tag mouse events correlating the mouse position with a logical entity that makes sense to the application.

Buttons are special panes. They may be momentary or 2-state. Clicking inside a momentary button generates a button pushed event. Clicking a two-state button changes its state. (and may cause a different bitmap to be drawn. (& use generates the event) Buttons may be draggable, with a bounding rectangle.

Dials are also special panes. They have a 16 bit integer as their state. They consist of a rectangular meter (optionally calibrated) and an indicator which is a draggable button.

Menus are a 2 level data structure interpreted by the UI Manager when the mouse button goes down over the menu bar. Menu events are sent back to application.

every event can be masked off
Events → a data structure passed by Get Next Event

REVOLUTION
in The Valley